D1408220

Plain Talks On Economics

Leading Principles and Their Application to the Issues of Today

By

Fabian Franklin

G. P. Putnam's Sons
New York & London
The Knickerbocker Press
1924

Made in the United States of America

CONTENTS

PART I

LEADING PRINCIPLES

CHAPTER I

PAGE

THE METHOD AND SPIRIT OF ECONOMICS . . . 3

The economist's way of thinking—The economist and the man in the street—How clear thinking averted a calamity.

CHAPTER II

THE IDEA OF THE MARGIN 9

Averages and deviations—The margin in agriculture—The margin and the value of land—How the "margin" connects "value" with "utility."

CHAPTER III

THE FOUR FACTORS OF PRODUCTION 16

Land, labor, capital, enterprise—What is capital?—Capital the result of saving—There might be capital without capitalists—Transportation and merchandising.

CHAPTER IV

DEMAND AND SUPPLY 23

What makes prices go up and down—How prices regulate production—How many tailors and how many barbers?

CHAPTER V

ILLUSTRATIONS OF DEMAND AND SUPPLY . . . 30

The price of wheat "fixed at Liverpool"—Hoarding in time of abundance—Hoarding in time of scarcity—Emergency rent laws.

Contents

CHAPTER VI

PAGE

VALUE 38

What economists mean by "value"—"Value" and "price"—Normal value—Normal value proportional to cost of production—Cost of production not uniform.

CHAPTER VII

MONEY COST AND REAL COST 46

Real cost consists of services—The service of capital—The service of labor—Different grades of workers—Compensation depends on scarcity—The case of the servant girl—Cost of living.

CHAPTER VIII

MONEY 54

Separation of employments—Difficulties of barter—What is money?—How gold and silver came to be the world's money—Money not only the medium of exchange but also the measure of value.

CHAPTER IX

PRICES 61

The price-level—Value of money and value of gold—Value of money and cost of production of gold—General purchasing power of money—The quantity theory of money.

CHAPTER X

GOLD, PAPER, CREDIT 70

Other things than coin that play the part of money—Paper money—Notes redeemable in gold—Irredeemable paper money—The banking system—The three factors that determine the general course of prices.

CHAPTER XI

LAND AND RENT 78

The landowner's share: rent—Rent of land and value of land—What makes rental value—Speculative value of land—Land and improvements.

CHAPTER XII

PAGE

ENTERPRISE AND PROFIT 86

No standard rate of business profit—Analogy between profit and rent—Prices not raised by rent of best land or profit of ablest manufacturers—A word about corporations.

CHAPTER XIII

CAPITAL AND INTEREST 94

Capital the result of saving—The rate of interest—The capitalist and the risk of enterprise—True interest and compensation for risk—Are the interests of labor and capital indentical?—What determines the rate of interest—Division of proceeds between capital and labor.

CHAPTER XIV

LABOR AND WAGES 103

The share of labor as a whole; the share of different kinds of labor—Grades of labor; wage-equality within a grade, wage-difference between grades—Trade unions and labor scarcity—Highly paid labor not necessarily dear labor.

CHAPTER XV

FOREIGN TRADE 109

Importing and exporting done by individuals, not by countries—Baseless fears about flow of gold—True nature of foreign trade—Free trade and protection.

CHAPTER XVI

THE LAW OF DIMINISHING PRODUCTIVENESS AND THE PROBLEM OF POPULATION . . . 118

Law of diminishing productiveness—Malthus and *The Principle of Population*—The controversy over Malthus—Population and standard of living.

PART II

ISSUES OF TODAY

CHAPTER XVII

OVERPRODUCTION 129

Purchasing power keeps pace with production—Not over-

PAGE

production, but misfit—Business psychology—A long-lived fallacy—The fundamental truth of the matter.

CHAPTER XVIII

MONOPOLY 141

Natural monopolies—Large-scale production and the tendency toward monopoly—Trusts and anti-trust laws—The check of potential competition—Competition not dead, nor dying.

CHAPTER XIX

TRADE-UNIONISM 152

Trade unions not necessarily monopolistic—Collective bargaining—Benefits of trade-unionism—Evils of trade-unionism—The strike—Fundamental causes of the advancement of labor—The reasonable attitude toward trade-unionism.

CHAPTER XX

COÖPERATION, PROFIT SHARING, ETC. 163

Coöperative production—Coöperative distribution—Labor banks—Profit sharing—Shareholding.

CHAPTER XXI

TAXATION: GENERAL REMARKS 173

Assessments for special benefits—Purposes of general taxation—Distribution of the tax burden—Taxation and the sense of justice—A discarded view—Taxation and the ability to pay—Practical effects must always be considered.

CHAPTER XXII

TAXATION: ITS VARIOUS FORMS 181

Taxes on commodities—Effect of import duties—The case of monopoly—Income tax, profits tax, inheritance tax—Progressive rates of income tax—The general property tax—Taxes on land and houses—Other aspects of taxation.

CHAPTER XXIII

PAGE

THE SINGLE-TAX DOCTRINE: ITS BASIS . . 195

Progress and poverty—Property in land unlike property in the products of labor—Holding land out of use—The single tax equivalent to confiscation.

CHAPTER XXIV

THE SINGLE-TAX DOCTRINE: OBJECTIONS . . 202

The ethics of land confiscation—The "unearned increment" —Land "held out of use"—Single tax and building enterprise—The farmer and his land.

CHAPTER XXV

PROTECTION AND FREE TRADE (*First Part*) . . 215

The tariff controversy—The labor-employment fallacy—The money fallacy.

CHAPTER XXVI

PROTECTION AND FREE TRADE (*Second Part*) . 224

The infant industries argument—Social and political arguments—Economic independence—Actual character of tariff legislation.

CHAPTER XXVII

CHANGES IN THE VALUE OF MONEY . . . 233

Imperfection of the gold standard—Debtors and creditors—Salaries and wages—The business cycle.

CHAPTER XXVIII

THE INDEX-NUMBER AND "THE STABILIZED DOLLAR" 241

Irving Fisher's plan—Meaning of "price level"—The index-number—"The stabilized dollar"—A legislative danger.

CHAPTER XXIX

FOREIGN EXCHANGE 251

Exchange and the gold standard—Normal fluctuations of the

Contents

PAGE

rate of exchange—Exports and imports and the rate of exchange—Balance of trade—"Triangular" exchange.

CHAPTER XXX

FIAT MONEY 261

What governments can and cannot do about fiat money—"Basing" of no avail without convertibility—Why bad money drives out good—The fiat-money plague in Europe—Inconvertible paper money and the rate of exchange—Essential vice of fiat money.

CHAPTER XXXI

LAISSEZ FAIRE 277

A practical maxim, not a scientific doctrine—Protection, usury laws, "speculation"—Mistaken opposition to factory laws—Anti-trust laws—Strong presumption in favor of *laissez faire.*

CHAPTER XXXII

SOCIAL JUSTICE 289

Vagueness of the term—Workmen's compensation laws—Minimum-wage laws—Specific merits versus abstract doctrine—Self-delusion or false pretence.

CHAPTER XXXIII

EQUALITY OF OPPORTUNITY 300

In what sense we do have equality of opportunity—Educational facilities and welfare laws—Unlimited scope of the abstract doctrine—What abolition of inheritance would mean.

CHAPTER XXXIV

SOCIALISM (*First Part*) 308

Socialist systems and the Socialist ideal—Is Socialism practicable?—The mainspring of productivity—A Socialist counter-argument—The waste of competition—The waste of Socialism.

CHAPTER XXXV

PAGE

SOCIALISM (*Second Part*) 320

The elimination of struggle—The pleasures of possession—Socialism and the family—Socialism and liberty—The ordinary man and the exceptional man.

CHAPTER XXXVI

ECONOMICS AND LIFE 333

Limitations of Economics—Economics and Ethics—The higher charms of life—Obsessions of the specialist—Great value, nevertheless, of the spread of economic truth.

INDEX 343

Plain Talks on Economics

Part I

Leading Principles

CHAPTER I

THE METHOD AND SPIRIT OF ECONOMICS

THIS is to be an elementary book on Economics, and yet not a text-book. My endeavor will be to give readers without previous knowledge of the subject a feeling of what Economics is like. I hope that many of them will get a real grasp of its most essential principles. Above all, I hope they will come to realize the difference between scientific thinking and unscientific thinking upon economic subjects. But I shall not set out with a lot of formal definitions, which is the natural thing to do in a text-book.

To begin with, I shall not define Economics itself. There are many possible definitions of Economics; what is meant by the term in this little book the reader will probably know fairly well when he has read it; if not, I doubt whether he would know any better if I started out with a formal definition.

What we are going to be concerned with is such matters as prices, value, money, rent, wages, profits, capital, interest, etc. But we are going to make no attempt to master the infinite intricacies of these things. On the contrary, we are going to try to concentrate our attention upon certain central facts which, as we shall see, have a dominating importance, and in comparison with which those intricacies are of minor significance. We shall find that what chiefly marks the economist's view of economic phenomena, as compared with that of the "man in the street," is not that the economist knows a greater multitude of facts, but that he knows their relative importance—that he seizes upon the facts which are vital, and by means of these possesses a clue to what would otherwise be a hopeless labyrinth.

How the Economist Thinks

The title of this chapter is "The Method and Spirit of Economics." It may be objected that there is no one "method and spirit" that can claim to be *the* "method and spirit" of Economics. Yet I use the definite article advisedly; for I have in mind the method and spirit which are at the heart of Economics as a science. The paramount object of that science is to discuss the *causation* of economic phenomena; and *the* method and spirit that I have in mind is the method and spirit preëminently adapted to the pursuit of that object. It may be impossible in a brief space to give a completely correct statement of that method and spirit; but one can indicate it with a fair degree of accuracy.

Most sciences, in order to get at the causes of

things, and find out how they operate, have to begin by going through a vast amount of laborious observation, or ingenious experiment, or both. This is true of all the physical sciences—astronomy, physics, chemistry, biology. If the foundations of economics had to be laid in this way, we might well despair of the case. For the subject-matter is too desperately miscellaneous to hold out much prospect of arriving at fundamental principles by mere piling up of observations; and experiment is out of the question, since we cannot subject multitudes of men and women, in their economic relations, to artificial conditions like those that we command in the physical or chemical laboratory.

What, then, does the economist do to get at his principles of economic causation? As against the disadvantages, just mentioned, under which he labors, he has one tremendous advantage. Unlike the physicist or the chemist, he *knows*, without the aid of any complicated inquiry, the nature of some of the chief factors that enter into the causation of economic phenomena. In fact, we *all* know them; and it may almost be said that the great achievement of the creators of economic science was not the discovery of causes, but the discovery of their importance. And the greatest discovery of all is the discovery that it is only by firmly fixing the mind on the question of *causation*, as distinguished from questions of mere *description*, that any headway can be made towards a vital understanding of economic phenomena.

What the Man in the Street Doesn't Do

It is interesting, for example, and for many purposes highly important, to know what has taken place, at various times and in various countries, about prices, or rent, or population; but all this miscellaneous information would give one no insight into the *essential nature* of what has taken place. The economist singles out the factors that are fundamental in these vast processes; and he finds that underneath all their complexities there runs a certain simplicity. He finds that certain great, simple, and practically irresistible forces determine in the main the course of economic events, however intricate and complicated these may be in detail. And the habit of mind which this knowledge produces constitutes the most vital difference between the economist and the man in the street when confronted with an economic problem.

When, for example, prices rise as they have done in recent years, the man in the street gets his mind filled with the thought of the greed of "profiteers"; the economist knows that the real cause of high prices lies far deeper. The man in the street might know it almost as well as the economist if he but fixed his attention on the right thing, the fundamental thing, instead of fixing it upon something which is conspicuous on the surface, but which plays hardly any part as a *cause* of high prices. What *does* play that part, we shall learn something about further on; but I will mention another and simpler illustration of the importance of fixing the mind steadily upon causation.

How Clear Thinking Averted a Calamity

In the midst of the war, our Government was confronted with a most serious problem in regard to the supply of wheat. Owing to the tremendous demand from the war-ridden countries of Europe, there was danger of a shortage in this country, and of the price of wheat going sky-high. I remember being told by a highly intelligent man—and one who knew a great deal about farming, too—that the Government ought to fix a maximum price of $1.50 a bushel for wheat; which was high enough, he said, to give the farmer a handsome profit, since $1 had always been regarded as a very good price. But what did the Government do? In order to keep the price down, it established not a *maximum* price but a *minimum* price; it told the farmers that they might sell their wheat at any price they could get, but if they could not get $2.20 the Government itself would give them that price for all the wheat they chose to offer to it.

What was the idea of this policy? It was that the true way to keep the price of wheat down was not by the direct process of *forbidding a high price*, but by the indirect process of *stimulating the supply*. The *cause* that threatened to send wheat up to $3 or perhaps $4 was not the greed of the farmer but the enormous demand for wheat. The way to counteract that cause was to match the enormous demand with an enormous supply; and the way to get an enormous supply was to encourage the farmers to raise an abnormally large amount of wheat by guaranteeing them an abnormally high (and yet not an extravagantly high) price for it. The method worked perfectly. But if the Government had done as my friend (and as the man in the street generally) would have advised it to do, and forbidden any higher price than $1.50, one of two things would have happened. Either the law would have been ignored, and the price gone up sky-high in spite of it, or the farmers would have raised nothing like the amount of wheat that was needed. Either of these things would have been a calamity; and in point of fact it is practically certain that *both* of them would have happened: thousands of farmers would have been discouraged by the law, so that the crop would have been nothing like as big as was needed; and in the situation thus arising the law would have been evaded in a thousand ways, with sky-high prices as the result.

This homely and simple example may serve to illustrate the vital importance of the habit of thinking of economic phenomena as the outcome of definite causation—of the working of definite and outstanding forces—and not as a mere series of statistical accidents.

CHAPTER II

THE IDEA OF THE MARGIN

BEFORE taking up any of the leading questions of Economics, I am going to direct attention to a notion that plays a very important part in economic thinking—the notion of the *margin*.

In a merely statistical or descriptive account of economic facts, one is apt to pay attention chiefly to *averages*. The average of a number of quantities is a middling quantity which, for some purposes, may be regarded as a fair representative of them all. It is a quantity such that if all the bigger ones were diminished down to it and all the smaller ones increased up to it, the total would be just what it was before. If of three million bushels of wheat, one million cost the farmers fifty cents a bushel to produce, one million a dollar a bushel, and one million a dollar and a half a bushel, the average cost to the farmers would be a dollar a bushel. If the total income of the 25 million families in the United States is 50 billion dollars, then the average income per family is $2,000; no matter how much greater than $2,000 may be the income of the very rich, nor how much smaller the income of the very poor.

Averages and Deviations

Evidently, even for purely descriptive purposes, the average may not be the most important or the most interesting thing to think about. In the case of incomes, for example, there is a much keener interest in the question of the *deviations* from the average than in the average itself. At the top of the scale there are incomes of a million dollars and more; at the bottom of the scale there are incomes of a thousand dollars and less; and both these extremes are more interesting—and at least one of them more important—to think about than the average itself. If, for example, in the next ten years the average income were to rise to $3,000 (I am supposing the purchasing power of the dollar to remain unaltered) the question whether we ought greatly to rejoice over this would depend on whether the increase was brought about chiefly through the raising of the distressingly low incomes, the raising of moderate incomes, or the raising of those that were already excessively high. The question of the average would be important; but the question of the deviations from the average would be even more important.

The Margin in Agriculture

But when we are concerned not with the mere description, but with the *explanation* of economic phenomena (which, as we have seen in Chapter I, is the chief object of economic science), it is neither the average nor the deviations from the average that we have most occasion to fix our attention upon. If you asked "the man in the street" why wheat usually sells for about $1.25 a bushel, he would be almost sure to say that it is because that is about the average cost of production (including transportation to market) plus an ordinary allowance for the farmer's profit; but the economist says *no*, the average has nothing to do with the case. And a moment's reflection will convince you that this is so; for, although farmers who produce wheat at a cost *less* than the average could well afford to go on producing it and selling it at a price fixed by the average cost, farmers who produce it at a cost *greater* than the average would have no inducement to go on doing so. The price, as a permanent thing, must be sufficient to pay practically *all* the farmers who raise wheat; it must be fixed according to the cost of production of wheat where that cost is heaviest; the cost, as economists say, at the *margin* of cultivation; which means cost on land of such low fertility, or such remoteness from the market, or both, that any lowering of the price would make wheat-growing on it not pay.

The Margin and the Value of Land

This idea of the margin first came into clear and prominent use in Economics through what is known as Ricardo's doctrine of rent. Adam

Smith, who laid the foundations of Modern Economics (or Political Economy) in his great work *The Wealth of Nations*, devoted much attention to the subject of the rent of land, and especially agricultural land. But in the chapters in which he deals with that subject there is no clear thread of thought. He makes many keen and interesting observations about various kinds of land and various kinds of produce, and sometimes almost hits upon the real thing that lies at the bottom of the whole question. But he never quite gets it; and the reader is left with a sense that he has been floundering. Ricardo, the greatest of Adam Smith's successors, puts his finger, with sure touch, upon the key of the whole situation.[1]

The difference between Ricardo and Adam Smith was not so much that Ricardo *thought* of the margin, but that he recognized the crucial *importance* of the margin; he saw that what determines the rental value of any piece of agricultural land is the degree of its superiority to land at the margin of cultivation. Land exists of all degrees of fertility and all degrees of advantage in point of nearness to markets, etc. At any given time, the demand for agricultural products is such that it will pay extremely well to cultivate certain grades of land, less well to cultivate certain other grades, and so on down until we come to a grade that it will just pay to cultivate if nothing has to be given

[1] It is proper to state that Ricardo had been anticipated in this matter by one or more less famous writers; but his name became affixed to the doctrine because he made it part of the structure of his great work *Principles of Political Economy and Taxation.*

for the use of the land. At this margin no rent, or practically no rent, is received; and the amount of rent yielded by any other land is determined by the amount of its superiority to the land at the margin. This fact is self-evident as soon as it is thought of; but a perception of the fact, and above all *a perception of its importance*, makes all the difference between a clear and fruitful view of the whole subject of the value of land and a murky view that leads nowhere.

How the "Margin" Connects "Value" with "Utility"

I shall give here only one more example of the idea of the margin. From the beginning, the foremost subject of economic discussion has been that of the relative commercial values of things that are bought and sold. One of the chief things that the economist has to discuss is why, for example, a pound of gold has as much value in the market as several thousand pounds of flour, a tiny diamond as much as a ton of steel. The explanation of these things constitutes the theory of value; and the very first thing that economic writers have always felt called upon to say is that the "value" with which the theory is concerned is a different thing altogether from value in the sense of usefulness or utility. The next thing they have felt called upon to say, is that even when they *do* speak of the utility of a thing in connection with value, they do not have in mind any inherent test of utility; they do not refer to the good the thing is capable of doing, either physical or moral; what they mean by utility is the capacity of satisfying human desires, whether these be good or bad, wise or foolish. If a woman prefers a bit of pretty lace to a warm coat, that is her affair; if a man would rather have a couple of packages of cigarettes than a good beefsteak, the economist may think he is foolish but he accepts the thing as a fact. But even with this point cleared out of the way—with "utility" defined simply as the capacity of satisfying human desires—the question still remains: what connection, if any, is there between "utility" and value, value in the market? Has a pound of gold as much capacity to satisfy human desires as five thousand loaves of bread? Has a tiny diamond as much "utility" as a ton of steel? The answer seems to be, plainly and emphatically, No. And with this answer economists were for a long time content; though, to be sure, they did point out various considerations which showed that there was *some* connection between "utility" and "value."

But at last the *exact* connection was firmly and clearly pointed out. The utility of any given article to any given person is not a constant thing; one loaf of bread a day has tremendous utility to a man, a second loaf has much less utility to him, a third loaf has perhaps no utility at all, and beyond that to have loaves of bread thrust upon him would be a positive nuisance. Accordingly the man would be willing to pay a big price, if necessary, for one loaf of bread, a moderate price for a second loaf, perhaps nothing at all for a third, and certainly nothing at all for any more. And so with each thing that he buys; the "utility" of successive instalments of it—their fitness to fulfill his desires—gets less and less; and he stops buying at the point where the utility of that particular kind of thing becomes less than that of something else which he can get for his money. That place of stopping is the *margin* for that particular kind of thing; and so you see that while the *total utility* of the food he buys for twenty-five dollars may be infinitely greater than the total utility of the diamond pin for which he pays the same amount, the *marginal* utility of the two things may be exactly the same. He would not on any account do without food altogether, and he would quite cheerfully do without the diamond altogether; but he would get less satisfaction (or so he thinks, at least) by spending twenty-five *additional* dollars on food than he gets out of the possession of the pin. Thus the economist's "value" turns out to be very closely related to "utility"—not, however, to utility on the whole, but to utility at the *margin*.

CHAPTER III

THE FOUR FACTORS OF PRODUCTION

THE supplying of the wants of mankind in an advanced stage of civilization is an appallingly complicated affair. If we were to attempt to follow it in all its details, or in a thousandth part of its details, we should find ourselves paralyzed and helpless. But it is not difficult to see that the supplying of these wants depends on four great factors—natural resources, labor, capital, and enterprise. We get our food, our clothing, our shelter, our comforts and luxuries of all kinds, by the use of *natural resources*, through the application of *labor*, with the aid of *capital*, under the guidance of *enterprise*.

It is perfectly possible for all four of these things to be furnished by one and the same individual. The farmer may own the land on which he lives, cultivate it solely with his own labor, own the implements with which he raises his crops, and determine for himself what he shall raise; in this case natural resources, labor, capital, and enterprise are all united in one and the same person. At the opposite extreme is the case of a great manufacturing establishment carried on by a man of splendid business ability who has no capital of his own, but commands the confidence of others. This man by his brains supplies the enterprise, and out of the fruits of his enterprise pays others for the natural resources, the labor, and the capital that are necessary to carry on the undertaking.

In what way the results of production are distributed among those who furnish the four factors that enter into it, will be discussed in subsequent chapters. But as to the *nature* of the factors themselves hardly any explanation is necessary, except in the case of capital. The part played in production by natural resources (such as farming land, mines, timber land, etc.), by labor, and by enterprise, nearly everybody understands fairly well. But most people have very hazy notions, or none at all, about the part played by what is called "capital."

What is Capital?

Many people think of the word "capital" as another name for "rich man," or "employer," or "the employing class"; many others think that it means money, or credit at the bank. But in fact capital plays a part in production which would still have to be played if there were no such thing as rich men, or an employing class, or money, or banks. Given your natural resources, your labor, and your enterprise or managing ability, there could still be but very little and very primitive production if nothing else were provided with which to carry on production. For the production of food, there must be ploughs and harrows and reapers and fertilizers and barns and livestock; for the production of clothes and shoes and furniture and the thousand comforts and luxuries of modern life, there must be factory buildings, and machinery, and a stock of raw material and of coal or other fuel; and besides all this apparatus of production there must be a supply of food and shelter and other necessaries to maintain the workers while the production is going on, and before its results are gathered in. These things—all the things which (in addition to natural resources, labor, and enterprise) are necessary for the carrying on of production—are what we mean by "capital."

Capital the Result of Saving

It may be objected that, after all, necessary as all these things may be, they do not constitute a *separate* agency of production, since they are themselves the result of labor and enterprise previously applied to the resources of nature. And if one chose to insist on this as a mere matter of *language*, there would be nothing to hinder. But in doing so, he would overlook a *reality* of the first importance. A specific *act*, over and above the application of labor and enterprise to the resources of nature, is necessary in order that there shall be capital.

That act is *saving*. If nobody saved anything for future use as a means of production, there would be no capital.

In an early stage of civilization, the principal instances of such saving, perhaps, were the acquiring of simple agricultural implements, the putting by of a certain part of the crop for seed, the raising of live stock for breeding, etc.; nowadays, the creation of capital by saving takes an infinite variety of forms. One of the principal ways in which people—rich or poor—provide capital seems, on the face of it, to be simply the laying by of money; they put money into the bank, or use it to buy shares in some corporation. But what they are really putting by is not money, but *capital*—bricks and mortar and steel and machinery and coal and all the other requisites of modern production. If they had spent the money for their immediate enjoyment, they would have spent it perhaps on cigars and silks and jewelry and automobiles and yachts; but when they turned it over to the bank or invested it in shares of a business corporation, the money was not used for any such purpose. It was used to provide the things that are necessary for carrying on the productive activities of the country.

There Might be Capital Without Capitalists

I think it well to say at once that to point out why capital is necessary, to show the part that it plays in production, and to insist that it is only by *saving* that capital can be obtained, is not to prejudge the question of Socialism versus Individualism. To say that *capital* is indispensable is not to say that the *capitalist* is indispensable; to show that capital is the result of *saving* is not to prove that it must necessarily be got by *individual* saving. It is open to the Socialist to contend that it could be got as well, or better, by *collective* saving—by the whole community putting aside for the maintenance of future production as much as may be necessary of the results of present production. But the fact which the Socialist cannot get away from (though he often either ignores it or attempts to deny it) is that capital *does* perform an essential service, and that, so long as this service is *not* rendered by the community as a whole, those who do render it—those who do furnish the capital—perform as essential a part in the work of production as do those who furnish the labor or the managing ability.

Transportation and Merchandising

Before closing this preliminary talk about the factors of production, it is well to make one very important remark concerning the nature and scope of production itself. When one speaks of production, or productive activity, one usually thinks of the farmer, or the miner, or the manufacturer—in short, of the man who "makes" things. But as a matter of fact nobody "makes" anything, in the sense of creating it out of nothing. The farmer does not produce a single grain of wheat, in the sense of creating it; he only moves certain grains of wheat and certain other particles of matter from one place to another in such a way as to enable the forces of nature to put a hundred grains where one was before. And so in general: when we "make" anything, what we do is to take what nature furnishes, and by applying various processes to it cause it to supply the needs of man. But in order to supply those needs it is just as necessary that the thing that is "made" be brought to the place where it is wanted, and to the man or woman or child who wishes to have it, as that it be "made" at all.

Everybody recognizes this more or less. Everybody sees that to haul coal up from the depths of the mine, to transport coal from the mine to the city or wheat from the farm to the mill, is just as useful work, just as productive work, as it is to dig the coal in the mine or to raise the crop in the fields. But the work done by the merchant serves exactly the same kind of purpose. He watches the demands of his customers, and sees to it, as best he can, that the right goods and the right amount of them—neither too much nor too little—are on hand for the people that want them. Possibly there might be some better way of doing this. But the world has gone on for some thousands of years without discovering it; and the service of the merchant has been as necessary to the world as the service of anybody else engaged in the vast and complicated process of supplying civilized mankind with what it needs or desires. The transportation of goods and the selling of them are in reality just as truly productive—that is, they just as truly serve the purpose of enabling human beings to have their wants satisfied—as are the processes that people usually have in mind when they speak of "production." It is therefore important in our economic thinking to keep in mind the broader meaning which the word "production" includes.

CHAPTER IV

DEMAND AND SUPPLY

In the foregoing chapter we saw that, vast and complex as is the system of production, there are just four fundamental factors that enter into it—natural resources, labor, capital, and enterprise. But this tells us only what goes to *make up* the system, and nothing at all about what *controls* it. With millions of human beings engaged in hundreds of different forms of activity, is it a mere matter of luck and chance what particular form their activities shall take, how much of one thing or of another shall be made, how many persons shall be engaged in one pursuit or another? Or, on the other hand, is there some intelligible thing that dominates the whole system?

Such a thing there actually is. People are not *commanded* to be shoemakers or farm laborers, to produce so many shoes or so much corn or cotton; nor is there any ordinance that tells how much they shall be paid for what they do or for what they make. But all the time there is something which decides, not exactly but pretty nearly, how much of one thing or another shall be produced, and consequently how many persons shall be engaged in producing it; and it decides these questions by deciding what price shall be paid for it. This thing, which runs through and dominates the whole system of man's economic activity, is known as *demand and supply*, and is often spoken of as "the law of demand and supply."

What Makes Prices Go Up and Down

The way in which "the law of demand and supply" works is, in essence, extremely simple. When eggs are fifty cents a dozen, there are a certain number of eggs that people will buy at that price. Now, if the number of eggs that are actually produced for sale is greater than the number that people are able and willing to buy at fifty cents a dozen, some of the eggs will remain unsold; and, rather than not sell them at all, some of the producers will take a lower price. On the other hand, if the number of eggs produced is less than the number that people are willing and able to buy at fifty cents a dozen, some of these people will have to go without, and, rather than go without, some will pay a higher price.

What is true of eggs is, of course, in like manner true of commodities in general. Whenever the price of a commodity is not such that *the demand at that price will just take off the supply*, there is a force at work that will compel a change of price: when the demand is less than the supply, the price will fall; when the supply is less than the demand, the price will rise.

You will observe, by the way, that it is at the *margin* that the matter is determined: in the first case, there may be many *consumers* who would be willing to *give* the old price, and yet the price will fall if the whole of their demand is not sufficient to carry off the whole supply; in the second case there may be many *producers* who would be willing to *take* the old price, and yet the price will rise if the whole of their supply is not sufficient to satisfy the demand. And this thing that happens at the margin fixes the price all the way through, because in the case of any commodity that is widely and freely dealt in, buyers will not pay a higher price if the thing can be bought at a lower, and sellers will not take a lower price if the thing can be sold at a higher.

Of course none of this is literally true. Actually some buyers do pay more than others, and some sellers do get less than others. But critics who allow this circumstance to interfere with a clear recognition of the inevitable working of the law of supply and demand are not—as they may flatter themselves they are—more accurate than the economist; they are only less intelligent. The inequalities they insist upon do, indeed, exist; moreover, some time must pass before the adjustment of price so as to equalize demand and supply takes place at all. But the economist knows all this perfectly well. When either of these points is of sufficient importance to merit serious consideration, he endeavors to take proper account of it; but he does not let minor deviations interfere with his fixing his mind firmly upon the central fact which evidently dominates the situation as a whole. Furthermore, it should be noted that mere inequalities of price do not constitute even a deviation from the rule if they are of a permanent nature. One regularly expects to pay a higher price on Fifth Avenue than on Third Avenue; but the Fifth Avenue price and the Third Avenue price, each for itself, is subject to the law of demand and supply.

How Prices Regulate Production

So much for price. But how about the *quantity* of any commodity that shall be produced? Does the "law of demand and supply" regulate that also? It does; and it does it through its control of price. In producing a given article, the manufacturers, or farmers, or what not, are counting (at least approximately) on getting a certain price for it; if it turns out that the supply thus put on the market is greater than the demand, the price falls; and when the price falls there is (if nothing else has happened that affects the matter) less inducement than there was before to produce the article. Accordingly, some persons will find it unprofitable or undesirable to produce it, or to produce so much of it as they did before. And just as the production of a given commodity is diminished by a fall of price, so it is increased by a rise of price.

The adjustment of production, however, takes place with much more difficulty than that of price; and accordingly we ought to speak of it as a thing that *tends* to take place rather than as a thing that *actually* takes place. Yet it would be a mistake to stress this point overmuch; in the consideration of economic questions, what tends to take place is almost always of greater importance—not only theoretical but also practical importance—than what actually takes place. And this for two reasons. First, because usually our knowledge of tendencies is the only thing by which we can guide our conduct: we cannot predict results as a whole but we can predict what kind of influence a given cause will exert upon the result. And secondly, because a tendency, while it may for a time be frustrated, will usually produce its full effect in the long run; and it is with long-run effects that the economist and the statesman is, in general, most deeply concerned.

How Many Tailors and How Many Barbers?

Through its dominant effect on prices, the law of demand and supply controls not only the relative quantities of the various *commodities* that shall be produced, but also the relative number of *persons* that shall be engaged in the various occupations. But here an error of vital importance would be committed if one were to ignore the tremendous gulf that separates callings of one kind from those of another. This gulf sometimes consists in inherent differences between man and man; sometimes in the difficulty, expense, and other obstacles that attend entrance upon a calling. It is not open to every one to be a tenor or a movie star; Carusos and Charlie Chaplins are born, not made. But, to say no more about callings that require peculiar native endowment, the possibility of entering any of the higher professions or of starting a career in the higher walks of business is, in the case of the poor, so great as to shut out all but the few who are exceptionally gifted or exceptionally energetic. Accordingly when we speak of demand and supply as governing the choice of occupation, it must be clearly understood that this takes place, in the main, only *within the several classes* into which men are practically divided by ability or circumstance.

But within these limits the action of supply and demand, though slower than in the control of production—and far slower than in the control of prices—is steady and sure. An excess of workers in any occupation tends to lower the price paid for their services in the same way as an excess of a given commodity tends to lower its price; lowering of the pay in one occupation makes other occupations more attractive; and, though the process may be slow, yet there will be a drift either of actual workers or of fresh beginners away from the occupation in question. And of course the opposite effect will be produced by a deficiency of workers. The process is not instantaneous, but it is going on all the time; the adjustment is not accurate, but in the way of a rough approximation it is thoroughly effective. If you doubt it, ask yourself how it comes about that we don't have twice as many tailors as there is any occasion for, and half as many barbers as we need?

For a first view of the subject, this will perhaps suffice. Demand and supply we shall have always with us; and in subsequent chapters important aspects of it will come up that have to be left undealt with here. One final remark, however, seems necessary by way of warning. The "law of demand and supply" applies only where there is competition. Where there is monopoly (that is, where the whole, or almost the whole, supply of anything is controlled by one person or by a group of persons acting together) prices may be fixed at the pleasure of the monopolists, or according to what they think is their interest. In a sense, to be sure, the law holds even here; for they cannot sell *any quantity they please* at any price they please. But they may prefer to get an excessive price for a small product rather than get a reasonable price for a large product; and the price they fix may be very different from what it would be if there were competition—that is, if a large number of people were trying to sell the same product at the same time, thereby subjecting themselves to the operation of the usual law of demand and supply.

CHAPTER V

ILLUSTRATIONS OF DEMAND AND SUPPLY

As was said in the foregoing chapter, the way in which "the law of demand and supply" works is, in essence,[1] extremely simple. But we shall understand it better, and appreciate its significance more fully, if we examine a few important concrete illustrations.

The Price of Wheat "Fixed at Liverpool"

I have often thought that it must be extremely irritating to our farmers to be constantly told that the price of wheat or cotton is "fixed at Liverpool"; whenever any (real or pretended) friend of the farmer proposes a scheme for helping him to get a better price for his crop, up comes somebody with a fine loud voice and says it's no use because of this queer thing about Liverpool. But really there is nothing to get angry about. Liverpool is only another name for demand and supply; you might as well get angry at the Atlantic cable. And of

[1] I say "in essence," because, in the application of the law to specific instances, highly complex considerations often enter.

course intelligent farmers know this. The fact is simply that American farmers produce more wheat and cotton than the American people consume; the surplus is shipped abroad; the price that farmers get for what is sold at home cannot be higher than the price they get for what is shipped to Europe; and the price they get for what is shipped to Europe must be low enough for the supply to be taken up by the demand. Liverpool does not *make* the price any more than the barometer makes the weather. But it is a great seaport at which wheat and cotton are imported into Europe from America and elsewhere; and it has naturally become a great market for the sale of these things. The traders there keep accurately informed, every day, of the state of supply and demand the world over; and the price is bid up and bid down accordingly. The thing is not at all a jug-handled affair, fixed up to hurt the American farmer; the Liverpool price is just as sure to *rise* if the supply is less than the demand as it is to *fall* if the supply is greater than the demand.

Hoarding in Time of Abundance

One of the complexities about supply and demand is that the supply of any article that is offered for sale at a given time is not necessarily the whole amount of it that has been produced, or even the whole amount that has been produced for sale. When the supply is exceptionally abundant, so that the price is abnormally low, many of the producers or dealers may think it a good policy to hold back their part of the supply and keep it for sale at a future time when the conditions will be more favorable to the sellers. When a farmer does this with his crop, or with part of it, nobody finds fault with him. We all feel that he does none too well even in ordinary times, and that if he can protect himself against abnormally low prices it is a very good thing.

But it is a mistake to suppose that this policy is always a good one for him. It is essentially speculation, and is subject to the risks of speculation. Many people think that if the farmers could borrow all the money they want to enable them to hold on to their crops when crops are big and prices are low, they would be saved from the distress that low prices bring upon them. But that is a mistake. The farmer can't be *sure* that conditions will be more favorable to him the next season, or the next after that; and nobody can afford to pay interest indefinitely on borrowed money. Moreover, if a big rise in price were *sure* to come, the professional dealers in wheat or cotton would be eager to buy up the crop from the farmer in order to make the enormous profit which such a rise would put into their pockets; this eagerness would bid up the price to something pretty near the future price which was so sure to come. If the price is *not* so bid up, it is because the dealers know that there is great risk of their losing instead of gaining by doing so; and it is their particular business to estimate the degree of risk that is worth taking.

Hoarding in Time of Scarcity

But while holding back supply by farmers in time of exceptional *abundance* strikes most people as quite justifiable, holding back supply by professional dealers in time of exceptional *scarcity* is denounced by nearly everybody as the extreme of wickedness. And nearly everybody is mistaken. It is, indeed, very wrong to create an artificial scarcity by "cornering" the market—that is, by a single person or a combination of persons getting control of the whole (or nearly the whole) supply and dictating their own terms to a helpless public. But when individual dealers—or speculators—in the ordinary pursuit of their business think it will be profitable to them to hold on to a certain number of bushels of wheat or bales of cotton or tons of sugar because they know that the supply is short and judge that it will continue to be short, they are —speaking generally—doing a service to the public as well as to themselves. It is true that the price, already too high, may thereby be made still higher for the time being; but consider for a moment what will happen next. Nobody makes money by merely *not* selling things; it is only when he actually *does* sell them that he gets his profit. If the dealer—or speculator—who has been holding back his wheat or cotton actually *does* make a profit by so doing, it must be because the scarcity when he sells is even greater than it was when he bought. By putting his supply on the market at this time of greater scarcity he is doing more to relieve the public need, and more to keep prices from soaring up to intolerable heights, than he would have done if he had sold in the first place.

It is true that the dealer *may* be mistaken in his forecast. But he is under heavy bonds not to make such a mistake; for if he holds back his stock for a higher price and the supply turns out to be big instead of little, the price will go down instead of up, and he will not only make no profit, but will probably suffer a disastrous loss. And, curiously enough, the same "nearly everybody" above mentioned commits an error about hoarding by private individuals which is precisely the opposite of the error he commits about hoarding by dealers or speculators. He thinks it is perfectly innocent, in time of scarcity, for a person to hoard sugar, or coal, or flour, for his own future use, although he thinks it wicked for a dealer to do so for future sale. Exactly the reverse is true. When, shortly after the war, there was a great scarcity of sugar and it was selling at 20 and 25 cents a pound instead of 8 or 10, the scarcity was greatly aggravated by hundreds of thousands of persons selfishly putting away considerable stores of sugar for their own private use, for fear the price would go still higher. Nobody knows how many millions of pounds of sugar may have been hoarded in this way, which would otherwise have been in the market for sale and would have brought the price down to a more moderate figure. The people that did this did it in entire ignorance of the facts of sugar production, present or prospective; in providing for their own individual comfort they were not helping to fit future supply to future demand. Unlike the dealers and speculators, they ran no risk of serious loss in case they guessed wrong; in fact they did guess very wrong, and did a great deal of harm to the public. The calculations of dealers and speculators, in holding commodities out of the market at a time of actual or impending scarcity, are part of that great process of adjustment of supply and demand upon which the whole system of production depends for its satisfactory working; hoarding by private individuals in time of scarcity is a selfish act which aggravates the scarcity and is entirely without excuse from the standpoint of the general welfare.

Emergency Rent Laws

A peculiar, and extremely interesting, case of supply and demand is that which relates to houses. From the standpoint of owner and tenant—and in our cities that is the standpoint of chief interest—we must think of supply and demand of houses as a matter of houses offered for rent on the one hand and persons wishing to occupy them on the other. Now, unlike shoes, or clothing, or food, which are used up soon after they are first produced, houses last many years; and the supply of houses at a given time consists of a great number that have been in existence for many years and a comparatively small number that are built from year to year to satisfy the fresh demand. But before a man decides to build a new house for rent he must take into account not only the rent the house is likely to command this year, or even the next few years, but the rent it is likely to command for twenty or thirty years, or perhaps longer. And this goes far towards explaining why the tremendous demand for houses, just after the war, though it drove rents up very high, did not result in causing a very great number of houses to be built to satisfy the demand. The cost of building (as measured in dollars) had risen tremendously, but that does not of itself explain the matter. The cost of making shoes had also risen tremendously, but there was no great scarcity of shoes; and this was because if it cost twice as much to make a shoe, the shoe was sold for twice as much, and that was the end of the matter. But if it cost twice as much to build a house and the landlord got twice as much rent for it, that was *not* the end of the matter; to make his investment profitable, he would have to have assurance that he would keep on getting twice as much rent for many years to come. This was the chief cause (though there were others, of course) of the housing problem that nearly all of our cities found so trying. And the difficulty was not relieved, but on the contrary was aggravated, by the emergency rent laws, which kept landlords from raising their rents beyond a certain amount. If landlords had been allowed to charge any rent they could get, and had felt sure they would not be interfered with by any restrictive laws, the very high rents that would have resulted would have encouraged a lot of people to build for the sake of the abnormal profits of the first few years, in spite of the fall of rents they would have to expect afterwards. It does not follow that the emergency rent laws were wrong; perhaps it was worth while to endure the scarcity of houses somewhat longer, rather than have the tenants suffer the hardships that unrestricted rents would have caused. The whole subject is too intricate to discuss here; there are many aspects of it that I cannot touch upon. But, whatever else there was in the case, this peculiarity about the demand and supply of houses was the central fact in the whole case; and for want of an intelligent grasp of it by Legislatures and by the public there was a great deal of disastrous floundering in dealing with the problem.

CHAPTER VI

VALUE

In the foregoing chapters, the word *value* has not appeared; "Demand and Supply" has been spoken of throughout as bearing upon *price*, which is the amount of *money* that is obtained for a given commodity or a given service. But if a yard of cloth sells for four dollars and a barrel of flour for eight dollars, the really significant point is that a barrel of flour sells for twice as much as a yard of cloth; and likewise for any two things, or any number of things, which we may compare with one another. What we are really after when we *get* the dollars is not the dollars themselves, but the things that can be bought with the dollars; what we really give up when we *spend* the dollars is not the dollars themselves, but the things which, at some past time, were given for the dollars.

In other words, buying and selling (including the buying and selling of services as well as of commodities) is at bottom barter. The use of money is a convenience of boundless importance; without it the interchange of commodities and services would be so clumsy, so difficult, so expensive, and so impossible to reduce to any kind of simplicity, that anything like the existing development of production would be utterly out of the question. And yet, while the *form* of barter is done away with, the *essence* of barter remains. On the surface, we exchange one thing for money, and exchange the money for another thing; at bottom, we exchange the things for one another. Money is indispensable in practice, and price is often the most convenient thing to talk about in theoretical discussion; but many deplorable errors are caused by the habit of thinking in terms of price, or money, when we ought to be thinking in terms of something more fundamental.

What Economists Mean by "Value"

By the *value* of anything we mean, in economic discussion, the capacity of that thing to command other things in exchange. But the idea is not easy to grasp with precision; indeed the definition is on its face vague; it requires explanation. We mean by value something not absolute, but relative. For example, in the case of flour and cloth, above referred to, we cannot say what the value of the flour is or what the value of the cloth is; but we *can* say that the value of a barrel of flour is twice the value of a yard of cloth. And so in general the *ratio* in which two things exchange for each other is their *relative value;* and it is only relative value that we undertake to say anything about when, in any economic discussion, we use the word value.

Now you may reasonably ask what object there is in introducing this somewhat difficult and somewhat slippery notion of *value* when the simple and familiar idea of *price* would suffice to cover the ground. Practically (you may well say) the only way we get at values is through prices; we don't exchange things for one another but for money; the value of one thing is twice the value of another when the price of the first is twice the price of the second.

"Value" and "Price"

All this is perfectly true; and the reason we nevertheless introduce the idea of value, as distinguished from price, is that it puts us in touch with something more fundamental than price, more fundamental than money. Supply and demand work out their results through the *medium* of money; but the vital thing which they determine is not the ratio in which various things exchange for *dollars*, but the ratio in which they exchange for *one another*. If all *prices* were doubled, all *values* (except the value of the dollar itself) would remain unchanged. You would get eight dollars instead of four for a yard of cloth and sixteen dollars instead of eight for a barrel of flour; but you would still get, as before, two yards of cloth for one barrel of flour. The *price* of a day's labor would be, say, six dollars instead of three, but its *value* would remain unchanged; the worker would get the same amount of bread and meat and clothing for his wages as he did before, neither more nor less.

Thus we see, to begin with, that value is more fundamental in its *significance* for people in general than is price; but this is not all that is to be said. Value is also more fundamental as a *cause* than price is. The *price* of a barrel of flour and the *price* of a yard of cloth—the number of dollars for which they will sell—are determined in part by the conditions affecting the production of cloth and of flour and people's desire for cloth and for flour, but also in part by conditions affecting the general purchasing power of *money;* and so for any two things we wish to compare. But the conditions that *underlie the supply and demand* of various things have essentially nothing to do with money; money is only the mechanism through which they work. The scarcity or abundance of things, the ease or difficulty with which they can be produced, the habits and desires of consumers in regard to the things—these are the forces that really determine supply and demand, and these have nothing to do with money. It is these underlying factors that cause the *value* of a barrel of flour to be twice that of a yard of cloth; given the same underlying factors a barrel of flour would exchange for two yards of cloth, whatever figures might represent the *price* of either.

Something has been said about these underlying factors in the preceding chapter; but it will be well to take another glance at them at this point.

Normal Value

Economists are in the habit of distinguishing between *market value* and *normal value;* market value being the value at any particular moment, as shown by the prices ruling at the moment, and normal value being a somewhat indefinite thing to which the market value tends to conform. Conditions may be such at a given moment that the value of a given thing is higher (or lower) than one would naturally expect, as compared with the values of other things, and we all feel that this won't continue very long—that the value is abnormal, that there is a normal value towards which it will gravitate. In these last few years, when everything has been upset by the upheaval of the greatest war in history, that feeling is not so strong as it used to be; but in normal times there is a fairly definite feeling about normal values.

Now, what basis is there for that feeling? The "man in the street" has the feeling as well as the economist; but the man in the street can give no reason for having it. The normal value, to him, is simply the value (or price) which he has been accustomed to; any other value is abnormal simply because it is unusual.

Normal Value Proportional to Cost of Production

But the economist—whose business it is to look into the causes of things—regards a certain value as normal not because it is *usual* but because any departure from it, up or down, *tends to be corrected* by causes that he can name. If, of two commodities, the price of one bears a larger proportion to the cost of producing it than does that of the other, those who control or direct capital and labor will have an inducement to put more into making the first and less into making the second. The supply of the first will be increased, that of the second diminished; accordingly, the price of the first will be lowered, that of the second raised. The normal values of various things are the values which this process tends to bring about; evidently, therefore, the normal values of things are *proportional to their cost of production.*

This statement, like all such statements in Political Economy, is open to the criticism that you can't be sure that the normal value is ever actually attained at all; and also to the criticism that even ideally the normal value is a very slippery thing because methods of production, and therefore costs of production, are continually changing. But these criticisms are trivial; nobody disputes their correctness, but they are of no importance. There is, however, a point of cardinal importance which must be noted if the statement is to have either theoretical accuracy or practical value.

Cost of Production not Uniform

The cost of production of anything not only *changes with time*, but in the case of most things is very far from uniform *at a given time.* For the cost of producing a thing depends—and in the case of some things, depends in a tremendous degree—upon the *natural advantages* under which it is produced; and the cost also depends on the degree of *skill and business ability* applied, which may vary almost as much as the natural advantages. Some coal is got near the surface of the earth, while some has to be got by deep shafts and tunnels; one mill may be run by water power which costs nothing, another may be run by steam power; one farm may require little or no fertilizer, another may need great expense to make or keep the soil fertile. Also, one factory may be run by a rare industrial genius, another by a mere plodder; one concern may be conducted with extraordinary business acumen, another in routine fashion. Now is it the *average* cost of production of an article that regulates its normal value? Obviously not. It is at the *margin* that the adjustment of supply to cost of production is effected. If the price falls so low that the production which is carried on under the least favorable conditions *doesn't pay*, the supply will be diminished because that part of the production will be abandoned; if the price rises so high that even the part produced under the least favorable conditions *more than pays*, the supply will be increased. Accordingly, when we say that the normal value of a thing is proportional to its cost of production, we must be understood to mean the *cost of production of that part which is produced under the least favorable conditions*. If we have to go down 1,000 feet for some of our supply of coal, the price of coal will have to cover that part, even though *some* coal is got by just scratching the earth. If Mr. Ford can turn out a certain automobile at $200, but other people can't turn it out so economically; if some of them can only turn it out at $250, some at $275, some at $300, and *if the demand is great enough to cover the whole output of all these manufacturers;* then Mr. Ford's automobiles, and those of all the intermediate people, will sell—or at least can sell—for $300. The normal value of the coal, the normal value of the automobile, is fixed by the cost of production of that part of the supply which is produced under the least favorable conditions.

This may strike you as hard lines for the buyer. But when we look at the matter from the demand side instead of the supply side, we notice a thing of the opposite kind. It is true that the price must be *high* enough to fit the *most costly* part of the supply; but it must also be *low* enough to fit the *least urgent* part of the demand. Producers whose cost of production of the thing is low *get* more than what they would, if necessary, be willing to take; but consumers whose desire for the thing is great *pay* less than what they would, if necessary, be willing to give.

CHAPTER VII

MONEY COST AND REAL COST

One of the chief difficulties about Economics is the difficulty of bearing in mind the real meaning of the words we use. You might think that this difficulty would be completely overcome by the writer of any work on Economics if he would state, in the shape of a formal definition, the exact meaning of every important term as he intends it to be understood. Many very able writers have pursued this plan, but their success in removing the difficulty has been far from complete.

We have seen that the normal value of any commodity is proportional to its cost of production.[1] In showing that this is so, we had reference to the *money cost*—the number of dollars that are expended in producing the thing; and in fact the truth of this proposition is so nearly self-evident that it was almost unnecessary to prove it by any argument.

[1] The cost of production of that part which is produced under the least favorable conditions; but for the sake of brevity we shall suppose this qualification understood, and not keep everlastingly repeating it.

Real Cost Consists of Services

But the real cost of producing anything is not the money that is laid out but the services for which that money is paid. First and foremost, there is the service rendered by labor, both hand-work and brain-work; secondly, and in most cases just as essential, there is the service rendered by capital. To produce a yard of cloth, or a ton of steel, or a steam engine, or a skyscraper building, a certain amount of work on the part of unskilled laborers, skilled laborers, and professional experts is necessary, and also a certain amount of capital has to be provided for the purpose and used for a certain length of time. Now the proposition that the value of various things is proportional to their cost of production in terms of *money* is extremely simple and almost self-evident; but we have still to examine the relation between cost of production in terms of money and cost of production in terms of services.

The Service of Capital

We will look first at the service of capital, because the case of capital is much simpler than the case of labor, as we shall see. The person that furnishes capital finds no very great difficulty in putting it to whatever use seems most profitable. It is true that capital is not money, but buildings, and machinery, and raw material, and whatever is necessary to maintain the workers while the process of production is going on. But these things are constantly being used up and replenished, and it is through the agency of money that this process is carried on. The man that supplies the capital with which to build or enlarge a factory, or with which to equip it with proper machinery, or with which to pay its running expenses until the goods it produces are completed and sold, provides all these things through the expenditure of money; and he can devote that money to supplying the capital for one purpose or another as he sees fit. Now if the returns on capital in one industry were much higher than the returns on capital in another industry, capital would tend to flow into the first and drift away from the second; and this process would be a very rapid one. The service of a given amount of capital for a given length of time will therefore, as a rule, command about the same return whether the capital be applied to one purpose or to another.

The Service of Labor

But when we come to labor, we have quite a different state of things. Those who furnish the service of labor are not free to choose in the same way as those who furnish the service of capital.

In the first place a man who has learned to do, or has become accustomed to doing, a certain kind of work cannot easily change to another kind, even though that other kind be not in itself more difficult. This, however, is a minor matter; it only makes the adjustment slow. If carpenters received three times as big wages as bricklayers, then[1] so many young men would go into carpentering and so few into bricklaying that the inequality would before very long disappear.

Different Grades of Workers

But there are inequalities in the compensation of different kinds of work which are so deeply rooted that they cannot be removed in any such way. Not all callings are open to everybody. Not everybody has the ability to be a lawyer, or a physician, or a mechanical engineer, or a skilled artisan, or the director of a factory, or the manager of a business concern; and not everybody who does have such ability has command of the time and money necessary to develop it. Accordingly, the population is practically divided into what may be called *grades* or classes. *Within each grade* there is a fairly close approach to freedom of choice of occupation, which leads, as we have seen, to something like equal pay for an equal quantity of work —with due allowance, too, for the hardship or disagreeableness of the work. But as *between one grade and another*, things remain as they may happen to be; there is no steadily working cause that tends to remove inequalities. The pay of a skilled mechanic may continue, year after year, and

[1] I am not taking account of obstacles caused by trade-union control; in this matter, as in all our discussions, we have to understand that if any person, or any body of persons, can maintain a monopoly—can keep other people out of their field—gross inequalities may persist indefinitely.

decade after decade, three times that of a drayman or a miner; the earnings of a competent lawyer or consulting engineer may likewise be three times that of a skilled mechanic; for there is no effective competition between the people who belong respectively to the grade of the unskilled workman, the skilled workman, and the professional man.

Compensation Depends on Scarcity

It would be a great mistake to suppose that these inequalities correspond in any way to the *merit*, or the *difficulty*, or *any inherent quality*, of the work in question. A chemist or a mechanical engineer gets ten times as much pay as a ditch digger or an elevator man, not because the chemist's or engineer's work is more meritorious, or more difficult—and certainly not because it is more disagreeable—but simply because there are comparatively few persons who can be had for the chemist's or engineer's job, and a great many who can be had for the digging of ditches or the running of elevators. It may require a thousand times as much ability to do the chemist's or the engineer's or the lawyer's work as it does to do the elevator man's; but *if everybody had that ability* the chemist and the engineer and the lawyer would get less pay than the elevator man, because nearly everybody would rather have their job than that of the elevator man. So the rates of pay that are current in one grade, as compared with another, depend on the demand for the services furnished by that grade taken as a whole and the available supply of these services; and so long as the general conditions of life remain substantially unchanged, very great inequalities between the grades will remain undisturbed.

The Case of the Servant Girl

An interesting exhibit of the actual state of things is to be seen in the remarkable change that has taken place in the wages of servant girls. Twenty or thirty years ago, in most of our cities, ten dollars a month was considered a good wage for a servant girl. If you had asked almost any mistress of a household why the servant girl got that and not a great deal more, she would have been almost sure to reply that it was because that kind of work was worth no more. Yet the same people are now paying forty, fifty, or sixty dollars a month (which, after allowing for the lowered purchasing power of the dollar, is still two or three times as high as the old wages), and the girls are working shorter hours and on better conditions. Surely this is not because the servant girls of today have more skill than of old; indeed, quite the contrary is the case. It is solely because servant girls are *more scarce* than they were; this itself being of course due to various causes, and especially to the opening of so many new opportunities for women's work.

Cost of Living

We must now leave this subject of cost of production, though it has been covered very imperfectly. But it will, I think, be useful at this point to say a few words about a subject which has filled people's minds to an extraordinary degree during the past ten years and more—"the cost of living." A vast amount of confusion, and a great deal of mischief, would have been averted if people, in talking about this subject, had kept in mind the distinction between money cost and real cost. If the price of everything had been doubled, and if at the same time all wages and salaries had been doubled, the real cost of living for wage-earners and salaried people would not have risen at all. In a way, everybody knows this; but many people don't think of it, and many who do think of it don't bear it steadily in mind. Multitudes of people actually thought, a few years ago, that living had been made harder for *everybody* by the high prices. Unfortunately it was only too true that it *was* made harder for millions of persons, because their incomes did not rise along with the prices; and it was, of course, no consolation to these persons to know that while *they* were suffering undeserved hardship through the high prices, *others* were enjoying undeserved good fortune through the same cause. But *real costs* had not risen; it did not take more labor, or more skill, or more machinery, or more of any other agency, to produce things than it did before. The adjustment of compensation had been frightfully disarranged; but if the fundamental conditions remained the same as before, then although the level of prices continued high, a readjustment was bound to take place which would restore things to something like their old relations.[1] An increase in the *real* cost of living is brought about, not by a rise of prices, but by an increase in the actual physical difficulty of obtaining things. Exhaustion of the soil, the using up of our resources of coal or timber, the necessity of getting supplies from a greater distance—such are the things that increase the real cost of living; and on the other hand the progress of science and invention, improved facilities of transportation, greater intelligence in our social and industrial arrangements diminish the real cost of living. An increase in the *money* cost of living is a very serious evil; but the evil tends to remedy itself. If the *real* cost of living had doubled as the money cost did, there would be reason for far more serious misgiving and lamentation.

[1] This does not apply to people with fixed incomes from bonds, annuities, or the like. Their revenue is so and so many dollars; and if a dollar buys only half as much as before, it means a dead loss, with nothing to check it.

CHAPTER VIII

MONEY

In all this talk about demand and supply, and value, we have been taking certain familiar facts for granted. A formal textbook, however simple, would naturally begin with a systematic account of these facts. But this little book is designed to be rather a series of plain talks than a textbook.

Separation of Employments

Above all, we have taken for granted the familiar but all-important fact of the *separation of employments*. People do not satisfy their needs by each one producing what he himself wants, but by each one producing, or helping to produce, some particular thing and obtaining all the things that he wants through the exchange of that thing for other things.

In the present advanced stage of civilization, what actually happens is, indeed, far more complex than this in form, but in essence this is what it is.

The worker in a woolen mill does not take a certain number of yards of cloth corresponding to his share in the making of it, and exchange it for other things; but his wages do in reality represent a certain number of yards of cloth, for it is out of the sale of that cloth that his wages are paid. In a much earlier stage of civilization we may conceive that each person made the whole of something and exchanged it for the various things which he needed for his own consumption. Even in this simple form an enormous advantage for everybody arose from the separation of employments; for it requires but little imagination to see how great an economy of time, and how vast an increase of skill, came from people devoting themselves each to some particular branch of production.

Difficulties of Barter

But it also takes very little imagination to see how difficult it must have been for people to exchange their products, one with another. If a man who made hats and wanted a pair of shoes had to look up a shoemaker who wanted one of his hats, he would have a hard time finding his man; and when he did find him it would be very difficult for them to arrange the terms of their bargain. And so on all round. Barter in the simple form indicated by this illustration was probably never carried on upon any large scale; the separation of employments never could have attained anything like its actual development if some means had not been found to get rid of the difficulties of barter.

The means by which the difficulty is overcome is *money;* and there are few things in the history of mankind more interesting, or more remarkable, than the universal use of money for this purpose. Necessity, says the old adage, is the mother of invention; and the fact that all kinds of people, having no relation to each other, have hit upon this same device of money is the best possible evidence of its supreme necessity as a means of effecting exchanges of all kinds of articles without resorting to barter.

What is Money?

But what *is* money? It is some one thing which everybody *takes* for what he has produced, and which in turn he *gives* for the things that he himself wishes to possess. Now money was not created by any act of government. People were not *compelled* to exchange things for money. Some particular thing came to play this remarkable part through inherent qualities which fitted it for the purpose. People voluntarily took money in exchange for what they had produced, because they were certain that they would have no difficulty in finding other people who would in turn take it for what *they* had produced. But how did this come about? How is it that some one thing took precedence of everything else in this respect? Let us see what qualities a thing must have in order that this should happen.

How Gold and Silver Came to be the World's Money

Imagine, to begin with, a thing that is *very widely desired* for its own sake: this fact will of itself have a strong tendency to cause it to be *universally desired*—desired just about as much by those who do not care for it for its own sake as by those who do: because if multitudes of all sorts of people *do* care for it for its own sake, it becomes comparatively easy for anybody to exchange it for whatever else he may wish to have.

However, this of itself is far from enough to cause the thing to play the part that money has played in the world. But suppose that besides being very widely desired, the thing is practically *imperishable;* that it contains much value in little bulk, and is therefore *easily transported;* that it is of perfectly *uniform quality*, so that no peculiarity of taste has to be consulted in disposing of it; and finally that it is capable of *exact division* into as small parts as one pleases. Obviously anything that has all four of these attributes would be wonderfully fit to serve as a medium of exchange. The person who had it could keep it as long as it suited his convenience; he could easily take it, or send it, to any place where it was wanted; he would not have to persuade the person to whom he offered it that it was of just the kind which that person desired; and he could use a little of it here and much of it there, just as the occasion might demand. For such a thing as this, anybody would be glad to exchange what he had produced, knowing well that he would have no difficulty in passing it on to other persons, each of whom would feel that *he* could pass it on likewise.

There are other things besides gold and silver which have some or all of these attributes to some degree, but there is nothing which has them *all* to anything like the degree in which they are possessed by gold and silver. And it is for this reason that gold and silver have been used as money by civilized people since the dawn of history. They were desired primarily for ornament and the display of luxury; this desire for them was widely enough entertained to satisfy the requirement first above mentioned; and they were so incomparably superior to anything else in the other four respects enumerated that in almost every country in the world one or the other of them came to be used as money—the thing *for* which everything else was sold, the thing *with* which everything else was bought.

Money not only the Medium of Exchange, but also the Measure of Value

Money, as was stated above, is some one thing which everybody *takes* for what he has produced, and which he in turn *gives* for the things he wishes to possess. If it did nothing but this—if it played no other part than that of a *medium of exchange*—it would still be of incalculable service to mankind. For it would overcome one of the two chief difficulties of barter, the difficulty of finding a person who wants to buy just what *you* want to sell, and at the same time wants to sell just what *you* want to buy.

But the other prime difficulty of barter is to agree upon the terms of the bargain. How many yards of cloth shall I give for a barrel of flour, or a hundred pounds of sugar, or a pair of shoes? At what ratio shall *any* two things exchange for each other? In other words, what, at any given time, is the *market value* of any one thing as compared with any other? And what are the *normal values* of the various things—the values toward which they may be expected to tend, in view not merely of the immediate state of demand and supply, but of underlying conditions? Obviously these questions would involve such complexity as to make any answer to them almost impossible, if we had to compare everything with everything else; but that complexity disappears if, instead of comparing everything with everything else, it becomes the universal practice to compare everything with some one thing.

And if some one thing is constantly used as the *medium of exchange*—if everything else is sold *for* that thing and everything else is bought *with* that thing—that thing is automatically used as the means of comparison; in other words, it becomes the *measure of value*. Nobody has to keep thinking of the relative values of cloth and flour and sugar and shoes; all that he has to keep track of in the case of each one of these things is the *price*, the amount of *money* for which it sells. We get at the value, not by directly dealing with all that multitude of ratios but by using the *price* of each thing as the *representative* of its value. We do not ask how many yards of cloth will exchange for a barrel of flour; but if a yard of cloth sells for four dollars and a barrel of flour for eight, two yards of cloth will exchange for one barrel of flour. And so in general: the value of anything is represented by its price; to know the relative values of any two things it is only necessary to compare their prices.

Thus we see that, through its use as a medium of exchange and as a measure of value, money brings about an infinite simplification of the process of exchanging things—services as well as commodities—for one another. That wonderful system of production and distribution with which we are as familiar as with the air we breathe would be impossible without it. From the time the child buys his first toy or his first stick of candy, the use of money as a medium of exchange and as a measure of value seems as natural to him as breathing. But in reality it is one of those devices of mankind whose workings, if we were not so familiar with them, would seem little short of miraculous. Of these devices, infinitely the most important is language; next after that comes the art of writing; and it is perhaps not going too far to assign to the use of money a place inferior only to these two in its marvellous consequences.

CHAPTER IX

PRICES

In the chapter on value, much was said about the difference between value and price. By the *value* of anything we mean the capacity of that thing to command other things in exchange; the *price* of the thing is the amount of *money* which can be got for it.

Obviously, however, price is itself an instance of value. The price of anything measures its value in comparison with money, and likewise measures the value of money in comparison with it. To say that the *prices* of all things are doubled is the same as to say that the *value of money* (its value in comparison with anything else) is halved; to say that the *prices* of all things are halved is the same as to say that the *value of money* is doubled. And so in general: a rise (or fall) of all prices is a fall (or rise), in the same degree, of the value of money.

The Price-Level

In actual fact, however, prices never rise (or fall) in this uniform way; some rise (or fall) more than others, and usually some rise while others fall. Accordingly, we look to the *average of all prices*[1] as the measure of the value of money. When that average rises—or, as it is often expressed, when the *price-level* rises—we say that the value of money has fallen; when the price-level falls, we say that the value of money has risen. What it is that determines the price-level—that causes it to be high or low, that makes it rise or fall—is one of the most difficult and intricate questions in Economics. It cannot be discussed thoroughly in this little book; yet I think we may find it possible to understand it in its essentials.

Value of Money and Value of Gold

Let us begin by reducing the question to the utmost simplicity of which it is capable. Let us suppose that all the money in use in our own country and in all the countries with which it has commercial dealings consists of gold coins; that in all these countries anybody who has gold can take it to the mint to be coined without charge, so that he gets back in the shape of coin precisely the same amount of gold which he handed in to the mint; and finally that all these countries permit the free exportation and importation of gold, both coined and uncoined.

[1] What we mean by the average of all prices is a somewhat complicated thing to define exactly, and I cannot go into it further here; but the general nature of such an average is obvious.

The first, and in a sense the most important, conclusion that can be drawn in this state of things is that the value of a coin is precisely the same as the value of the gold which it contains, neither more nor less. A gold dollar contains 25.8 grains of gold, nine-tenths fine (i.e., 23.22 grains of pure gold); and a gold dollar will buy just as much of other things as 25.8 grains of uncoined gold will buy, neither more nor less. And the same is true, of course, of the coins of other countries. A pound sterling contains 4.86 (strictly 4.8665) times as much pure gold as a gold dollar does; and it follows that a pound sterling will exchange for 4.86 dollars. A franc contains .193 times as much gold as a dollar does, and it follows that a franc exchanges for 19.3 cents.[1]

All this is important, but it is so simple as to be self-evident. Very different is the question of the relation that the dollar bears, not to uncoined gold, nor to the gold coins of other countries, but to *things in general*, and this difficult question we must now look into.

Value of Money and Cost of Production of Gold

If a barrel of flour normally sells for twice as much as a yard of cloth, this is because the cost of

[1] The slight variation from these ratios which takes place, owing to the expense and delay of transporting gold from one country to another, is here ignored. This variation may be either up or down, according as the gold is more urgently demanded in our own or in the foreign country.

production of the flour is twice that of the cloth; but why do the cloth and the flour sell for eight dollars and four dollars, rather than eighty dollars and forty dollars, or eighty cents and forty cents? Has cost of production anything to do with that? It has. Gold is itself constantly being produced by mining and by the processes of metallurgy; and its production requires the application of labor and capital just as does the production of iron or steel or wheat or bread or cloth. The value of the dollar is the same as that of 25.8 grains of uncoined gold, nine-tenths fine; and the normal value of the uncoined gold is, like that of any other commodity, proportional to its cost of production. If the normal price of a barrel of flour is eight dollars, this is because the cost of production of the gold that goes into eight gold dollars is the same as the cost of production of a barrel of flour.

Here, however, we must pay the most careful attention to that understanding about the cost of production which, for the sake of brevity, we often omit to mention. The value of gold is determined not by its cost of production *in general*, not by its *average cost* of production, but by the cost of production of *the part that is produced under the most unfavorable conditions;* and in the case of gold this consideration is of the utmost importance. If prices rise—if you can get *less* of things in general for a given number of dollars, and therefore for a given amount of gold—it will no longer pay to produce gold under the worst conditions under which it *did* pay to produce gold before; the least remunerative mines will be abandoned, because the gold got out of them will not suffice to cover the expense of keeping them in operation.[1]

Thus we see that there is a correspondence between the price-level and the cost of production of gold, i.e., the cost of production of gold where the cost is greatest; or to use a most convenient term, the cost at the *margin*. But it would be misleading to say simply that the cost of production at the margin *determines the price-level;* for, while this is true, it is equally true (as appears from what has just been said) that *the price-level determines* where the margin shall be.

General Purchasing Power of Money

So far, there is nothing really peculiar about the matter. The price-level represents the *general purchasing power* of the dollar, or in other words, represents the value of the dollar, and therefore the value of the gold in the dollar; and what has thus far been said amounts essentially to the

[1] This fact, which has always been pointed out in economic theory, has recently been brought out practically in a most striking way. When prices went up so enormously a few years ago, the people interested in some of the gold mines tried to get Congress to give them a bonus to enable them to keep on working the mines. It would have been wrong (for plenty of reasons) to grant the bonus; but the assertion that it didn't pay to work the mines without it was quite correct. Now why didn't it pay, when it had paid before? The mines were no harder to work, they were no more remote from markets, and gold had not fallen out of use; but *prices* of all kinds had risen, and therefore the same amount of gold could no longer pay for the labor, materials, machines, etc., necessary to produce it *at those mines*.

statement that the value of gold corresponds to its cost of production in the same way as does the value of anything else. But in the case of money, there is *another correspondence* much more important, much more far-reaching in its consequences, and the like of which does not exist in regard to commodities. The gold in the dollar is, to be sure, itself a commodity; but, besides being a commodity, the dollar is something else. In the case of a barrel of flour, or a yard of cloth, or a pair of shoes, or an automobile, the demand for it turns entirely on the desire of people to possess that particular thing; and that desire is distinctly limited by the specific use to which it can be put. The same is true of *gold as a commodity*—as a thing to be made into watches or rings or tooth-fillings or pens or gilding; but in the passing of *money* from hand to hand the consideration of the uses to which the gold that it contains may be put does not enter at all. What people value *money* for is solely its power to command other things in exchange. They prize it not for itself, but for what it can buy; and if they save it, instead of spending it at once, they save it for the sake of its capacity to buy things in the future. In a modern country like ours, moreover, the amount of sheer hoarding that is done is a small matter; people who save money do not keep it in a stocking or a strong-box, but deposit it in banks or invest it in securities. And the people to whom they thus entrust it—banks, railroad corporations, governments, or what not—purchase things for the money, or lend it to still others who do so. A certain amount of money is, however, held on to by nearly everybody; the shopkeeper holds a certain amount in his till, the private individual keeps some on hand in the house or in the shape of a checking account at the bank, the bank itself has to keep a certain amount as a reserve so as to be fully prepared to meet all demands which there is any likelihood of being made by its depositors.

The Quantity Theory of Money

Now in any country, at any time, there exists a definite condition of things as to the extent and kind of its industry and commerce, the habits of its people in the transaction of business, the extent to which credit is resorted to, the ratio of the amount of money which people feel it necessary to have immediately accessible as compared with the whole amount of their possessions or the magnitude of their business—in a word, there exists a certain condition as to all those institutions and habits which determine what is called the rapidity of circulation of money, and the proportion of the amount of money that lies idle to the amount that circulates. These characteristics of the nation being given, it will require a certain *definite amount of money* to carry on the business of the country at *a given scale of prices;* and if that scale of prices be raised or lowered, the amount of money required to do that business will be greater or less in the same proportion. If, then, the aggregate amount of money in the country is increased or diminished, prices will rise or fall correspondingly.

While one readily sees, in a general way, that this must somehow be so, it is not quite obvious how the adjustment is brought about. Let us suppose, then, a given scale of prices to exist, and the amount of money in the country to be such as that scale of prices requires; and then let us suppose an increase of 20 per cent. in the amount of money. It is evident that, on the old scale of prices, some of the money will not be required either for the transaction of business or for the keeping up of the usual reserves, whether in banks or strong-boxes or lying loose in people's pockets. This surplus idle money will seek a use. And it can find no use except in the purchase of things of one kind or another. The pressure of this new supply of money seeking a use will raise prices—possibly in a very irregular manner, but still will raise them. This process will continue until the level of prices, taken as a whole, will be raised by an amount sufficient to make use for all the money that has now become current; and this will not happen until the general level of prices has been raised by 20 per cent.

I must remind the reader that we have, in this chapter, been discussing prices on the supposition that there is only one kind of money—gold coin; and upon that simplest supposition we have arrived at what is known as *the quantity theory of money:* Given the nature and extent of a nation's industries, and the business methods and habits of its people, the *value of money* in that country varies inversely as its *quantity;* in other words, an increase or decrease of the quantity of money in any proportion involves a rise or fall of prices in the same proportion.

CHAPTER X

GOLD, PAPER, CREDIT

I AM afraid that the foregoing chapter has been a little difficult, even though it simplified the problem of money by assuming that there was only one kind of money, namely gold coin. Nevertheless, we must go into still deeper water before leaving the subject of money, after which we shall again take up subjects of a less intricate character.

Other Things Than Coin That Play the Part of Money

To understand, even in an elementary way, the problem of money and prices, as it exists in the modern world, it is essential to take account of other things than gold which play the part of money. And I do not refer to a different commodity, such as silver, which may serve as money in a silver-standard country in precisely the same way that gold does in a gold-standard country. For simplicity, we are going to assume throughout that, in the countries we are dealing with, there is only one substance out of which the standard money of the country is coined. But we are going to consider the various devices by means of which transactions that call for the transfer of money are effected without the use of actual coin.

By means of these devices a given quantity of gold in a country is made to suffice for the transaction of a vastly greater volume of business, upon a given scale of prices, than would be the case without them. The existence and development of these devices, therefore, operates to raise prices just as an increase in the stock of gold money would do: if, for example, a given amount of gold money can, in consequence of these devices, effect the transaction of three times as much business as it could effect without them, the price-level will be three times as high as it would be if such devices did not exist.

Paper Money

The simplest of the additions to the stock of gold money is what is generally known as "paper money"—notes, issued by the government or by banks, which circulate as money. In this country we have become so familiar with paper money that most people never think at all of the gold for which it is a substitute. It is all the more desirable, therefore, that we should understand its real character and the functions which it performs.

There is one kind of paper money that is not really an addition to the stock of gold money at all, but merely a convenience. This is the gold certificate. A ten-dollar or hundred-dollar gold certificate is a piece of paper which simply *represents* ten gold dollars or a hundred gold dollars that have actually been deposited in the United States Treasury and which are retained there in full, ready to be handed over to any person who presents the certificate. The certificate is more convenient to handle, and in that way facilitates business; but it is not a real addition to the volume of money circulating in the country.

Notes Redeemable in Gold

Very different is the case of notes—whether issued by the government or by banks—which are *redeemable* in gold on demand and yet against which an equal amount of gold money is not actually kept on hand for the purpose of redemption. Experience shows that keeping a comparatively small percentage of the aggregate value of the notes as a *reserve* for their redemption is quite sufficient to assure all holders that they can get gold for their notes if they wish; and accordingly, so long as the honesty of the government and the banks is unquestioned, a given volume of gold dollars can be made the basis of the circulation of notes for several times that number of dollars, which are regarded by everybody as being for all ordinary purposes just as good as gold.

Irredeemable Paper Money

Of a totally different nature is the issue of paper money which is not redeemable in gold—either because no promise to that effect is made in the note or because the government or the banks fail to keep their promise. Important as a discussion of such paper money is, especially in view of the frightful experiences of European countries since the Great War, we must forgo any close consideration of it here. Two things, however, must be obvious to any one who will apply the reasoning in the last chapter which led to the "quantity theory of money." First, that if irredeemable paper money is to circulate on a parity with gold—in other words so that a paper dollar will buy just as much as a gold dollar—the quantity of that paper money must be limited. Secondly, that after you pass the limit of quantity (whatever that may be) at which the irredeemable paper money will circulate on a parity with gold, there is nothing to prevent its value from sinking to any conceivable depth if more and more of it is issued. Short of zero, there is no limit to the depth to which that value will fall if the money goes on being issued without limit. We had that experience in the early days of our own country; the phrase "not worth a Continental" still survives as a memento of the worthlessness of the paper money issued by the Continental Congress. And to-day the Austrian krone, the Polish mark, etc., to say nothing of the ridiculous Russian ruble and the preposterous German mark, are shocking examples of the same thing.

The Banking System

These few words it seemed advisable to say about irredeemable paper money, which may get entirely away from the gold standard; but this was a digression. What we are discussing is the devices which, while maintaining the gold standard, enable a given amount of gold to effect a far greater volume of business than it would if the gold itself had to be transferred in every transaction. Of these devices, one that is far more potent even than the issue of circulating notes is the vast credit system of modern times, and especially the banking system. A person (individual or corporation) who keeps an account at a bank may either deposit money there, which is entered to the credit side of his account, or may obtain credit by depositing commercial paper (drafts or promissory notes) or securities (stocks or bonds). The bank credits him with a certain number of dollars, but it does not have to keep anything like that quantity of money in its vaults; a small fraction of that quantity suffices (for reasons we cannot enter into) to make quite certain that the bank will be able to pay out all the dollars that will actually be demanded of it in the course of business. The great bulk of business transactions are settled not by actual transfer of currency (either coin or paper) but by the entering of certain figures on the books of the various banks. And even the banks settle with each other chiefly by balancing their accounts through the medium of that great modern institution, the clearing-house.

Just in so far as business transactions are settled by the mere entering of certain figures on the debit or credit side of a banker's books; just in so far as, instead of handing over a bag of gold in payment of a purchase or a debt, A writes an order on his banker which B deposits with *his* banker, the result being the entering of a certain amount to the debit side of A's account at his bank and to the credit side of B's at his; just in so far as the banks themselves, instead of settling their accounts, each one directly with each other one by the transfer of cash, only settle their aggregate net balances through the clearing-house, which requires incomparably less cash to be actually handled:—just in so far as all this highly developed mechanism of credit and finance enables a small amount of gold to effect exchanges which would otherwise require a large amount, the need of actual gold for the transaction of a given volume of business upon a given scale of prices is enormously reduced. It is none the less true that, *given the state of development of this mechanism*, a country will require, upon a given scale of prices, a definite quantity of basic money with which to transact its business. The application of the quantity theory is not essentially altered; only, of course, the quantity of money corresponding to a given scale of prices is vastly less than it would be if this machinery of credit did not exist or were less highly developed.

The Three Factors that Determine the General Course of Prices

In view of all that has been said concerning money and prices, in this and the preceding chapter, it is plain that there are three great fundamental factors that affect the general course of prices. Increase of the volume of production, and of the trade that naturally goes with it, tends to lower prices. Increase of the volume of gold which forms the basis of the monetary circulation (or rather of the combined volume of that gold and the paper money which circulates on a parity with gold) tends to raise prices. Increase of the scope and potency of the system of banking and credit, which multiplies the amount of business that can be done with a given amount of money, likewise tends to raise prices. Of course, a *decrease* in any of these factors has the opposite effect. But assuming that there is an *increase* in all three cases —which usually happens in such an age of industrial and commercial progress as we have been familiar with—we see two factors tending to raise prices and one tending to lower them. What will be the net outcome it is impossible to say—it all depends on the relative rapidity with which the three processes go on. The progress of discovery and invention, the improvement of agricultural methods and of industrial organization—these things have, during the past half-century, brought about an enormous increase of production; but there has also been a great increase in the supply of gold, and a still more remarkable development of credit and the banking system. On the whole, if any conjecture is permissible, it would be that (apart from the readjustment of prices after the profound disturbances caused by the Great War) the general course of the price-level will, for a long time to come, be upward rather than downward.

Finally, we must observe that while upon a long view these fundamental factors determine the course of the price-level, very important temporary fluctuations of the price-level are brought about by quite a different kind of causes. Especially should it be noted that the recources of banking and credit may, without any change in their nature or in people's habits concerning them, be stretched to their utmost capacity or used with extreme care and reserve, according to the temper of hopefulness or the reverse that may prevail in the business world at the time. Thus we may have ups and downs of the price-level without any of the three fundamental factors being changed; but it still remains true that they control the whole result. The fluctuations brought about by changes in the temper of business are deviations from a level determined by those three fundamental factors; and if those factors were different the like deviations would take place, but from a different level.

CHAPTER XI

LAND AND RENT

In Chapter III we saw that the supplying of the wants of mankind depends on four great factors—natural resources, labor, capital, and enterprise. The person who furnishes any one of these things in compensated by a share of the product. We have now to try to get some idea of how the share of these four classes of participants in production is determined.[1]

The Landowner's Share: Rent

In the present chapter we shall consider the compensation that goes to the landowner for the

[1] As was pointed out in the chapter referred to, all four of the factors may be furnished by one and the same person, as in the case of the small farmer who owns his land, cultivates it solely with his own labor, owns the implements with which it is worked, and conducts the business at his own risk. But in our discussion it will be supposed throughout that the landowner, the workman, the man who furnishes the capital, and the man who undertakes and controls the enterprise are separate and distinct persons. If a person combines in himself any two or three, or all four, of these characters, his share of the product may be expected to comprise the share that would have fallen to each of them if he had been a separate person.

use of his land. This subject was touched upon in Chapter II, as an illustration of the importance of the idea of the margin; and indeed the essence of the matter was there given. But we shall now go into it a little more fully.

What is paid to the landowner for the use of his land is called rent, both in common talk and in the language of economists. In common talk, however, the word rent is applied likewise to what is paid for the use of a building, or a typewriter, or a piano, or what not; but in dealing with essentials economists usually mean by rent not the price paid for the use of things like these, which have to be produced by human effort, but the price paid for access to *natural resources*, or, as they usually put it, the use of *land*. And the reason is, that the rent of land is governed by a specific principle of the first importance, while the price paid for the use of houses, or anything else that is produced by human effort, involves no peculiar principle at all.

Rent of Land and Value of Land

If you ask "the man in the street" why the owner of a piece of land gets a thousand dollars a year as rent from the user of it, the chances are that he will say that it is because the land is worth ten thousand dollars. But the fact is precisely the reverse. The land does not rent for a thousand dollars a year because it takes ten thousand dollars to buy it; on the contrary, it takes ten thousand dollars to buy it because it is worth a thousand dollars a year to somebody to have the use of it. What you pay for the use of a piano (apart from compensation for wear and tear) depends on how much the piano is worth to sell, and that in turn depends on the cost of production of the piano; but in the case of land there is no cost of production. A plot of land 25 × 100 feet in the financial district of New York City may be worth a million dollars while a plot of the same size in an adjoining county is worth only a hundred, solely because the advantages to be derived from the use of the one are worth ten thousand times as much as those to be derived from the use of the other. It is not the selling price of the land that determines the rental value, but the rental value that determines the selling price.

What Makes Rental Value

But what is it that determines the rental value of land? The essence of the answer to this question was briefly given in Chapter II, where Ricardo's doctrine of rent was cited as a signal example of the importance of the idea of the margin in economic theory; but there will be no harm in repeating here, with a little expansion, what was there said. Land exists of all degrees of fertility and all degrees of advantage in point of nearness to markets, etc. At any given time the demand for agricultural products is such that it will pay extremely well to cultivate certain grades of land, less well to cultivate certain other grades, and so on down until we come to a grade which (on account either of its low fertility or its disadvantage of situation) it will just pay to cultivate if nothing has to be given for the use of the land. At this margin the land will command no rent, or practically no rent; and the amount of rent that any other land commands is determined by its superiority to the land at the margin. If one piece of land will yield just barely enough to pay, at the customary rates, for the labor and capital devoted to its cultivation, and another yields a thousand dollars a year more than this, the rental value of the first piece will be nothing, and the rental value of the second will be a thousand dollars a year.

Nor is the case of urban land—building lots in cities—essentially different, though it presents itself in a somewhat different way. There is a limited amount of land of such character as to present the greatest advantage for the uses of urban life, whether residential or business uses; and the same is true of land of every lesser degree of desirability, until we get down to land which is practically of no advantage at all for city uses—land such that nobody would pay anything whatever for the privilege of building on it. Such land as this has no rental value at all as city land (though it may possibly have some value as country or farming land); and the rental value of the city land varies all the way from nothing or next to nothing at this margin to the enormous rates commanded by the most advantageously situated city property. Just as in the case of agricultural land, these rates are a *differential* matter; they measure the superiority of the particular land in question over land at the margin.

Speculative Value of Land

At this point it will be well to go back for a moment to the question of the *selling* value of land. It was stated above that "it is not the selling price of the land that determines the rental value, but the rental value that determines the selling price." This is quite true; yet it is necessary to take into account a factor which, for the sake of simplicity, was left out of account; and this factor, while present in all cases, plays a far greater part in the case of city land than in that of agricultural land. When a man buys a piece of land he is influenced not only by an estimate of the uses to which it can *immediately* be put, but also by the price for which he thinks it likely it may be sold in the future—or, as it is usually expressed, by its *speculative value.* If a piece of land, either agricultural or urban, can be used now with a profit of $1,000 a year over and above the normal return upon the capital and labor expended by the user, the land will command a rent of $1,000 a year; and if (after allowance for taxes, etc.), the possession of a piece of land commanding this rent is supposed to be worth $10,000 the selling price of the land will naturally be $10,000. But if there is reason to believe that the rental value of the land will be much higher twenty years from now, buyers may be glad to pay

$15,000 or $20,000 for it, even though at first the income from the land will not justify that price. In the case of a growing city, this is one of the chief factors in the selling price of land; and on the outskirts of the solidly built-up sections that is especially the case. There are large areas of vacant land which it would be folly to build upon today, because tenants could not possibly be found who would pay enough rent (for house and lot together) to compensate the builder, even if the builder paid *nothing whatever for the land;* yet this land commands a selling price, and sometimes even a high selling price. But this fact does not contradict the principle stated above; the selling price is still based on the rental value—only it takes into account the probable *future rental value* as well as the present rental value, which in some instances is nothing at all. It is a case of speculation; a word frequently used as though it were necessarily an odious and anti-social thing, whereas it is often not only a legitimate but a highly useful phase of business. The "speculator" in land takes chances of loss as well as gain; if he holds on to the vacant land until he thinks the right time has come to build on it or to sell it, he has in the meanwhile (often for ten, twenty, or fifty years) to pay taxes on it, besides forgoing all interest on his purchase-money. That the process is by no means sure to result in a net gain is sufficiently proved by the fact that great quantities of vacant land are always in the market at almost insignificant prices. Anybody with money to invest can buy them, and yet they are not gobbled up by shrewd investors, as of course they would be if the game were as profitable as some writers seem to think.

Land and Improvements

One more point, and a very important one, must be briefly touched upon before we leave the subject of the rent of land. We have been considering land purely as a natural resource and as though nothing had been done to it by the application of human effort. Let us now briefly consider how the question is affected by the existence of improvements which have become permanently attached to the land. In the case of agricultural land, these may be largely in the shape of drainage, clearing, fencing, etc., which have made the land more available for agricultural uses, as well as in the shape of buildings. In the case of city land, the permanent improvements are chiefly houses, though there may also have been grading, etc. Now the Ricardian law of rent—that differential law which we have been discussing—does not, *on its face*, apply to things that are the result of human effort; the price normally paid for the use of these things, though it is also called rent, is governed by their cost of production. Nevertheless *when the improvements have once been made* and have become permanently attached to the land, the rent of the whole thing, *land and improvements together*, is governed solely by that law of rent which we have been talking about. If, for example, you have built a fine private residence upon a lot in a good section of the city which has since gone down in the world and become a slum, the rent you can get for house and lot together, and likewise the price you can sell it for, depends solely on the value of the uses to which in the new circumstances it can be put, which may be very little indeed; and it won't make a particle of difference whether the house cost a thousand dollars to build or a hundred thousand. And of course the same thing is true of agricultural improvements permanently sunk in the land.

In the case of city houses, however—at least in growing cities—the cost of production *does* usually enter decisively into the determination of rent in spite of this. The building of houses for the accommodation of great multitudes of people is a regular business; and if the rents of those already built are not high enough to encourage the building of new houses, such building will decline in quantity or stop altogether, and the shortage of houses thus resulting will drive rents up until they again somewhat correspond to cost of production. The rent of any *particular* house is unaffected by what may have happened to be its cost of production; but the *general level* of house rents is decisively affected by the prevailing cost of production of houses.

CHAPTER XII

ENTERPRISE AND PROFIT

NEXT after land, or natural resources, it would seem fitting to take up labor, as the most essential of the three remaining factors of production; then capital; and last enterprise, which is the factor that comes to play a cardinal part only when production and exchange have become pretty highly developed. But it happens that, for purposes of exposition, it is desirable to take up the subject of enterprise and profit (the enterpriser's share of the product) next after land and rent (the landowner's share).

This is because, while interest (the capitalist's share) and wages (the workman's share) are determined in a somewhat definite way by standard rates for a given quantity (so much a year for the use of a hundred dollars of capital, so much a day, or a month, for the performance of such a kind of work), the case of the profits of enterprise is more like the case of the rent of land; it is a differential matter.[1] And it will conduce to simplicity to get

[1] This view of business profits is one of the important contributions made by the eminent American economist, Francis A. Walker, to economic theory.

both of these differential factors out of the way before we take up the question of the share that goes to capital (interest) and the share that goes to labor (wages and salaries).

No Standing Rate of Business Profit

There is nothing like a standard rate of earnings for business ability—the ability to conduct with success a business enterprise, either industrial or commercial or financial. Even when this kind of ability is paid for in the shape of salary, there can hardly be said to be a standard rate; yet there is something like a standard rate. It may be said, for example, that a first-rate business manager, a first-rate organizing and directing expert, of the kind that a great concern in this country seeks to employ in its highest positions, will receive somewhere between $10,000 and $100,000 a year: a wide range, to be sure, yet persons in the business will know pretty accurately at what point in the range a given individual belongs—what salary he will command. But for the man who conducts the business as his own enterprise[1]—the entrepreneur

[1] When we speak of the enterprise as his own, we do not mean that he necessarily owns the whole, or even any part, of the capital invested in the enterprise. He either owns it, or sufficiently commands the confidence of others to obtain the use of it; and in the latter case he pays for that use, either in the shape of interest at a fixed percentage or in the shape of a share in the expected profits. Whichever of these things may be the case in any individual instance, we must think of the *profits* of the enterprise as something distinct from the interest on the capital used in the business—just as it is distinct from the wages and salaries received by those who do the work. The *profit* is what the entrepreneur gets *as such*, over and above the rent, interest, and wages that go to

as he is called by most economic writers—the case is very different.

Of the persons who undertake to carry on business enterprises, a considerable proportion get little or nothing in the way of profit, and there are some who cannot even make ends meet—who sustain a loss instead of making a profit; on the other hand, there are many who make very large profits, and a few whose profits are such as to dazzle the imagination. No one dreamed that the business of selling all sorts of little things at five and ten cents could be made the basis of one of the splendid American fortunes until Mr. Woolworth accomplished that feat; and this success in the field of merchandising is cast into the shade by Mr. Ford's unparalleled profits in the field of manufacture.

Analogy Between Profit and Rent

Now into the determination of business success or business failure—the determination, too, of the degree of the success—an element of chance undoubtedly enters, and we ought never to forget this entirely. But on the whole, and for an understanding of the matter in the large, we may look upon the outcome of an enterprise as being in general determined by the ability of the entrepreneur. All degrees of managing or business ability exist, and persons of all these degrees of

the landowner, the capitalist, and the workers respectively; though it may happen that the entrepreneur is himself landowner, capitalist and worker as well as entrepreneur.

ability undertake business enterprises. In the fierce competition of our times, it may be said that all those entrepreneurs who do not come up to a certain degree of ability and energy are driven to the wall, and before long disappear from the field, and have to earn their living in other ways. Just above this degree are the entrepreneurs who may be said to be at the *margin*—it is almost a toss-up whether they shall continue in business or not, but they *do* just barely continue. This class may be said to make practically no *profit* at all; what they get out of their business is just about what they could expect to get as wages or salaries if they were employed by others instead of carrying on their own business. How far down this margin shall be depends on the demand for the things furnished by the business, and the supply of persons capable of carrying it on with various degrees of ability; just as we saw in the matter of farm land that the margin depended on the demand for agricultural products on the one hand and the quantity and accessibility of land of various degrees of fertility on the other. And, like the rent of land, the profits of enterprise range all the way from zero at the margin to whatever may result from the superior ability (or combination of ability and good luck) of any particular entrepreneur.

This differential—the difference between the next-to-no-profits of the business man who just barely manages to keep going and the great profits of the highly successful business man—may, as we have seen, be enormous. Whether it is just that such differences of reward should exist, whether it is expedient that they should be interfered with by law—these are questions of public policy which we are not at present engaged in considering. What we are trying to do here is simply to get an understanding of what actually happens—whether just or unjust, expedient or inexpedient—under the play of free competition.[1] And the consideration of profits, as well as that of rent, in the light of the idea of the margin, gives us the fundamentals of such an understanding.

Prices not Raised by Rent of Best Land or Profit of Ablest Manufacturers

We see, namely, that neither the rent of the best land nor the profit of the ablest manufacturer or merchant operates to raise the price of the thing produced or dealt in. So long as the demand for wheat is such as to require a resort to land of a given degree of infertility or remoteness in order to get the whole supply demanded, the price will have to be sufficient to make it worth while to raise wheat on that land; and *all* the wheat will sell for that price, since there is nothing to make a pur-

[1] Throughout this book, free competition is understood to exist, unless the contrary is stated. If big profits are obtained by means of monopolistic control, the whole case is entirely altered—not only as to any question of justice, but also as to what actually happens; for profits derived from monopoly may have no relation whatever to superior ability. It goes without saying that the justice and expediency of interfering with monopoly rest on a wholly different basis from that which applies to the case of free competition.

chaser pay more for the wheat from the poor land than from the good land. The *owner* of the good land gets the benefit of the difference—it is this that makes the rent of land; but the wheat itself costs no more to the consumer. It may be argued that the community as a whole ought to get the benefit of the difference; that is a large question on which a great deal may be said. But whether the community as a whole gets the rent or the landowner gets it, the rent of the land does not increase *the price of wheat.*

And so in like manner for profits. As has been said in a previous chapter: If Mr. Ford can turn out a certain automobile at $200, but other people can't turn it out so economically; if some of them can only turn it out at $250, some at $275, some at $300, and *if the demand is great enough* to cover the whole output of all these manufacturers; then Mr. Ford's automobiles, and those of all the intermediate people, will sell—or at least can sell—for $300. At the price of $300, Mr. Ford may make an enormous profit; but his big profit is not the *cause* of the $300 price; on the contrary the $300 price is the *cause* of the big profits. The price is $300 not because Mr. Ford gets a big profit but because the *marginal* manufacturer cannot turn the car out for less.

A Word About Corporations

We have been talking of the entrepreneur as if he were a single individual. Of course, if a business is carried on by a partnership of two or more persons, the case is not in any way altered. In modern times, however, a large proportion of all the great business undertakings are carried on not by single individuals, or partnerships of two or three individuals, but by corporations. The enterprise is the joint concern of hundreds or perhaps thousands of persons, each of whom owns a specified fraction of it. The ownership is divided into shares; and if there are a million shares, the owner of one share receives one one-millionth of the profits if there are any, and suffers one one-millionth of the loss if there is a loss. This state of things does not make any vital difference in the application of the principles above set forth; a corporation's business, like that of an individual, may be well-conducted or ill-conducted, and accordingly (though here, too, the element of chance enters and cannot be entirely ignored) may be highly profitable or not profitable at all—may show results ranging all the way from enormous gains to bankruptcy and extermination.

There is, however, one difference in the two cases which, even in a rudimentary survey, demands a word. In a highly successful corporation, it is very apt to be the case that some one person (or some two or three persons) is the real mover of the enterprise and the creator of its prosperity; and his share in the profits is determined, not by any fixed rule applying to all cases, but by an understanding or arrangement to which all the shareholders assent as a reasonable recognition of his contribution to the common success. This recognition may take the shape either of a very large salary—such as would hardly be paid to any one who was simply an employee—or by the assignment to him of a large number of shares in the enterprise, over and above any salary he may receive for his services.

These few remarks have been made about corporations, lest it should seem as if their existence had been overlooked; but they do not affect the essentials of the question of profit.

CHAPTER XIII

CAPITAL AND INTEREST

THE person who furnishes capital for the carrying on of an enterprise receives his compensation in the shape of *interest.* Before taking up the question of how the amount of this compensation is determined by the play of economic forces, it will be well to remind ourselves of one or two things that have already been said in preceding chapters. By the term capital we do not mean money. Money *represents* capital, capital is *measured* in terms of money; just as any other form of wealth may be represented by money and measured in terms of money. Capital consists of those things which enable production (including transportation, merchandising, etc.) to be carried on—buildings, machinery, raw material, the tracks and rolling stock of railroads, the food and clothing that workmen consume during the process of production, etc.

Capital the Result of Saving

And all this capital is the result of saving; in order that the capital should be in existence *now,* and available for the purposes of production, it was essential that some persons in the past should have abstained from consuming all that they had acquired; and in order that the capital shall be maintained (for it is constantly being worn out, or used up in the processes of production) it is essential that there shall be a continuation of such abstinence. If everybody lived "from hand to mouth" there would be no capital; and on the other hand if there were no capital everybody would have to live "from hand to mouth," or nearly so, for production would be very meagre.

The Rate of Interest

Another thing that has been mentioned in a previous chapter is that the service of a given amount of capital for a given length of time will command about the same return whether the capital be applied to one purpose or another; because if the returns on capital in one industry were much higher than in another industry, capital would flow into the first and drift away from the second. This return, this compensation for the service rendered by the use of capital, is called *interest;* and it is measured by percentage. If the man who furnishes $100 of capital gets $10 a year for the use of it, he is said to receive 10 per cent. interest on his investment; and what has just been said about equal returns for different uses of capital is equivalent to saying that there is, at any given time, something like a standard *rate of interest* on capital, the same in one employment of capital as in another. What it is that determines that standard rate we shall make some endeavor to understand presently. But first we must take notice of a most important element which greatly complicates the question of interest on capital —the element of risk.

The Capitalist and the Risk of Enterprise

We have been distinguishing between the entrepreneur and the capitalist—between the man who undertakes the business, with all its possibilities of loss and gain, and the man who supplies the capital with which it is to be carried on. These may, of course, be one and the same person; but when they are two separate and distinct persons we have been talking as though the capitalist played a part wholly different from that played by the entrepreneur. It was desirable to do this for the sake of simplicity; but in fact this complete distinction of function is very seldom realized.

If A wants to start a business enterprise, and B, having confidence in A's ability and integrity, supplies him with the needful capital, B may become either a partner or a creditor of A. If it is arranged that B shall have a certain share of the profits, he is a partner; if it is arranged that B shall have a fixed return on the capital he has invested, he is a creditor. In the first case B is an entrepreneur besides being a capitalist, and his returns from the business are obviously a combination of profit (or loss) and interest. In the second case his returns may be regarded (and usually are regarded) simply as interest.

But when we look more closely into the matter, we find that this is not a satisfactory representation of the facts in the second case. Although B may feel very fairly satisfied of the safety of his investment—feel confident that he will get the stipulated percentage on his capital every year and get back the principal at some time in the future—yet there is always more or less danger that these expectations will be disappointed. If at any time A should fare ill in his business (either through his own fault or through unexpected changes in conditions beyond his control), B may not get the stipulated interest when it falls due; and if this should continue, and things should keep going from bad to worse, B will not only fail to get his interest, but may lose the whole or a large part of the capital he invested.

True Interest and Compensation for Risk

Accordingly, when a person who has invested money in a business enterprise carried on by others receives a certain percentage on his investment, this must be regarded as partly interest and partly compensation for risk; and since there is a very large range of variation in the element of risk, the rate of interest (that is, what is *called* interest, but is really a combination of true interest and compensation for risk) varies very widely in different uses of capital. Thus money lent to the

Government of the United States may command only 4 per cent. interest, at the very same time that the usual rate of interest on commercial loans is 6 per cent., and that bonds of railroad and industrial corporations vary all the way from 5 to 8 per cent. The man who lends to the United States Government feels, humanly speaking, absolutely certain that he will get interest and principal without fail, when it falls due; even an extremely slight degree of doubt on this point is enough to make a marked difference in the rate of interest at which he is willing to lend his money; and when it comes (as it does in a great many cases) to material doubt as to getting the interest when it falls due and some real danger of losing the principal itself (in whole or in part) a great difference in the rate of interest is necessary to overbalance the risk.

But, these considerations about risk having once been set forth, we shall, in the remainder of the discussion, understand by the rate of interest that rate which may be regarded as really paid for the *use* of capital, exclusive of what is paid to cover *risk*. So understood, the rate of interest is fairly uniform in the various applications of capital at a given time; and we must now consider what it is that determines this rate. And this brings us to the question of how the results of production, over and above what goes to the landowner as the rent of superior land, and to the entrepreneur as the profits of superior business ability, are divided between interest on capital and wages of labor. This is perhaps the most difficult of all the elemental problems of theoretical economics, and has been the subject of endless controversy. We shall get but a very imperfect idea of its solution, and must dismiss it with brief treatment.

Are the Interests of Labor and Capital Identical?

But before coming even to that, there is one very important remark that it seems desirable to make at this point. It is often said that the interests of labor and capital are identical, and that the trouble between them is due solely to misunderstanding. I should be very glad to subscribe to this comfortable doctrine, but I cannot. Nevertheless there is a most important truth of which that doctrine is an overstatement, and which we should constantly bear in mind.

The interests of capital and labor *are* identical in so far as concerns the *aggregate product*. Capitalists and workers alike gain by an increase in the total production, and any policy on the part of either that tends to reduce that total is an injury to both. But there remains the question of the *division* of the product between capital and labor —between interest on the capital on the one hand, and wages and salaries for the labor on the other. *Given* the productivity of a nation—*given* the total product—the question of the rate of interest on capital is essentially a question of what *proportion* of the product (after allowance for rent and profits) shall go to capital and what proportion to labor.

What Determines the Rate of Interest

Now it is quite conceivable that people might be so constituted that they would save simply for the assurance of their future and would entrust their savings to others who would use them productively, even if no compensation in the shape of interest were offered to them as an inducement. Indeed, there must be many persons at the present time who would do this if they could do no better. But it seems clear that nothing like enough saving would be done to provide the vast amount of capital required for the carrying on of modern productive activity, if all that the saver could look forward to was to get back at some future time the capital which, in the interval, he had gone without the use of. And so long as that full amount of capital cannot be obtained without the inducement of interest, every person who furnishes capital will be able to get the prevailing rate of interest even though he might, if necessary, have been willing to accept a lower rate, or none at all.

Thus the rate of interest seems to be an instance of the ordinary working of the law of supply and demand; but the case is not quite so simple as we have put it. For no one can say just to what extent the mere desire for security in the future might cause a lowered or raised inducement to produce exactly the opposite of the usual effect. If the rate of interest were very low, for example, it might cause a really very large number of persons to save *more*, instead of saving *less*, because a greater amount of saving would be necessary in order to provide the income they are anxious to have; and in like manner a very high rate of interest might cause them to save *less*, instead of saving *more*. Still, experience seems abundantly to show that, within those limits which alone need to be considered for practical purposes, the accumulation of capital, as a whole, is slackened by a fall in the rate of interest and stimulated by a rise in the rate of interest—that what actually takes place is substantially what was described in the preceding paragraph. This is especially demonstrated whenever there has been (without any such frightful upheaval and dislocation as was brought on by the World War) destruction of capital on a great scale, by war or otherwise; a temporary rise in the rate of interest suffices to bring about a rapid accumulation of capital to take the place of what has been destroyed; and when this has been effected the rate of interest falls to its old level.

Division of Proceeds Between Capital and Labor

With a given normal rate of return on capital, the rest of the total product (after deduction of what goes as rent to the owner of superior natural resources and what goes as profit to entrepreneurs of superior ability) goes to the workers in the shape of wages and salaries. The distribution is not accidental. If less were paid out to the workers, more would be left for interest on capital; this would stimulate the supply of capital, and the competition among the owners of the capital to find a use for it would cause an increase in the demand for labor, a rise of wages, and a fall in the rate of return on capital. On the other hand if more were paid out to the workers, less would be left for interest on capital; this would slacken the supply of capital, and cause a lessened demand for labor, a fall of wages, and a rise in the rate of return on capital.

Accordingly, we see that, while there is a certain antagonism between the interests of labor and capital in the division of the total product between them, that division is pretty definitely determined by natural causes. It may, however, be argued that if the workers were to form an effective combination which would dictate the rate of wages and salaries for all the various kinds of work, they could extort from the capitalists a large part of what, under free competition, goes to the capitalists as interest. This cannot be denied with positiveness; but there is strong reason for believing it to be impossible. It all depends on whether people on the whole would put as much capital into productive enterprise with a lower rate of return for its use as they do with the actual rate; and it seems plain, as we have seen, that they would not.

Finally, just a word about another possibility. As was pointed out in an early chapter, there might be *capital* without *capitalists;* in a communistic or socialistic order of society, capital might be provided by the community as a whole instead of by individuals.

CHAPTER XIV

LABOR AND WAGES

WE have now discussed the share of the total product which falls to three of the four fundamental factors of production—natural resources, labor, capital, and enterprise—leaving to the last the factor of labor. This order was adopted, of course, solely because it seemed best adapted to an understanding of the whole question, and not at all on account of any consideration of the relative importance of the four factors. Indeed, it is plain that the part played by the other three is only that of increasing the productivity of labor: the richer the natural resources, the more abundant in quantity and the more highly developed by science and invention the capital, and the abler the conduct of enterprise, the greater will be the product which will result from a given exertion of labor. But it happens to be the case that the discussion could best be carried on by considering the rent of land, the profits of enterprise, and the interest on capital before coming to the wages of labor.[1]

[1] By this term we are to understand not only the pay of workmen, skilled or unskilled, which is usually called wages, but also the pay of salaried employees of all grades.

The Share of Labor as a Whole; the Share of Different Kinds of Labor

In considering the share of the product falling to labor, we have to pay close attention to two very different aspects of the subject. There is the question of how much of the total product falls to *labor as a whole*, and there is the question of how much falls to *one kind of labor as compared with another*.

Both of these questions have been touched upon in previous chapters, as they came up naturally in connection with other subjects. In Chapter XIII we saw that workers as a whole and capitalists as a whole have a common interest in the increase of the total product; and we also saw that while they have opposed interests in the division of the product between them, this division is determined by economic forces whose operation it is impossible to counteract to any serious extent except by a coercive combination on the part of all the workers. The workers (even supposing they all combined) could not press down the share going to capital *and keep it down*, because the resulting discouragement of productive saving would prevent capital from being kept up, and thus throw labor out of employment.

A parallel argument may be made in regard to a combination on the part of all the owners of capital to press wages down; but, for reasons that I cannot enter into at this point, the argument has not, in our time, the force that it once had. However, the same conclusion follows *practically* from a different consideration: An effective combination of all capitalists for this purpose is impossible; the attempt would break down from the mere fact that a combination to extort high returns for capital at the expense of labor would not have behind it any moral force such as, rightly or wrongly, attaches to a combination to extort high wages for labor at the expense of capital. Millions of persons, glad to avail themselves of the opportunity for gain, and not having the fear of public condemnation to deter them, would use their capital just as they saw fit, and the combination would before long break down completely. Of course, even in the case of labor an all-embracing combination is almost impossible; but in the case of capital it is utterly out of the question.

Grades of Labor; Wage-equality within a Grade, Wage-difference between Grades

So much for the division of the total product between capital as a whole and labor as a whole. As to the relative compensation of one kind of labor as compared with another, this subject was discussed with some fullness in Chapter VII. It was there pointed out that great inequalities exist in the compensation of different kinds of work, owing to the fact that the population is practically divided, by differences either of ability or of circumstance, into different *grades* or classes. *Within* each grade (as was there explained) there is something like equality of compensation in the various occupations that belong to that grade; but *between* the different grades—as, for example the unskilled workman, the skilled workman, and the professional man—there may be any amount of difference in compensation. And the difference is determined, not by any absolute or inherent difference of *quality*, but solely by differences of *scarcity:* the rates of pay that are current in one grade, as compared with another, depend on the demand for the services furnished by that grade taken as a whole and the available supply of these services.

Trade Unions and Labor Scarcity

One or two remarks, however, should now be added to what was said in Chapter VII. The statement there made, and here repeated, that compensation is about equal in the various occupations belonging to a given grade of labor, was based on the supposition of free competition—the supposition that no *artificial* obstructions were placed in the way of a person's choice of occupation. Now experience has shown that particular occupations can be so controlled by powerful organizations, called trade unions, as greatly to limit the number of persons who can enter those occupations; and as this limitation brings about a scarcity of the particular kind of labor in question, it may result in bringing about, and maintaining indefinitely, a much higher scale of pay in that occupation than what is offered in other occupations of the same grade. But it would be a mistake to suppose that this contradicts what was said above about the futility of an attempt to force a rise of *wages in general* at the expense of the return on capital. Labor can be made scarce in a *particular* occupation by trade-union rules which keep laborers out of it; it cannot be made scarce in *all occupations* by any such process, since the man that is shut out of one occupation has to find another to earn his living by.

Highly Paid Labor not Necessarily Dear Labor

There is another point that must not go without mention. We have been saying that the more there is paid in wages the less there is left as a return upon capital. Of course this assumed a given degree of development of the arts of production; as the arts advance there is a bigger total to divide between labor and capital, and both receive the benefit. But besides this, the important point must be noted that an increase of wages may *of itself* mean increased productivity. A low-wage workman may mean an underfed and ill-housed workman; and such a man cannot do as much work, or as good work, as a well-fed and properly housed one. And not only physical but mental and moral superiority may be the result of good wages; and these things too—apart from being good in themselves—may mean increased efficiency of the worker. There can be no question that the high wages of American labor, as compared with most European labor, have in large measure meant not so much more *taken from* what goes to capital but so much more *put into* the total product: highly-paid labor may not mean dear labor, for the work may be so good as to be cheap at the price. Not to recognize this would be a most serious mistake; but we must not make the opposite mistake, either. Higher wages do not *necessarily* mean either more work or better work; indeed cases are by no means unknown where they have meant less work and worse work. What will be true in any particular case can only be decided by good common sense, or experience, or both.

CHAPTER XV

FOREIGN TRADE

WITHIN the limits of this book, it will be possible to devote to the subject of foreign trade only a very brief and imperfect treatment. But instead of apologizing for the inadequacy of the treatment, I shall begin by apologizing for treating the subject at all. For it might be argued with considerable force that in an elementary discussion of economic principles no notice ought to be taken of the question whether the parties to a trade are citizens of the same country or of two different countries. And some of the reasons why people do take notice of it are certainly bad reasons.

Importing and Exporting done by Individuals, not by Countries

The bad reasons are chiefly two. The first arises from the habit of thinking of a country as though it acted as a unit in its international trade. But the buying and selling that goes on between one country and another consists of thousands of separate transactions, decided upon by private individuals, each actuated by his own interest.[1] If Jones, a Chicago merchant, buys a bill of goods from a manufacturer in Birmingham, England, rather than from one in Providence, R. I., he is guided by precisely the same considerations as he would have been if he had preferred a manufacturer in Bridgeport, Conn., to the Rhode Island man. The people of Illinois never bother their heads about how much they collectively buy from Massachusetts people; they never ask how much Illinois imports from or exports to the rest of the United States. They are perfectly satisfied to let the thing take care of itself; they do not personify their State as an importer or exporter; they know perfectly well that importing and exporting, as between Illinois and the rest of the country, is nothing in the world but buying and selling by a lot of separate people in Illinois, in the daily pursuit of their own interest and convenience. But precisely the same thing is true of exporting and importing between our country and the rest of the world; and yet when we think of that, some deep-seated habit or instinct causes us to think of the country as a whole as doing the importing and the exporting, and to be troubled in our minds as to the consequences. I don't say there is no reason for giving attention to the matter; but the first point to be noticed is that foreign trade is not in

[1] Of course there are occasional transactions between Governments, but this is too unimportant a factor to trouble about.

its *essence* different from domestic trade, and that, like domestic trade, it consists of thousands of separate transactions, each of which is entered upon voluntarily by buyer and seller alike, and each of which is therefore presumably to the benefit of buyer and seller alike.

Baseless Fears about Flow of Gold

The second of the bad reasons for viewing foreign trade in a different spirit from domestic trade is closely allied to the first. I refer to the idea that a country must always view with alarm any outflow of gold from it to other countries, and regard with satisfaction any inflow of gold from other countries to it. This notion has far less potency in the public mind than it had in former times; but for centuries it was one of the chief influences in shaping the economic policy of nations. That it has now been so largely outgrown is one of the most solid results of the teachings of the economists of the past century and a half. It would be highly interesting to discuss this subject in some detail; but a few words will suffice to indicate the essentials of it. The quantity of gold[1] which a country needs for carrying on its business is not an absolute thing; as we have seen, it is related to the price-level. Given the nature and extent of the country's business, and the character of its system of banking and currency, a

[1] We shall suppose all the countries in question to be on the gold standard.

certain quantity of gold will be needed *at a given price-level;* an inflow of gold will tend to raise the price-level, an outflow will tend to lower the price-level. But if the price-level in our country is raised, this will increase the inducements for us to buy goods from other countries, and diminish the inducements for the people of other countries to buy goods from us; and this increase of our imports of *goods* and decrease of our exports of *goods* tends to make it necessary for us to send gold out of the country in order to balance our accounts. And the like is true in the opposite case. This is a very imperfect statement of what it would require considerable space to set forth satisfactorily; but it suffices to indicate the essence of the matter—that gold is automatically distributed among the various commercial countries in the quantities which are needed for carrying on their business: any excess produces a rise of prices which drains gold out; any deficiency produces a fall of prices which draws gold in.

True Nature of Foreign Trade

But now, having got it well fixed in our minds that trade with foreign countries is of essentially the same character as trade within our own country; that it isn't the United States that buys from England or France, but Jones of Chicago that buys from Robinson of Nottingham or Jourdain of Lyons; and also that we needn't worry over any danger of having too little gold in the country or wish to have any more than naturally comes to it or stays in it—having got rid, therefore, of certain false notions that muddle many people's minds—let us ask ourselves what points there are about foreign trade which really *do* demand attention.

In the first place, then, although the trade between our own country and other countries is made up of separate transactions between private persons, and although it is safe to assume that each of these separate transactions is advantageous to both parties, it is not only natural, but proper, to look at the thing also from the standpoint of the nation as a whole, provided we think straight and steer free of fallacies. Taking the nation as a whole, what is the nature of its gain from foreign trade? What determines the character of the trade itself—why does one nation export wheat and import cloth, while another nation exports cloth and imports wheat?

If we wish to have a real answer to this question, we must think in terms of real cost, not of money cost, and we must look upon foreign trade as consisting essentially of an *interchange of commodities* and not as an *exchange of commodities for money.* The real cost of production of the wheat, or the cloth, or any commodity, is not the money laid out, but the human effort devoted to its production; and the real payment for all the commodities that a country imports consists not of money but of the commodities that it exports. For the sake of simplicity we shall imagine that there are only two such commodities, say wheat and cloth; the principle would be the same if there were any number.

Now if we export wheat to England and import cloth from England, it might in the first place be thought that this must be because we enjoy an advantage over England in the production of wheat and England enjoys an advantage over us in the production of cloth. But in fact we might export wheat and import cloth even if we had an advantage over England in the production *both of wheat and of cloth*, provided our advantage in raising wheat was greater than our advantage in making cloth. The thing that decides the matter is not whether we can make more cloth than the Englishman with a given amount of effort; but whether by *raising wheat and exporting it to England* we can get more cloth than we could get by the same amount of effort devoted to *making the cloth ourselves*.

This may seem a little difficult to follow; but it is really precisely what we are perfectly familiar with in every-day life. A skilled watchmaker may also be a better hand at chopping wood, and shoveling coal, and doing rough work generally, than the man he pays to do these things for him; but his superiority in the making of watches is greater than it is in these other employments; and he has others do these things for him because he can get more of them done for a given expenditure of labor on the making of watches than he could by expending the same amount of time directly on the rough work. And likewise a given country exports those things in which its productive superiority is greatest (or its inferiority least) and imports those things in which its productive superiority is least (or its inferiority greatest). And the nature of the gain is obvious.[1]

Free Trade and Protection

We have been tacitly assuming, in all this, that the citizens of a country are free to buy goods wherever they find it to their advantage to do so; and the doctrine of free trade rests on the proposition that any restriction of this freedom interferes with the gain which naturally attends the exchange of commodities between nations, as has been above set forth. If the government requires the payment of a duty of thirty per cent. upon the importation of a given article from a foreign country, it will not be imported unless the advantage of importing it exceeds this percentage in addition to the cost of transportation. To the extent that it thus operates to prevent trade taking its natural course, the duty entails an economic loss upon the country; it prevents its activities from flowing into those channels in which its productive advantages are greatest. The object of a duty on a given commodity, apart from serving as a source of government revenue, is to protect the home

[1] Nothing has been said about the cost of transportation. Of course that has to be taken into account, but the way in which it operates is evident. Importation and exportation will not take place if the advantage of the interchange of goods is too small to cover the cost of transportation and still leave something to the good.

producers of that commodity against foreign competition; and the question of protection versus free trade has, throughout almost the entire history of our country, been one of the leading issues of national politics.

Upon that issue I will here say only a few words. There are solid arguments for protection; but intelligent protectionists should frankly and squarely admit the soundness of the free-trade position so far as regards the immediate economic effect of a protective tariff duty. The sound arguments in favor of protection rest not upon a denial of immediate economic loss but first upon an assertion of future economic gains that make that loss worth while, and secondly upon considerations that are social and political rather than economic. Under the first head comes chiefly the "infant industries" argument—the argument that an industry which cannot be carried on to advantage in its early stages may become thoroughly self-sustaining if protected for a time. Under the second head there are two principal arguments. One is the "diversity of employments" argument—that it is worth while for a country to suffer some economic loss rather than be limited and specialized by confining its activities to those pursuits in which it has the greatest economic advantage. The other is the "economic independence" argument—particularly that dependence on importation from foreign countries for any vital need of the nation is a peril to the country in time of war. To weigh all these considerations is the province of the statesman rather than the economist; but it has seemed proper to make this brief mention of them in connection with our elementary survey of the subject of foreign trade.

CHAPTER XVI

THE LAW OF DIMINISHING PRODUCTIVENESS AND THE PROBLEM OF POPULATION

IF there were an unlimited quantity of good agricultural and mineral land in the world, and all of it easily accessible to people in places where it was desirable to live, there would be no problem of population—that is, no economic problem of population; mankind could increase and multiply and have no concern about the difficulty of getting fed and clothed and housed and warmed. And the same thing would be true if, from a given piece of agricultural or mineral land, men could extract twice as much by putting in twice as much labor and capital, ten times as much by putting in ten times as much labor and capital, and so on indefinitely. But neither of these things is so. There is only a limited amount of land that it pays to cultivate at all; and into the land that it does pay to cultivate it does not pay to put more than a certain amount of labor and capital. Even within easy reach of any great city there are large tracts of land which are left unused, for the simple reason that it is of such poor quality that it could not be made to yield, with a given expenditure of labor and capital, as much as is yielded by the worst land that is actually under cultivation. And upon the land that *is* actually under cultivation, the agriculturist soon finds that if he were to put more labor and capital into the working of it, he would not get returns that warrant the expenditure. By better manuring and more thorough working of his farm he may raise a larger crop on the same number of acres; and it is even possible, for a while, that each additional hundred dollars that he invests in fertilizers, and each additional day's work that he puts into the cultivation, will yield a bigger return than did the next preceding hundred dollars or the next preceding day's labor. But evidently a point is soon reached when, instead of additional doses of capital or of labor bringing increasing or even equal results, they will bring diminishing results. If the land yielded twenty bushels of wheat an acre as the result of a given expenditure of labor and capital, it is possible that twice the labor and capital will cause it to yield forty bushels an acre; but it is quite certain that five times the labor and capital will not be rewarded by a yield of a hundred bushels an acre.

Law of Diminishing Productiveness

The same kind of thing is true throughout the whole domain of agriculture, forestry, and mining —the "extractive industries," as they are called.

In the condition of things existing at any given time, it is impossible to increase the supply beyond a certain point without *increasing the cost per unit* of the thing supplied. This fundamental fact about the extractive industries, this *law of diminishing productiveness,*[1] is the basis of some of the most vital of all the teachings of Economics. You will recognize that it was at the bottom of the explanation of agricultural rent in a former chapter, though it was not there stated so broadly or so emphatically; and we are now going to see its bearing upon an even more vital question, the question of population. And as the doctrine of rent bears the name of Ricardo, so to the principle of population is attached the name of Malthus, another of the great founders of the science of Economics.

Before going into the question of population, however, it will be well to fix more clearly in mind the meaning of the law of diminishing productiveness itself. You must note particularly the words with which the statement of the law above given opens. *In the condition of things existing at any given time,* you cannot increase the supply of food,

[1] No such law applies to the manufacturing industries. On the contrary—speaking generally—in turning raw materials into manufactured goods, the greater the quantity the less the cost per unit; for machinery and organization can be made more effective the larger the scale upon which the manufacture is carried on. This contrast between the two great branches of production accounts, in large measure, for the fact that, while the masses in our time are supplied at small cost with conveniences and luxuries which were beyond the means of any but the rich in former times, the difficulty of obtaining the primary necessities of life has not been diminished in anything like the same degree.

etc., beyond a certain point without increasing the cost per unit; but that point may be carried farther and farther on in the process of time, through the advance of scientific knowledge, mechanical invention, methods of organization, facilities of transportation, etc. Thus the methods of today enable far larger crops to be raised with a given amount of labor than was the case a hundred years ago. But it still remains just as true as it was then that there is a definite limit—and one not very far off—beyond which we cannot increase the supply without increasing the cost per unit. It would be a mistake to forget the part which progress in the sciences and arts that bear upon agricultural production is capable of playing; but it would be fully as serious a mistake to forget that at any given stage of that progress the extent to which agricultural production can be economically carried is strictly limited.

Malthus and "The Principle of Population"

The cardinal proposition to which Malthus compelled attention is that the capacity of population to increase is of *an inherently different nature* from the capacity of the earth, or of any particular portion of the earth, to furnish the corresponding increase of subsistence. Under favorable circumstances—as for example in the American colonies or States in Malthus's time—population doubles (by natural increase, exclusive of immigration) in a moderate number of years, say twenty-five; at the end of this twenty-five years there is nothing *in the nature of man* to make impossible another doubling in the next twenty-five years; and so on indefinitely. Therefore, if people continue to have the same habits in regard to marriage and child-bearing, and the external circumstances continue to be equally favorable, population will increase in a *geometrical progression*, being regularly doubled every twenty-five years. Thus, if the population of a country at a certain time was 10 million it would, at successive intervals of twenty-five years, become

20, 40, 80, 160, 320, 640, 1280, 2560 million.

But it is quite plain that the supply of food to be obtained from a limited area already fairly cultivated cannot long keep up any such ratio of increase; no matter how rapidly inventions may be made, nor how greatly human efficiency may be improved, the supply of food cannot possibly be kept up to the tremendous demands of a geometrical progression even of a far lower rate than that supposed above. And the same thing is true of the world as a whole, from and after a time when a large proportion of its entire cultivated area has been brought under effective cultivation. Accordingly, in a country which derives its food supply from its own land and is fairly well populated, it is impossible that such a rate of increase as has actually taken place under favorable conditions should be maintained for a long period; and even if the whole world, as it is now populated or as it was populated a hundred years ago, be taken into account, only a very moderate extension of the period would result. It follows that mankind is faced with the necessity of either keeping the rate of increase of population far below what it may easily be and often has been, or lowering its standard of living, or both.

The Controversy over Malthus

This proposition is so self-evident, and so simple, that it may seem astonishing that it should have given rise to unending and bitter controversy. Such, however, has been the case; and, as so often happens in economic controversy, while the trouble has been partly caused by misunderstanding, incompetence, and perversity, it has come in large part from failure to realize that the questions at issue turned not so much on acceptance or rejection of any clear-cut proposition as upon differences of emphasis. Malthus's great work on *The Principle of Population* was an extensive and many-sided discussion, full of information as to facts and of sagacious interpretation of the facts; and he found in the experience of mankind abundant illustrations of the impossibility of combining a rapid increase of population with the maintenance of a high standard of living. He pointed out that experience as well as theory showed that if population was not checked by prudential habits in the matter of marriage and child-bearing, it was bound to be checked by war, pestilence, or famine, or to result in a general condition of poverty and want. Upon the inevitableness of these hardships in case population was not kept within bounds by prudential habits, he laid so much stress that many have labored under the impression that he had declared that the great bulk of mankind was in fact bound to continue forever in a state of poverty, and that the standard of living for the masses could never rise much above what it was. This was not at all Malthus's position, nor was it a necessary corollary from his "principle of population." But it is true that Malthus did not place anything like sufficient stress upon the possibility that *a raising of the standard of living* might itself operate as a most potent *cause of limitation* of population. He did not ignore this possibility; but he did not in anything like sufficient degree recognize the part it is capable of playing.

Population and Standard of Living

Since Malthus's time, there has been a great change in the habits of a very large part of mankind in the matter of marriage and child-bearing. The desire to maintain a high standard of comfort, and even of luxury, has come to play a greater and greater part in life, and there is no telling to what point its influence on population may be carried in the near future. This is by no means a matter for unmixed satisfaction. Of all the joys of life, of all the things that make for its richness and beauty, of all the elements that go to the building up of fine and generous character, none can be placed higher than the experiences that go with the bringing up of a family of children. In all the principal modern countries, there has been going on for many decades a marked lowering of the birth-rate; and he must be a very determined optimist who sees nothing to regret in this. It undoubtedly does result in a higher standard of material comfort, and often of intellectual opportunities, than could otherwise be attained; but these things are not the whole of life. Mr. Roosevelt was certainly an optimist if ever there was one; but he found in what he called "race suicide" ground for bitter regret and vigorous denunciation.

And yet the fact must be faced that mankind as a whole has no choice but between some kind of restriction of numbers and a low material standard of living. Moreover, the case is intensified by the fact that the advance of medical science and of public-health methods has so reduced the death-rate that the maintenance of the old-time birth-rate would result in a rate of increase of the population far more rapid than that same birth-rate caused in past times. Thus it is seen that the whole problem is involved in difficulties and perplexities so profound that none but a very rash man could undertake to formulate any simple solution of it. The nearest approach to a suggestion in that direction that the present writer can venture to make is the expression of a hope rather than of a judgment. If people could be got to appreciate more keenly the solid joys of a cheerful and modest home life, and to be less eager for objects that do not offer anything like such deep or abiding satisfaction, the question of population would take care of itself as well as can be hoped in this imperfect world. If those who are in circumstances of moderate comfort would not set their standard of comfort (or luxury) too high, and at the same time those who are in real danger of distressing poverty would set their standard high enough, population would not increase so rapidly as to press upon the possibility of subsistence, and yet would be kept up in a manner as nearly satisfactory as the nature of the problem permits.

Part II
Issues of Today

CHAPTER XVII

OVERPRODUCTION

"It is an ill wind that blows nobody good" is a proverb very much older than the modern industrial system. Long before there was steam or electric power, long before there was a factory system or any organization of large-scale manufacture, people were in the habit of saying that a hail-storm was a good thing for the glaziers, and a big fire a good thing for the carpenters and builders. The fear that there may not be enough work to go round beset people's minds in the old days, as well as in these times when trade-unions adopt rules designed for the purpose of "making work."

Let us try to understand just how much there is of superficial truth, and how much of fundamental error, in this feeling. There is no subject upon which economic writers have had to expend more effort in clearing up popular error; and this has been true ever since Political Economy has been the object of serious and systematic thought. But in recent times a fresh difficulty has been put in the way. In addition to the old instinctive fear of the workman that, if there is too much production, he may lose his particular job, attention is directed to the great fluctuations of business, the periodical return of general "hard times" and widespread unemployment with which the world has been so familiar for a hundred years. Some very keen thinkers and writers—especially Socialistic writers—have regarded the recurrence of commercial crises and periods of business depression as proof that the resources of modern capitalism have become so great, the development of modern invention and business organization so stupendous, that overproduction has become a standing evil—a permanent disease of the industrial system; and they regard the recurrence of crises and industrial depressions as being at once a proof of the existence of the disease and the means by which the progress of the disease is checked from time to time.

We will begin by examining this view first; for while it relates to more complex matters, it is easier to deal with than is the simpler notion of the wayfaring man about the need of "making work."

Purchasing Power Keeps Pace with Production

The economist holds that there cannot be in any true sense such a thing as general overproduction; that what looks like overproduction is in reality only maladjustment of production; that the aggregate supply of things produced can never, *simply as an aggregate*, outrun the demand for things—because, first, the *desire* of mankind for things in general is *unlimited*, and secondly the *purchasing power* to back this desire is *created by the production itself*. But those who hold the overproduction view above indicated maintain that, while this sounds like good theory, the phenomena of hard times prove it to be false. Here we have, they say, great stocks of goods that cannot be sold at remunerative prices; abundant supply all round, but insufficient demand. And they go farther; they assign a cause for the connection between hard times and overproduction. They point out that the desire for the accumulation of wealth takes the form, in our time, of a tremendous pressure in the search for profitable investments; that consequently capital is embodied in the form of industrial plant—buildings and machinery—to an extent having no proper relation to the demand of consumers; that, being once put into this form, its owners find it necessary to keep the plant running at a loss rather than let it lie idle; that thus there is constant danger of production not to satisfy demand but to keep machinery going. And they say that in this circumstance is to be found the essential cause of the recurrence of periods of business depression and widespread unemployment. For when a manufacturer finds that his goods have greatly outrun the demand for them, he is compelled to shut down his plant or at least slow up production; this throws many men out of employment; being thrown out of employment, these men can no longer keep up their demand for goods; thus the evil feeds on itself, spreads wider and wider, business depression causing unemployment and unemployment causing business depression, so that the evil becomes general—nation-wide, perhaps world-wide.

Not Overproduction, but Misfit

The scientific economist admits that there is much truth in this picture; but he denies that it proves what the upholders of the overproduction theory say it proves. For he sees no reason to believe that the *magnitude of the aggregate production* has anything to do with the case. If manufactures were carried on upon half the scale that they now are, there is every reason to believe that the same fluctuations of business would occur—as indeed they did occur when methods of production had not advanced to anything like half their present efficiency. The reason for the fluctuations lies in the very nature of business enterprise, together with the necessary imperfections of human calculation. Manufacturers and merchants naturally seek to avail themselves of all the opportunity that, in any given condition of things, appears to present itself in their particular line of business; and when everything looks prosperous some will be sure to be oversanguine as to the extent of that opportunity. In this way, in one line and another, there will be an oversupply—a supply greater than the demand in that particular line; and a concurrence of many such overestimates will result in stocks of goods remaining unsold, shutting down of factories, unemployment—in short, that self-propagating wave of depression that was described above.

Business Psychology

And in the propagation of this wave an element enters which has not yet been mentioned, but which is the most powerful of all—the element of business psychology. When once the idea spreads that business depression is impending, business men naturally become seized with a fear of loss which is sure to be, by many, as much exaggerated as was the hope of gain when times were good; and thus many people are thrown out of employment not because of the diminution of demand already experienced, but because of the fear of such diminution in the near future. It is this *diminution of production* that really makes the trouble so serious; for diminished production means diminished purchasing power, and therefore *diminished demand*, every whit as much as it means diminished supply. The wonder is that the trouble is ever got over—but it *is* got over, largely through the restoration of a better psychological condition in the business world. Into this extremely difficult question of "business cycles" of alternate exaltation and depression, I cannot enter further; but it is plain that their occurrence is caused not by the *magnitude* of the total production, but by the impossibility of *adjusting* production to the exact circumstances of the time. There is not the faintest reason to suppose that this impossibility would be in any degree lessened if production were carried on upon half its actual scale. If there were any fundamental truth in the overproduction idea, the stupendous increase in the productive power of machinery during the last hundred years would make trouble of a far more constant and deep-seated nature than that which appears in the shape of alternate periods of prosperity and depression.

A Long-lived Fallacy

Let us now look at the older and more common form of the overproduction idea—that which regards a hail-storm or a fire as not altogether a bad thing, since it creates work for glaziers or for carpenters and builders, and which sees in trade-union rules for "making work"—that is, for diminishing the effectiveness of labor—a means of preventing unemployment. The fallacy which underlies this view is remarkably persistent; it is almost impossible to get it out of people's heads. Some years ago I came across a most interesting illustration of this. Immediately after the great earthquake at Messina, the London *Spectator* seized upon the opportunity which that catastrophe afforded to give its readers a lesson in Political Economy, in the shape of an article on the "Economics of Destruction." Referring to the vast amount of work that would have to be done in clearing away the débris from the site of what once was Messina, with a view to ultimately raising on that site or near it a new city, the *Spectator* said:

The workmen employed on the gigantic task will certainly be congratulating themselves on their good fortune in securing employment likely to last for some years, and other people looking on at this scene of busy industry will be tempted to say: "After all, the earthquake was not altogether a bad thing. It has made work for these men and their families." We venture to prophesy that a good many people will make this remark, and will be quite convinced in their own minds that it embodies a real truth. For by the time that the work of reconstructing Messina is well in hand the horrors of the earthquake will to a large extent have passed out of memory, and the minds of the onlookers will be influenced by what they see, not by what they have forgotten.

It is the old story, on a larger scale, of Bastiat's broken window-pane. The amiable onlooker, seeing the pane broken, remarks that it is an ill wind that blows nobody any good, for the breaking of the pane will make a job for the glazier. This philosopher of the street, fixing his mind only on the thing which he immediately sees, forgets to ask who would have had a job if the window had not been broken. The householder who is the victim of the accident may be in need of another pair of shoes or of stockings for his children, and the money which he has to spend in replacing the pane makes it impossible for him to procure these gratifications. The job which the glazier gets involves the loss of a job to the bootmaker or the hosier. Thus the breaking of the window-pane means no increase whatever in the sum total of national employment; it merely means a redistribution. And that is not the end of the story.

If the pane had not been broken and the shoes had been bought, the householder would have had the double enjoyment of a pair of shoes and of a pane of glass, whereas now he has only the pane of glass.

The *Spectator's* prophecy as to the persistency of the fallacy was soon shown to be correct. In the next number of the paper, there appeared a letter from an evidently highly educated correspondent, who challenged the *Spectator's* position as follows:

> In your article on "The Economics of Destruction" you are surely too hard on the "philosopher of the street," as you call him, who remarks, when a window-pane is broken, that it is an ill wind which blows nobody any good for it will make a job for the glazier. Surely he is right. You say he fixes his mind only on what he immediately sees, and forgets to ask further questions. Now, as I agree with him, I may also call myself a philosopher of the street, and I will point out that I see all that you point out about the loss to the householder, and I see something further which you apparently overlook. It is true that the owner of the window-pane, inasmuch as he has had to pay the price of the repair to the glazier, cannot buy with it shoes or stockings for his child. But, on the other hand, the glazier, whose child may have been without shoes or stockings, is now able to buy them. It is, as the philosopher of the street observes, an ill wind that blows nobody any good—the householder has lost, the glazier has gained. Of course, if the glazier has been prevented from doing another job, which increases the wealth of the world, there is a net loss of wealth; but this is unlikely.

The probability is that he would have been at leisure, and in that case the wealth of the world is the same as before the window was broken—one man has done a job he would not otherwise have done, and there has been a small redistribution of wealth in consequence.

To this argument the *Spectator* made the following reply:

> If our correspondent's argument is sound, he ought to begin to do his best to dissipate poverty and unemployment by smashing windows, blowing up houses, burning furniture, and, in fact, carrying havoc and destruction into every trade where there are unemployed. Under his theory, there can be no national disasters. Occurrences like the Messina earthquake are merely redistributions of wealth, and the countries that endure them are not in reality suffering. The truth is, of course, that you cannot destroy the things that people need, and the men and women who supply these things, without reducing the wealth of the world. Scarcity can never be the source of abundance.

I have given all this space to these quotations for two reasons. In the first place a sharp controversy of this kind, centering upon a specific illustration, is apt to make a deeper impression than could be produced in any other way. But there is also another reason. While the *Spectator's* reply does well enough as a *reductio ad absurdum*, it does not squarely meet the difficulty in the other man's mind. It has been wisely observed that the disproof of a fallacy is never fully satisfactory until it shows not only that the thing is false, but just where the departure from truth to error occurs; for nearly every persistent error rests upon a partial foundation in truth. So it is in this instance. The writer of the letter rests his case on the supposition that if the pane of glass had not been broken, the glazier would have been idle; and if this view is fundamentally sound then his argument is sound, let the consequences be what they may. And in that case the trade-union man is right, too, when he wants to "make work" by diminishing the output of the workman; and the protectionist is right in wishing to compel his countrymen to do a greater amount of work than they would naturally have to do to get the things they need; and the perennial dread of general overproduction is not based on delusion, but on reality.

These people are all in one boat; but they are all wrong together. The supposition that the glazier would have been idle if that particular pane of glass had not been broken may be correct in any individual case; it may on its face be correct in a million individual cases; we may even admit, for the sake of the argument, that it is true in every *individual* case; for all that, it is absolutely false in the *general* case. Each separate glazier may wait until some particular pane of glass is broken before he can get a job; and yet it doesn't follow in the least that if twice as many panes of glass were broken every year as there actually are there would be fewer idle glaziers. On the contrary it is safe to say that there would be just about *twice as many idle glaziers* at any given time as there are now; simply because, with the average demand for glaziers twice as big as it now is, there would be *twice as many glaziers.* There isn't the slightest reason to suppose that the work would come in with any greater *regularity;* there would be slack times and rush times for glaziers, just as there are now. And if windows were never broken at all, the consequence would not be that there would be a lot of unemployed glaziers starving for want of work; it would simply be that a lot of people who have learned the glazier's trade would have learned some other trade.

The Fundamental Truth of the Matter

I hope it will now be easy to see what the fundamental truth is about the danger of unemployment, of there not being enough work to go round. At any given moment—in any given situation—there *is* a certain amount of danger of any particular person, or set of persons, being thrown out of work; and it is natural that workingmen, to whom unemployment is a terrible evil, should be anxious about it. But that danger arises from a *want of fit* between supply and demand, from an *irregularity* in adjusting the one to the other, and not from supply *as a whole* being too large. There is no limit to the desire of people for *things in general*, and the increase of production simply has the result of enabling them to fulfill that desire in greater and greater measure. Misfits are bound to occur, but there is no more reason to expect them to occur with a *large total* than with a *small total* of production.

Take any one of the striking labor-saving inventions of the past hundred or hundred and fifty years, and see what has come of it. Steam and electricity and a thousand forms of automatic and other machinery make it possible to turn out perhaps ten times, perhaps a hundred times, as much of cloth, or shoes, or transportation, or watches, or sewing, or paper, or printing as could formerly be turned out with a given amount of labor; but has this reduced the employment of labor? Not at all; the result has simply been that people are far more abundantly supplied with clothes and shoes and dresses, that instead of watches being a luxury almost everybody has a watch, that there is a hundred times as much travel as there was a hundred years ago, that forty-page newspapers have taken the place of four-page ones and have ten times as large circulation. Not all these things are unmixed blessings; but that is not the point. What we are concerned with here is the question of overproduction; the question of the need of "making work." If there were any real ground for the fear of overproduction, any real justification for the policy of "making work," the inventions of the past hundred years, instead of increasing (as they have done) the material comforts of the whole population, would have had the result of permanently throwing three-fourths of the population out of employment.

CHAPTER XVIII

MONOPOLY

In the discussion of Demand and Supply, Prices, Wages, Interest, etc., in Part I of this book, everything rested on the supposition of competition. Every now and then, it seemed desirable to remind the reader of this supposition and to point out that in the absence of competition the conclusions arrived at would not hold. If, for example, a particular person or group of persons are so placed that they alone can supply a given commodity, the price which they can get for it does not necessarily have any relation to its cost of production, and may yield quite abnormal gains to those who supply it. And likewise if a particular person or group of persons are the only ones who can furnish a particular service, the rate at which that service is remunerated may be vastly higher than that received by others in similar occupations. There are many examples of this kind of monopoly which have always been familiar. In the case of commodities the most striking instance is that of the owner of a patent; here the exclusive power to furnish the article is actually conferred by law, the object being to stimulate invention. In the case of services, some of the notable instances are those of a great pianist, or singer, or actor, or surgeon, or lawyer; the ordinary working of competition has little if any relation to the payment which these exceptional individuals may command for their services.

It would be interesting to discuss these and other special examples of monopoly; but we shall have to confine our attention to those larger aspects of the question of monopoly which have in recent years come to be of commanding public importance.

Natural Monopolies

During the past four or five decades, certain developments of modern economic activity have tended powerfully toward bringing about monopoly where before there had been competition. In a certain class of enterprises, indeed, this condition had shown itself long before that time; and it will be well to say a word about this class before discussing the more general subject.

So marked is the character of this class of enterprises that they have very properly been called *natural monopolies;* because free competition in these cases is either impossible, or, if possible, would be absurdly wasteful. The supplying of water or gas to a city is one of the oldest instances of this class of enterprises; to duplicate the plant by which either of these necessities is supplied would be a monstrous waste, and could not in any case result in genuine competition. At most there might be two, or possibly three, gas companies supplying the same consumers; and though these might for a while make a show of competition—or possibly even a sincere attempt at it—they would be sure to get together upon some understanding, so that real competition would come to an end. And when this time came, they would naturally expect to get returns on the entire capital they had invested, which might be two or three times as great as there had been any necessity for.

Obviously the right way for the municipality to deal with these enterprises—*public utilities*, as they are called—is to grant to some one corporation the exclusive right to furnish the service in question, or else to furnish the service itself. In the case of water—partly because of the simplicity of the service, and partly because of its absolute necessity—practically all municipalities furnish their own supply; in the case of gas (and likewise of electric light) the service is usually supplied by a private corporation. But when any public utility is supplied by a private corporation, the rates at which it is furnished are controlled by law; and thus, while the wasteful absurdity of attempted competition is avoided, the public are by no means at the mercy of the monopoly.

Telegraphs, telephones, and railroads are instances of natural monopoly, not always quite so sharply marked as those of the water supply or gas supply of a city, and yet clearly enough cases in which ordinary competition is quite out of the question. In the case of railroads, particularly, when there are two or more different roads connecting two great cities, they may all perform useful, and even indispensable, service in the traffic on their respective routes, without any unnecessary duplication, and yet offer competitive service as between the great cities which they connect. But since at the utmost there can only be two or three, or perhaps four, such lines, there cannot permanently be full-fledged competition. Even if there be no formal compact between the companies, they are bound to act upon some understanding as to rates rather than that each of them should cut off its own nose to spite the other's face. It is only when there is a field open to an indefinite number of competitors that genuine competition can be expected; and this cannot be the case where, as in the instance of railroads, the entry of any new competitor would mean an enormous investment of capital which would wastefully duplicate what already exists. Accordingly, intelligent upholders of the merits of competition long ago ceased to wish to bring railroads under the sway of ordinary competitive principles; while looking to competition as an influence in the railroad situation, they recognize that the main reliance for securing good railroad service at reasonable prices must be some form of public regulation. Of course, here too there is the alternative of government ownership and operation; and the question of its merits and demerits as compared with the ownership and operation of railroads by private corporations is a prominent subject of political controversy.

Large-scale Production and the Tendency toward Monopoly

So much for "natural monopolies"; but the tendency towards monopoly in other fields, which has been so marked a development of the past few decades, is of a character at once far broader and far less simple. It does not rest upon any such impossibility to maintain competition, nor upon any such enormous economic advantage in the elimination of competition, as exists in the case of "natural monopolies." The tendency towards monopoly which we are now to consider arises from the advantages which large-scale business enjoys over small-scale business, in these days of highly-developed machinery and organization.

In the case of agriculture, as was pointed out in the chapter on the "law of diminishing productiveness," a man working a given piece of land cannot put more than a certain amount of capital and labor into it with advantage; after a certain point is reached, every additional investment becomes less and less productive. But in the case of manufacturing, or of commercial or financial business, the opposite state of things is encountered. There is something like a law of *increasing* productiveness —not continued indefinitely indeed, like the law of diminishing productiveness in agriculture, but continued in many instances to a very advanced point. Up to a very high point the bigger the business—especially in the case of manufacturing—that a concern handles, the less the cost per unit of product. The fixed charges do not increase in proportion to the business; the expenses of management do not increase in proportion to it; the larger the business the more perfect can its organization be made; and in many instances machinery of a far more effective kind can be employed for a big output than for a small one.

Besides these large and obvious advantages, there are many others that are connected with matters of detail. Some of these relate not so much to economies in the actual process of production as to advantages in commercial competition. Such are the capacity to fill orders promptly, the convenience to customers of having all grades, sizes, etc., obtainable from one and the same establishment, the ability of the big concern to purchase materials at the most advantageous times and in the most desirable quantities, etc.; to say nothing of any *unfair* advantages extorted by the pressure of superior wealth. All these numerous advantages, taken together, are, in some lines of business, so great as to drive out of competition all except very large establishments; and, from the nature of the case, a very small number of these very large establishments may be sufficient to supply the entire demand. But as soon as the number of competitors in a given field is so small that combination among them is easy, combination in some form is almost certain to be attempted, sooner or later; and it is doubtful whether, in such cases, any amount of legal prohibition of combination can be made thoroughly effective. In such cases as this, it may be said that competition itself has had for its final outcome the extinction of competition: the little concerns having been driven out by real competition, the big concerns that survive are too few to keep up genuine competition.

Trusts and Anti-Trust Laws

But it is a mistake to suppose that this process is so absolute that competition is necessarily doomed to extinction, or even that it must cease to be a factor of the first importance. That mistake was made by a great many important persons, including writers on economic questions, some twenty or thirty years ago. They argued that the advantages of large-scale business in all the principal lines of production were so great that it was futile to fight against monopoly, and that the only sensible thing to do was to accept it and make the best of it.

But that view was an extravagant one. The situation in regard to large-scale production—even in such extreme cases as those of sugar-refining, iron and steel making, or beef-packing—is by no means parallel to that of the "natural monopolies," where a duplication of plant would be sheer waste. The economies of large-scale production, though they may be very considerable from the standpoint of competition (because even a *little* lower price may be sufficient to put a competitor out of business) may be no very large fraction of the total cost of production; and furthermore the competitors were often driven out not so much by the actual economies of their bigger competitors as by unfair practices of various kinds. The big monopolies, or near-monopolies, in this country came to be known as Trusts; and the anti-Trust laws (of which the chief one was enacted in 1890) were designed in large part to prevent these unfair practices, and have in considerable measure succeeded in doing so. More important in this respect than the anti-Trust laws themselves have been the laws which have stopped the giving of "rebates" by railroads; for one of the chief of the unfair advantages that had been enjoyed by the Trusts (above all by the oil Trust, the Standard Oil Company) was the making of special arrangements with the railroad companies which placed upon their competitors heavy burdens from which the Trusts were exempt.

The Check of Potential Competition

The fact that the economic advantage of the big concern is not overwhelmingly great (especially when unfair practices are stopped, or reduced to a minimum) has very important consequences. In the first place, the big concern—let us say Trust for short—can never feel that it has an absolute monopoly; even if no competition, or no genuine competition, exists, there is always the *possibility* of competition, and this *potential competition* is a check upon any desire that the Trust might entertain to squeeze all it could out of the public.

To understand just how this affects the case, let us see how the possessor of an *absolute monopoly* would act, supposing him to be actuated solely by the desire to make his gains as big as possible. Even then, he would not put up the price to the highest possible point. For though he has control of the supply, he has not control of the demand; if he sets his price extremely high he may make a big profit on every unit of his product that he sells, but he may be able to sell only a very small number of the units. An absolute monopoly, if operating solely for its pecuniary interest, would fix upon that price at which the *profit per unit* multiplied by the *number of units sold* would make the biggest possible total. This is called making the price *as high as the traffic will bear;* by which is not meant that if you made the price higher there would be no traffic, but that the *diminution in the amount of traffic* would more than make up for the *increase in the price.*

Now it is evident that none of our great industrial Trusts do anything of the kind. Whether they would do so if they had no fear of competition, we need not trouble our heads to conjecture; they are so very far from doing it that we may be quite sure their actual conduct is determined by the knowledge that to go much above the price which would arise under competition would be very dangerous—that it might at any moment turn *potential competition* into *actual competition*, which it would be extremely costly to deal with.

Take the case of the American Sugar Refining

Company, for example. Its price for refined sugar is such as to give it a fraction of a cent a pound profit; and if it increased the price by twice that fraction, which would double its profits per pound, this would cut down the number of pounds consumed by only a trifling amount. And the same kind of thing is true of the great Chicago meat-packing concerns, the United States Steel Corporation, etc. None of these is in anything like complete actual possession of the field; but even more important than the presence of the actual competitors are the possibilities of potential competition. The whole situation is vitally different from that of absolute monopoly.

Competition Not Dead, Nor Dying

The belief that competition is on its last legs is by no means so fashionable nowadays as it was twenty or thirty years ago. So far from rapidly obtaining full possession of the great fields of large-scale staple production, the domination of monopoly even in those fields is probably less complete than it was then; and outside those fields competition continues to be thoroughly alive. In the case of articles that are produced in great variety, giving room for individuality in taste, or skill, or knowledge of particular forms of demand, no such advantage is possessed by a gigantic concern over its comparatively modest competitor as in the case of such a business as sugar, oil, or steel.

And it must be remembered that so long as competition occupies a very large part of the entire field of business enterprise, its influence is sure to affect also that part of the field which has been taken possession of by monopolistic or semi-monopolistic combinations. Many fortunes, and big fortunes, are still being made in lines quite outside the monopoly régime; and so long as there exist great resources ready for new investment, in the hands of persons who are not part of the Trusts or combinations, these combinations have constantly to reckon with the possibility of dangerous competition, and therefore must keep their exactions within moderate limits.

CHAPTER XIX

TRADE-UNIONISM

In the foregoing chapter, upon the subject of Monopoly, nothing was said about Trade Unions. These bodies are organizations of workingmen whose members bind themselves to act together upon questions of wages, hours, conditions of labor, etc.; and inasmuch as they control admissions to the body, it is evident that, if sufficiently powerful in any particular trade, or group of trades, they may obtain a monopolistic command of it. For they may keep down the number of persons who are permitted to become members, or to learn the trade as apprentices working alongside the full-fledged members; and if they refuse to work with non-union men, they may, in case they control the whole, or almost the whole, supply of labor in the trade, by various means make it practically impossible for employers to carry on their enterprises with any other than union labor. When this state of things exists, the trade union is a monopoly; and wages in the calling so affected may be raised far above the competitive level—

the level at which similar labor is paid in other callings.

A condition of somewhat this kind exists in many fields, a very conspicuous instance at this time being that of the building trades; one of the main causes of the high cost of building, and consequently of the scarcity of housing, in New York and other great cities, is the extremely high rate of wages which the building-trade unions are able to exact, as a consequence of the limitation of the number of workers in these trades which their rules have brought about.

Trade Unions not Necessarily Monopolistic

But, while trade-unionism *may* aim at monopoly, it does not necessarily do so; the subject is much broader than the mere question of monopolistic extortion which may form one phase of it. Indeed, it is so broad that, though a separate chapter is here devoted to it, we shall be able to consider only a few of the most important aspects of the question, and even these only in an elementary way.

The primary and essential purpose of trade unions is not *monopolistic limitation* of the number of workers who may *enter* a trade, but *united action* on the part of those who *are in* the trade. Instead of each worker making his own bargain with the employer, and running the risk of non-employment or discharge in case he is not willing to accept the employer's terms, the workers take their position as a unit, and stand or fall together.

Collective Bargaining

This process has received the name of *collective bargaining;* but it ought to be observed at once that there may be collective bargaining without trade unions. All the employees in a single establishment might form a union of their own—and they sometimes do—and agree to stand together for such terms as they collectively decide to be proper; but this is not what trade-unionists mean by collective bargaining. The object of the trade union is to establish rates of pay, hours, etc., which shall be insisted on by *all workers in the trade* in a given locality or a given region—sometimes a great city, sometimes a considerable section of the country, sometimes perhaps the whole country. When this has been accomplished, any particular employer, in making terms with his own employees, is virtually dealing not only with all of them collectively, but with the whole body of union workers in the trade throughout the region which the union covers. If he wants, for example, to put wages down below the point fixed by the union, or if he is unwilling to raise wages when the union demands that they shall be raised, he will not only lose the workers he has been employing, but he cannot replace them by others unless he is able to pick up workers that do not belong to the union at all. And, if the union is very powerful, this last may not only be a difficult thing, but may, by various means at the disposal of the union, be made practically impossible.

Now in this situation there is something that smacks of monopoly, to be sure; yet, so long as there is no limitation either on the number of apprentices or the number of full-fledged workers who may join the union, the essence of monopoly is lacking. Without this limitation of numbers, it is impossible for the union to establish, except perhaps temporarily, highly excessive wages—that is, wages far above those that are paid for similar work in other occupations. If such wages did become established for a time in a given trade, there would before very long be a rush of workers into that trade far beyond the demand for such workers; and with a lot of workers unemployed, there would be such pressure to get work on some terms that it would be quite impossible for the union to maintain the high wages it had been insisting on. Accordingly, where a union does not restrict the number of persons who can enter a trade, it is bound, as a matter of good policy, to limit its demands to a point not very different from that which open competition would establish.

Benefits of Trade Unionism

Turning aside, then, from the question of monopoly, or near-monopoly, let us ask what benefits trade-unionism confers upon the workers when it does not give them a monopolistic advantage.

Of these benefits the most evident and indisputable is the prevention of injustice to individuals. Quite apart from any question of the general rate of wages, the individual worker, if acting by himself, is subject to the caprice not only of the owning employers, but of those subordinates to whom they assign authority over their employees; and the protection which the trade union affords against unjust and arbitrary treatment—in the shape of discharge, fines, or other hardships—is one of the great benefits which it has conferred upon the workers.

Another phase of the union's influence, perhaps even more important, is the pressure which it is able to exert in favor of good conditions relating to sanitation, comfort, etc. Improvements of this nature are often refused or delayed not so much because of their actual costliness as because of mere inertia or indifference; and in overcoming this inertia or indifference the union may greatly benefit the workers without imposing any serious burden on the employers. The same thing may be said of the shortening of hours of labor in cases where such shortening of hours does not reduce production; and there *are* such cases, though the claim that shortened hours do not reduce production is often made where it is not really justified by the facts.

Besides these benefits, which lie outside the question of the rate of pay for a given amount of work accomplished, the action of the union may benefit the workers by bringing about more promptly a rise of wages which the forces of competition—the action of demand and supply—would bring about of itself, but would bring about more slowly. One of the most important points in a wise conduct of trade-union policy is to form a correct judgment of the possibilities of the situation; to make a move for higher wages at the time when the state of demand and supply is such that higher wages might be expected as the natural result of the conditions. At such a time, and especially if the union has in the past shown itself reasonable by not making untimely demands, employers may be expected to yield at once to a powerful union what they would concede only slowly and grudgingly to the demands of employees acting either individually or in small groups.

Besides all these things, which are the direct and immediate result of union activities, we must take account of the broader human effect of the organization of labor. The habit of working together in promotion of the common welfare, in matters in which the members are so deeply concerned, develops a capacity for coöperation which may be turned into many channels, and which may, in the long run, have consequences of the most vital importance; and, apart from this, the sense of human power, of being something more than a mere cog in the wheel of industry, of having a voice in the settlement of large questions, tends to raise the stature of the worker as a human being.

Evils of Trade-Unionism

So much for the benefits of trade-unionism; we must now take a glance at some of its evil effects. To begin with the last point above mentioned, its influence upon the worker as a human being. Collective action has, as has just been said, an elevating effect; but when it takes the shape, as it very largely does in trade unions, of suppressing or minimizing differences of personal character and ability, there is a loss of individuality (to say nothing of loss of efficiency) which it would be difficult to overestimate. As a general rule, the unions seek to establish fixed standards of work as well as of pay; they seek to prevent any worker in a given trade from doing more, or at least much more, than any other. In so far as this may be necessitated by the very nature of unionized labor, it might be passed over as a necessary evil, the price that has to be paid for the benefits of collective action. But the rules which unions make in regard to limitation of output per man are often made not because they are necessary to prevent overworking of employees by employers, but in pursuance of the policy of "making work." The fallacy underlying this policy was explained and commented on at considerable length in the chapter on Overproduction; and there can be no doubt that the pursuit of that policy by trade unions is the cause of a vast amount of waste, from which the working people themselves suffer in common with the community as a whole. In addition to these things may be mentioned the high-handed and often outrageous methods by which non-union men are coerced or intimidated, and prevented from obtaining employment; and finally the frequent abuse of power by the chiefs of the labor organizations, who, if either corrupt or overambitious, force their followers into strikes which are unjustified by the facts and which inflict grievous loss not only upon the workers as well as the employers, but also upon the general public.

These remarks about the actual workings of trade unions are far from covering all their aspects, either good or evil; they merely touch upon some of the most important. Before leaving the subject, however, it will be well to say a few words about the effect of trade-unionism upon the general condition of labor.

The Strike

The great weapon of the trade union is the *strike*. The strike may be a powerful weapon, even in its simplest form; namely, when the workers in a particular trade, organized in a strong union, *refuse to work* unless their demand be granted. The difficulty of replacing the old workers by new may be so great that, rather than suffer the loss which it entails, the employers give in. To the simple strike in this form is often added the *intimidation* of non-union workers ("scabs," as they are called); the *boycotting* of resisting employers, that is, refusal of union workers (in other trades as well as that immediately affected) to have anything to do with those employers; and the *sympathetic strike*, which is a strike of workers in allied trades, to back up the original strike by spreading its inconvenience over a wider field and thus bringing outside pressure to bear upon the resisting employers, that the disturbance may be brought to an end by a settlement.

Fundamental Causes of the Advancement of Labor

It has often happened that through these means advances in wages and shortening of hours have been obtained when without them the concession would not have been made. But it does not follow, as many imagine it does, that the use of the strike, or even trade-unionism as a whole, has been the cause of the great advance in wages, and the great improvement in the condition of labor, which has taken place in the present and the preceding century.

There is very good reason for believing that the enormous growth of capital, and the increase of productiveness through the wonderful progress of science and invention, would have resulted in substantially the same advance of the condition of labor that we have witnessed if there had been no such thing as a trade union—provided only that the laboring population had not increased more rapidly than it has done. In so far as trade-unionism has had the effect of raising the standard of living of the masses, and through that raising of standard has kept down the increase of the whole working population, it has contributed toward raising the general level of wages; apart from this there is little reason to believe that it has exercised any important influence on that level. In a particular trade, the union may be able to keep people out and thus keep wages at an abnormal level in that trade; but this does not raise the general level of wages, for the workers excluded from the monopolized trade crowd other trades all the more; so that this circumstance does not contradict the general proposition.

The Reasonable Attitude toward Trade-Unionism

One who bears in mind these fundamentals of the trade-union question may still be puzzled to decide the rights and wrongs of any particular case; but he will at least have a thread of thought to guide him. He will not give his approval to a strike upon the mistaken supposition that the strike is the great instrument without which labor would be unable to improve its condition; he will approve it only as a prompt and effective means of accomplishing an adjustment which is reasonable and natural in the circumstances, but which without the strike might be thwarted by unreasonable resistance on the part of the employers. And he will have a fair insight into the question of union labor as against non-union labor. He will see that unionism, so long as it is not all-pervasive—that is, so long as it has to take into serious account the existence of non-union labor—confers great benefits through collective action and yet leaves us, in large measure, the benefits of competition; but that if unionism became supreme, the benefits of competition would be completely wiped out.

The case is in many ways similar to that of the Trusts, or great combinations of capital. In regard to these we jog along in a compromise way, not attempting to wipe out everything that savors of monopoly, and yet preserving much of the advantages of the competitive spirit. And so in like manner, the man of sense accepts the good along with the evil of trade-unionism, knowing that it is part of the inevitable order of the time, and confident that on the whole the good outweighs the evil; but on the other hand, he insists that the rights not only of the non-union man, but of the public at large, shall be maintained as against any pretensions of trade-unionism to complete domination of the labor world.

CHAPTER XX

COÖPERATION, PROFIT SHARING, ETC.

UNDER the modern organization of production, the compensation of labor, except in the case of the small farmer who works the farm he owns or rents, almost always comes to the worker in the shape of wages at a fixed rate. This rate is usually so much a day, sometimes so much an hour, or so much a week; in many cases, however, the worker is paid not by days or hours, but by "the piece"—so much a ton of coal mined, so much a garment turned out, etc. But whether paid by time or by the piece, he is paid at a fixed rate—a rate arranged in advance between him and his employer. He has no share in the shifting fortunes of the business; he gets his agreed wages, neither more nor less, whether the business does well or ill. He does not share the benefit of exceptional profits, and he does not suffer the hardship of unlooked-for losses. Of course, in the long run his wages, and even the possibility of his being employed at all, depend, broadly speaking, on the prosperity of the business; but there is no direct or definite connection between the amount he receives for his work and the gains either of those who supply the capital for the enterprise or those who undertake and carry on the enterprise.

Throughout the past hundred years, or thereabouts, in which the modern industrial system has been growing to its present vast dimensions, a great deal of thought has been devoted to the possibility of giving the manual workers a more direct interest in the fortunes of the undertaking in which they are employed; and there have been a considerable number of instances in which plans have actually been put into operation for this purpose. These have taken chiefly two forms, one of them being *coöperation*, the other *profit sharing*. Some of these experiments have been successful, others have broken down. Neither plan has made much headway; both have thus far been found to work successfully only in cases where the human element—the good will and ability of those carrying it on—has been of exceptionally high quality. Nevertheless, there are many who hope that there is a great future for coöperation, or for profit sharing, or both; and certainly the success of either, as a means of improving the condition of the working people and above all as a means of creating better relations between labor and capital, would be heartily welcomed by well-meaning people in general.

Coöperative Production

In principle, by far the most important form of coöperation is that in which the workers actually own and manage the enterprise—say a manufacturing concern—in which they are employed. In this case they are their own employers—that is, the group as a whole is the employer of the individuals who form the group. I say that this is the most important form of coöperation *in principle*, because wherever it exists it completely alters the situation of the manual worker, by merging his interest as an employee with his interest as an employer; his pay comes not from the fulfillment of a bargain that his work shall be compensated at a fixed rate but from the actual gains of the business. Just how these gains are to be divided among the workers is, to be sure, a matter of arrangement; but that is, comparatively speaking, a question of detail. Upon some plan regarded as equitable, each worker receives a return on the capital he has put into the enterprise, and a payment for his particular labor; but the whole that is thus to be divided is determined by the degree of success or failure that has attended the enterprise.

But while this is *in principle* the most important form of coöperation, it is also the one most difficult to carry out *in practice*. The difficulty of providing the necessary capital is itself very great; but still greater is the difficulty of securing the necessary managing ability and business skill; and even if all these things be provided, there is the further difficulty of maintaining that harmony within the group which is necessary to secure continued operation of the enterprise. And when one considers how enormously this last difficulty must be aggravated when things go badly—when gains dwindle or perhaps are converted into losses—it is easy to see why this fundamental form of coöperation has made but little headway. The future may possibly bring about a great development of this form of coöperation; but as yet there has been but little sign of any such development, and the few instances of lasting success have been those in which a start was given by able and high-minded owners who have turned a thoroughly established business over to their employees, and have inaugurated a system that was calculated to perpetuate the good management and good will which are essential to continued success.

Coöperative Distribution

Vastly easier, but also vastly less important, is coöperation in a matter that affects the worker's outgo, instead of his income—not how much he gets for his work, but how he spends what he does get. A remarkable movement was started in England about 1850, by an association of workingmen known as the Rochdale Pioneers' Society, to establish retail stores owned and operated by the very persons who bought their goods at the stores; and from a very small beginning this movement has grown until now the business of the workingmen's coöperative stores in England runs high up into the millions.[1] The stores are carried on by efficient

[1] The plan has been worked in this country also, but has never, until recently, attained large dimensions. Within the past few years, however, it seems to have gained a new and important start in some parts of the country.

managers appointed by the owning society and serving for moderate salaries; the object is to turn over to the members the profits which would otherwise go to retail dealers carrying on business for their own gain. The excellent plan is pursued of selling goods at the ordinary retail price, so that there may be no danger of loss, and then distributing the profits at the end of every year, or every quarter-year, each member receiving an amount proportional to the total amount of his purchases during the period. The capital invested in the business is also owned by the members; and before the distribution of profits there comes a distribution of interest on the capital which each member has contributed. Excellent as the scheme is, it is evident that it is not *in itself* of vital importance. As a matter of fact, the gains returned to the purchasers average about 10 per cent. of the amount of their purchases; and even this, it must be remembered, is reckoned upon standard retail prices and not upon any special low prices such as are often offered by ordinary retail stores. Nevertheless, there is much value in forming the habit of coöperation and the habit of investment—for the members largely invest their share of the profits in the business itself, and this has been the great source of its remarkable growth—and many still point to the success of the Rochdale Pioneers and their imitators as reason for looking for greater and more vital results from the coöperative principle. But we must not forget that coöperation of this kind, which does not affect the worker's vital interests and does not involve him in any scheme controlling his daily life and labor, is a vast distance away from the kind required for coöperative production.[1]

Labor Banks

An extremely interesting development of coöperation which has recently taken place in our own country is the establishment of labor banks—banks carried on by labor unions, the capital being subscribed by members of the union and the bank being conducted by the union itself as owner. There is no reason why these institutions should not be successful, in the same way as the English coöperative stores have been; prudent and capable management is, indeed, necessary to secure success, but there are no great inherent difficulties in the way of obtaining such management. Like the coöperative store, the labor bank, though it may prove very useful to working people, is not a thing that can vitallyaffect their condition; it is a side matter, not a matter involving the character or control of their daily life and work. But every successful attempt at coöperation, even if not of a fundamental character, does suggest the possi-

[1] The great English coöperative stores do actually carry on some branches of manufacturing; supplying themselves with certain goods at their own factories instead of buying them from other manufacturing concerns. But this is not a case of coöperative manufacturing, as described in the earlier part of this chapter; for, in the factories carried on by the coöperative store, the workers are wage-employees, like those in any other factory. They are not *their own employers;* their employer is the Society that runs the coöperative store.

bility of coöperation of the more vital kind, and is calculated to encourage attempts of more far-reaching importance.

Profit Sharing

Another scheme for improving the position of the worker is that of *profit sharing*. While coöperation seeks to combine the resources of the workers among themselves, profit sharing seeks to effect a combination of interest between the workers on the one hand and their employer on the other. The employer remains in complete possession, and usually in complete control, of the business; the workers continue to receive a fixed wage; but in addition to that wage they receive a stipulated share of the profits of the business—say, half the profits. At the end of the year, the profits of the business are reckoned, and half of the amount is distributed among the employees, each receiving a sum proportional to the wages he has earned. Thus if the profits of the business have amounted to $100,000, the workers get $50,000 of this as an addition to the wages they have received during the year; and if the total of these wages has been $400,000, say, then any employee who has earned $2,000 in wages receives in addition one two-hundredth of the $50,000, or $250.

The great benefit of this arrangement is that it gives the workers a direct interest in the prosperity of the business; if, by fidelity, energy, and alertness, they can cause the profits to be $200,000 instead of $100,000, the $2,000 man just mentioned will get $500 instead of $250 as his share of the profits.

This advantage is so evident, and is so in accord with the interests both of employer and employed, that one is tempted to think that the profit-sharing plan offers a solution of the whole problem of good relations between labor and capital. But unfortunately experience does not give much support for such a belief. The idea is by this time nearly a century old, and a great deal has been thought and written about it; but the plan does not spread, or at least does not spread at all rapidly. The reasons for this are doubtless many; and in large part they are the same as those which have stood in the way of the spread of coöperative production. One of the obstacles is the problem of what shall be done when—as sometimes happens—the year shows loss instead of profit; the workers would, as a rule, be neither willing nor able to refund part of their wages. This can, indeed, be guarded against by holding back some of the gains in the fat years as a provision for the needs of the lean years; but one can readily imagine the complaints to which such a policy may give rise. As in the matter of coöperation, a high degree both of ability and of mutual confidence and good will is necessary to the success of the profit-sharing plan. It must also be mentioned that workingmen, and especially trade-union leaders, are apt to look with disfavor upon the profit-sharing idea because they suspect that the real purpose of the employer may be to "speed up" his workers—to get more work out of them than he could otherwise get, and more than is good for them physically. In addition to these obstacles, there is that of the complexity of modern business accounting; unless there is thorough confidence on the part of the workmen in the soundness of the accounting methods, dissatisfaction with the results of the plan may at any time threaten its breakdown.

In spite of all these difficulties and limitations, it would be quite unjustifiable to conclude that it is impossible for either coöperation or profit sharing to have a great future. Both are worthy of serious and persistent endeavor, and the slowness of their growth up to the present time does not prove that with the growing prosperity and the growing intelligence of the working people, they may not be developed upon a scale far beyond anything which has thus far been attained.

Shareholding

Finally, something should be said about a resource that is clearly within the reach of any well-paid wage-earner and which offers no complexity or difficulty. Without pre-arrangement of any kind, without entering into compacts with anybody, he can become part owner of any one of a thousand enterprises by simply investing his savings in them. Nearly all the great business enterprises of the country are conducted by corporations, and the wage-earner, like anybody else, can buy the shares of these corporations at the price which they command in the open market. Whether this is a wise policy in any particular case is, of course, always open to doubt; very probably in most cases he would do better to entrust his savings to a savings bank, or buy perfectly safe bonds, and get a modest but sure return on his investment in the shape of interest at four or five per cent. But the point is that, with the high wages now prevailing in many occupations in this country, the wage-earner can, if he chooses, become a shareholder, and ultimately a substantial shareholder, in any one of a vast number of business enterprises.

It is the practice of some great corporations to encourage their own employees to invest in the stock of the corporation itself; and there are cases in which this policy is carried to a much more important point by combining it with the profit-sharing plan. This is done by giving the wage-earners their share of the profits not in the shape of cash, but in the shape of shares of stock to an equivalent amount; and the result of this, in the course of years, is that the workers may gradually become owners of the whole stock, or of so much of it as to give them control of the corporation.

Thus it will be seen that, while no confident prediction of a great future can be made for any of the means by which the wage-earner can become in addition something of a capitalist or entrepreneur, yet the elements of such a future exist, and afford ground for hopeful interest in their development.

CHAPTER XXI

TAXATION: GENERAL REMARKS

THE subject of taxation involves a vast number of questions, both theoretical and practical. It is the purpose of this chapter only to point out a few of the broadest aspects of the subject; and of the next briefly to discuss some of the chief points concerning the principal forms of taxation in actual use.

Assessments for Special Benefits

It will be well, perhaps, to begin with a few words in regard to a kind of taxes which are wholly different in character from the great body of taxes—namely taxes levied for special benefits, which it is felt should be paid by the persons who receive those special benefits. Such *special taxes* are often not spoken of as taxes at all, but as *special assessments*. Perhaps the most important of these are assessments levied against the owners of real estate for improvements directly affecting their property, such as the grading or paving of the street on which it fronts, the opening of a new street in the neighborhood which increases the value of the property, etc.

The discussion of such special taxes has almost no relation to the general subject of taxation; the assessment of them is really a matter of compensation for specific value received, and differs from an ordinary business transaction only in that the receiver, a private party, is compelled by public authority to perform his part of the bargain whether he desires the benefit or not, and whether or not he is satisfied with its price. In this element of compulsion the special tax, or special assessment, is like any other tax; apart from this it is wholly different.

Purposes of General Taxation

In the case of taxation in general, there is not only the element of public compulsion, but another even more profound difference between it and private bargaining. Not only does the government—local, State, or national—not ask the individual whether he wishes to pay or not; it also does not regulate *how much* he is to pay by the amount of benefit he receives from the things for which the tax-money is expended. There is no exact or fixed line that determines what things shall be paid for by special assessments and what by general taxes. A large number of the purposes to which the proceeds of general taxation are applied *might* be regarded as proper subjects for special assessment; and where the line is drawn depends on the general feeling of the community as to the proper functions of government.

Probably the most important, and certainly one of the most interesting, instances of the steady change in the ideas prevailing on this subject is that of public education; especially as illustrated in the case of England. A hundred years ago it was not there thought the business of government to provide education, at least beyond the most rudimentary stage, to the people in general; and it was only by very slow stages that the point was reached at which it was generally recognized that government should furnish a very considerable measure of education to all children, without charge to their parents. This principle once recognized, the cost of the free schools must necessarily be met out of the proceeds of general taxation, and not by levying a special assessment on parents in proportion to the benefit they (that is, their children) get out of the schools. In our own country this principle has been recognized from the earliest period in our history; though the scope of its application has grown from the modest beginnings of early days to that exhibited in the great system of public education which we now know, and which forms one of the chief objects for which State and local taxes are expended.

Of course police—the preservation of order—is a far more primary object. The repairing and lighting of streets, the building of sewers, the acquiring and maintaining of parks and playgrounds, the support of institutions for the insane and feeble-minded, the maintenance of boards of health and sanitary inspection, are among the most important of the other objects which are universally recognized as part of those functions of government which serve essential interests of the community as a whole, and which must be paid for out of the proceeds of general taxation. In the case of the national government, the maintenance of the army and navy, and of the necessary agencies of internal order such as courts, comes first of all; but in addition to these, in our country, there has been a vast extension of governmental activity into fields in which it has been felt that the public welfare could not otherwise be effectively served—the improvement of agriculture, the management of public lands, scientific activities like those of the Geological Survey and the Weather Bureau, etc. The total of governmental expenditure, national, State, and local, in all these varied directions, has become enormous; and there is every reason to believe that their scope will be still wider in the future.

Distribution of the Tax Burden

It would be going beyond any purpose contemplated in this book to discuss the question of what limits it is best to set to the functions of government, and accordingly to the aggregate amount of expenditure which must be provided by general taxation for the fulfilment of these purposes. But assuming that a certain amount has to be raised by taxation, we shall briefly consider the broad principles which should govern the distribution of the tax burden.

Taxation and the Sense of Justice

Perhaps the foremost requirement that nearly everybody would lay down for a system of taxation is that it should conform to the general sense of justice. But, though this requirement is truly fundamental and of the first importance, it is extremely vague; it is preëminently a case of Captain Jack Bunsby's favorite saying that "the bearings of this observation lays in the application on it." One result of it, to be sure, is simple enough; taxes should be so laid as to make no arbitrary discrimination—to bear alike upon all persons in like circumstances. This nobody disputes; but it does not get us very far. The difficulty arises only in regard to persons in different circumstances—the rich and the poor, the landowner and the business man, the spendthrift and the miser.

A Discarded View

It is not very long since many persons maintained the view that a man ought in justice to pay an amount proportioned to the benefits he derives from the existence of government, and especially to the protection it affords to his property or his income. This view has, however, long been almost universally abandoned; and one reason for its abandonment is that there is no possible way to measure that benefit. But that is not the only reason. A more fundamental objection is that every man's stake in the government is primarily his share as a human being in the maintenance of the safety and general well-being of the community of which he is a member. His taxes are not to be regarded as mere payment for the protection of his property, or even of his life, but as the amount which it is proper for him to contribute to the upholding of the social order of which he forms an integral part, and whose value to him is as incomputable as the value of the air he breathes. Today hardly anybody disputes this; and, in so far as any general principle of justice is held in view, it is the principle that everyone should be taxed according to his ability to pay.

Taxation and the Ability to Pay

But, though this principle is more sound than the principle of payment according to benefit received, it is very far indeed from being a perfect guide even from the standpoint of justice, and still more so from the standpoint of practicability; and this for many reasons.

One is that ability to pay is very difficult to define, and still more difficult to measure by any clear rule; but there is another reason even more important. Though the satisfaction of the general sense of justice is an important object, it is not the only object to be held in view in levying taxes. In taxation, as in other matters of government, we must bear in mind not only the result *intended*, but also the results that *will actually flow* from a given course. Moreover, when we speak of a given tax being "just," we do not mean that it is calculated to bring about a state of ideal justice, such, for example, as is aimed at in the schemes of many Socialists; whatever the merits of these schemes, they involve a change in the whole social order, whereas the purpose of taxation must be regarded as that of obtaining the revenue necessary for governmental purposes, in such a way as not only to do as little *injustice* as possible, but also to do as little *harm* as possible, in a community living under the existing social order.

Practical Effects must always be Considered

If we were to attempt to determine all questions of taxation *solely* by the consideration of ability to pay, the result, in the existing social order, would be full of harm, and even full of absurdities. It might possibly be shown, for example, that a man who made enormous business profits in a given year was better able to give up to the government ninety-five per cent. of his income than an ordinarily prosperous person was to give up one per cent. of his; but the levying of the ninety-five per cent. would disastrously interfere with enterprise, while the levying of the one per cent. would be completely harmless. This is of course an extravagant supposititious case; but it serves to bring out the principle.

And there is another disastrous effect, hardly less serious, which would be produced by taxing people literally according to their ability to pay. If only the very rich paid taxes—even assuming, for the sake of the argument, that such a plan was workable and would yield all that the government required—the people at large would find it hard to realize that taxation was any concern of theirs, and the consequence would be that there would be no effective check on governmental extravagance. It is practically of the very first importance that everybody should feel some appreciable part of the weight of taxation; that everybody should have a direct interest in the efficiency and economy with which the tax money is expended. And, imperfect as all tax systems necessarily are, they do attempt to take into account, as they should, all the great practical considerations which bear upon the actual working of the taxes.

CHAPTER XXII

TAXATION: ITS VARIOUS FORMS

One of the most important questions about a tax is whether the person who pays it really does pay it or shifts the burden to somebody else. In the first case the tax is said to be a *direct* tax, in the second an *indirect tax*. Apart from the property tax, the most important instances of direct taxation are taxes on *income*, on *business profits*, and on *inheritances and bequests*. Nearly all indirect taxes are essentially taxes on consumption—taxes which, whoever pays them in the first place, are really and ultimately paid by the consumer of the thing upon which the tax is based. A tax on *property*, which has always been the chief tax levied by our local governments, and one of the chief taxes levied by our States, is, from the standpoint of the lawyer, a direct tax; but from the standpoint of the economist it requires special consideration, and cannot be simply set down as a direct tax in the same sense as an income tax or an inheritance tax. A very brief discussion of these various forms of taxation must suffice here, the purpose being solely to bring out the most salient points. And it will be best to begin with indirect taxes.

Taxes on Commodities

When a tax is laid on the manufacture or sale of a particular thing, the manufacturer or dealer pays the tax in the first instance, but it is not really a tax upon him, but upon the person who actually consumes or uses the thing. If, for example, the Government requires the manufacturer of a certain grade of cigars to put a one-dollar stamp on every box of 100 of these cigars he makes, that dollar becomes just as much a part of the cost of production of the cigars as are the wages he pays his workmen or the price he pays for the tobacco; it is not really a tax on the manufacturer at all, but on the consumer of the cigars. In like manner a duty laid on the importation of foreign goods is a tax on the consumer, not on the importer; to the importer it is as much a part of the cost of the goods as is the price he pays for them to the foreign manufacturer or dealer, and it is accordingly included in the price he has to charge for the goods when he sells them.

Effect of Import Duties

An extremely important point in this connection is the effect of an import duty on the price not only of the imported goods but also of like goods made at home. If the duty is not so high as to be prohibitive—that is, to exclude the foreign article altogether—consumers of the article will have to pay the higher price not only for the imported goods but for the like domestic goods. If, for example, a duty of 10 cents a pair is laid upon the importation of a certain kind of stockings, this will not only cause the importers to charge 10 cents a pair more, but will enable the domestic manufacturer to get 10 cents a pair more for them than he otherwise could. Thus the burden upon the consumers consists not only of the tax on the foreign goods, which they have to shoulder, but also of the enhancement of price of the domestic article.

When the duty is so high as to be prohibitive, no tax is actually collected at all; the burden then consists *entirely* in the enhancement of price of the domestic article caused by the removal of foreign competition. What the enhancement will be, however, is a matter that cannot be told at all from the amount of the duty. If, for example, we were to impose a duty of $10 a yard on the importation of cloth, no cloth would be imported; but of course the price of cloth in this country would not be raised $10 a yard.

Finally, it should be observed that even when the duty is not prohibitive, it is not correct to say that the cost is raised by exactly the amount of the duty. The importer *does*, indeed, add the duty to the price he pays abroad for the goods, and reckons it as part of the cost of the goods; but it may be that the foreigner accepts a somewhat lower price than he otherwise would for the goods, because the enhanced price here diminishes the total demand for them. This same kind of remark applies, indeed, to the effect of consumption taxes in general; but it is not quite so important as it may at first sight seem. For if the high price diminishes demand and thus somewhat lessens the increase of price which the tax would otherwise cause, then by the same token the increase of price that *does* take place has the effect of preventing people from getting the goods, or getting as much of them as they otherwise would. In other words, consumers suffer a deprivation of the goods, in addition to whatever increased price they pay for the goods they do get.

The Case of Monopoly

When we say that a tax laid upon the production or sale of a given article is not paid really by the producer or dealer, but is shifted by him to the consumer, we must remember that the cause of this shifting lies not in the mere *desire* of the producer or dealer to be reimbursed for the tax, but in the *forces that determine price* under a system of competitive production. It is the competition of different producers of the same thing that keeps its price[1] proportional to the cost of production. In the case of an *absolutely monopolized* article, there-

[1] That is, its *normal* price. It must always be understood that the price may temporarily differ greatly from the normal price; and indeed that in all these general assertions one is speaking of what *tends* to happen, of what upon the average or in the long run will happen, and not of the price which actually prevails from day to day, owing to all sorts of passing fluctuations in demand and supply.

fore, there is no reason to assert that a tax laid upon it will be shifted. The price of such an article is not determined by its cost of production; the monopoly fixes it at whatever point it thinks fit. An absolute monopoly (as we have seen in Chapter XVIII), if it seeks to get the greatest possible gains, makes the price of what it furnishes "as high as the traffic will bear"; and when a tax is laid on, it cannot arbitrarily add the tax to that price. Whether the tax will fall wholly on the monopoly or be in part shifted to the consumer is a complex question, turning on the degree in which an increase of price cuts down the demand.

Curiously enough, the popular notion about monopoly prices is apt to be exactly the opposite of the truth. It used to be said by many people, whenever Mr. Rockefeller made one of his great donations to charity or education, that he would be sure to raise the price of oil by enough to cover the gift. This was of course upon the assumption that the Standard Oil Company was a monopoly, and could do what it pleased with the price. But if it could do what it pleased with the price, there was no reason why it should not have raised the price before just as well as after; and yet nobody seemed to think that Mr. Rockefeller had been making a gift to the public by refraining from doing so. And it is the same way with a tax; the person who can shift the tax to the consumer is not the person who is in a position to make the price anything he pleases, but the person who has to regulate his price by the cost of production.

Income Tax, Profits Tax, Inheritance Tax

Let us consider now some of the chief forms of *direct* taxation—taxes which are really paid, or at least which are intended to be really paid, by the persons upon whom they are directly levied. Of these the property tax—which, until recently, was in this country incomparably the most important—requires very special examination; we shall therefore consider first the other three principal forms of direct tax—taxes on income, taxes on business profits, and taxes on inheritances and bequests. All these are truly direct taxes—their burden really falls upon the persons on whom they are levied. When a tax is laid upon a commodity, the producer of that commodity feels at once that he can—often even that he must—raise its price, because it costs not only him but *all his competitors* just so much more to produce the article and put it on the market. But nothing of the kind is true of an inheritance tax, an income tax, or a profits tax. In the case of a tax on inheritances or bequests this is too plain to require any elucidation; in the case of the other two a few words of discussion may be useful.

Take the case of a clothing manufacturer whose income (untaxed) has been $100,000 a year, and suppose now that an income tax of 10 per cent. is levied upon him. He would, of course, be glad to screw up the price of his goods enough to make up the difference; but he has no reason whatever to believe that everybody in the trade has been taxed any such amount, or perhaps any amount at all.

So, too, with a profits tax; if of that $100,000 income $50,000 has come to him in the shape of profits made in his business, it does not in the least follow that everybody else in the business has been taxed on a corresponding amount. On the contrary, some people make big profits, some no profits at all, on the same amount of business; and those competitors who have made little or no profit can make the goods just as cheaply after the profits tax was imposed as before.

Progressive Rates of Income Tax

These considerations apply with even greater force to *progressive* taxation of income and profits than to ordinary taxation of them. The most obvious way to tax incomes or profits is to levy a tax *proportional* to the amount of the income or profits: a five per cent. tax, say, on all incomes, or all above a certain small exempted amount; and likewise in the case of profits. But it has of late been thought well to require persons of large income to pay more than persons of small or moderate income, not simply in *proportion* to the size of the income, but at *a higher and higher rate*, the higher the income is. Under the present income-tax law of the United States, there is a "normal tax" upon incomes not exceeding $6000, and a surtax of from 1 to 50 per cent. upon all of a person's income above $6000; the surtax gradually rising for each additional portion of income until it reaches 50 per cent. for an excess over $200,000, and remains at that rate for all above that sum.

Manifestly a tax thus levied, based as it is upon the condition of affluence of each particular individual to whom it applies, cannot be shifted; it is quite outside the range of action of those forces of business competition which bear upon prices through cost of production. And the same thing is true of a profits tax which is levied at a higher rate the higher the profits are; such a tax as the "excess profits" tax levied during the Great War and continued for some time after. The ground on which these taxes are advocated is that they are a fair application of the rule of taxing people according to their ability to pay; and it must be admitted that they do fall heavily—as they are intended to—upon the persons on whom they are directly levied.

It is often asserted by opponents of such taxes as these that they do not accomplish the purpose for which they are intended, but are shifted to the people at large just as commodity taxes are shifted. This view will not stand examination; it is impossible for the people on whom progressive income or profits taxes are levied to pass them on by any definite act, as commodity taxes are passed on by simply raising prices to correspond.

Nevertheless the contention that the public does lose indirectly, as well as gain directly, through these taxes, is by no means without foundation. If the taxes act as a serious discouragement to enterprise, or if they put a handicap on precisely those persons who are of the greatest help in promoting the general prosperity, it is quite possible that the unseen loss incurred by the community in this way may outweigh the obvious gain obtained by it from the taxes themselves. It is not that those who are taxed relieve themselves of personal loss by passing it on; but it may be that their personal loss entails an equal or greater loss to the people at large. The excess-profits tax, though entirely justified as a war measure, was felt by nearly all competent authorities to be doing far more harm than good after the war; this being a tax which acted with peculiar force as a handicap to business enterprise and business ability. The objection does not apply with anything like equal force to the progressive income tax; but here too, when the rate goes beyond a certain point the evil effect may far outweigh the good.[1]

The General Property Tax

We come now to what used to be regarded in this country as *the* direct tax *par excellence*, the "general property tax." In the old days, it was felt that the best measure of a man's ability to pay that could be found (and certainly the simplest and most uniform) was the amount of his possessions of every sort and description: his lands and houses, his furniture and jewelry, his horses and carriages—and for that matter his stocks and bonds,

[1] In our country, the question of very high rates on large incomes is complicated by the fact that there exist great quantities of securities, issued by the national, State, and local governments, which are wholly exempt from taxation. This creates what may be called an accidental difficulty, quite apart from the inherent merits of the question, caused by the possibility of escaping those high taxes altogether.

though these, now the most important, were in the early days of the country a minor factor.

But there is nothing upon which all men whose opinion is worth considering are more thoroughly agreed than that the "general property tax" is in its working not only vicious but absurd. Some of the reasons for this I will indicate in a few words. First, the amount of a man's possessions is a very poor index of his ability to pay, for it may have very little relation to his income; secondly, it is often impossible to arrive at a sound valuation of a man's possessions; thirdly, the assessment of that value gives an endless amount of opportunity for dishonesty, either on the part of the person taxed or of the assessing officers or both; fourthly—and most important of all, ever since the early part of the last century—the levying of the same rate of tax on stocks and bonds as on houses and lands takes so huge a percentage of the income on the stocks and bonds that people simply *will not pay the tax*, no matter how much evasion, or even false swearing, it may take to avoid it. The general property tax has been abandoned in some of our principal States, and modified so as to be comparatively rational in others; and where it has been retained unmodified on the statute books its operation is little more than a farce.

Taxes on Land and Houses

But there is one part of the general property tax which is on quite a different footing—the tax on real estate, on land and houses. This was always the most important part of the general property tax, and it continues to be the chief source of revenue for our local governments—cities, towns and counties. Let us now consider a tax levied at a uniform rate on the value of all the land and houses in a given city,[1] and examine how it operates—who really pays the tax? Most people answer this question very simply by saying that the tenant pays the tax; that the landlord is sure to pass it on to him. But the case is not quite so simple as that.

The rent that is paid for a house must be regarded as consisting of two parts—one part being a return to the owner of the house upon the capital invested in the building of the house and the other a payment made on account of the desirability of the site on which the house is built.[2] Now these two parts are governed by wholly different principles. A tax levied on the site-value cannot be shifted to the tenant, because the amount he pays for that turns not on cost of production at all, but simply on desirability, and the desirability is neither increased nor diminished by the tax. But, an objector may say, the desirability is what determines the rent of the house too; nobody is any more willing to pay a high rent for the house than

[1] For the sake of brevity, our discussion will be confined to city real estate, but evidently the same considerations apply to non-urban property.

[2] There is of course a third part, namely the amount necessary to cover repairs, superintendence, etc., and in the case of modern apartments the expense of running elevators, etc.; but it is best to regard this third part as an addition to what may be called the net rent—the return the landlord gets after these expenses are covered.

he is for the site just because a tax has been clapped on it. This is true enough, as far as it goes; but it overlooks an essential point. The site is there, of itself; the house won't be there unless somebody builds it. And if a tax is put on the house, it won't pay anybody to build it unless, in addition to the normal return on the capital he puts into it he gets enough to enable him to pay the tax. The house tax is like a commodity tax, a tax on production; it operates as an increase of cost, and raises rent just as a tax on cigars or whiskey or stockings raises the price of these things. But the lot is there; it doesn't have to be produced; the supply of lots is not diminished by taxation nor increased by the absence of taxation. Thus we may say that, broadly speaking, the land tax falls upon the land owner, the house tax upon the tenant.[1]

I say "broadly speaking," because it must always be remembered that economic generalizations of this kind do apply only "broadly speaking," and not to every particular case. All that we mean is that the general level of rents, the general course of rents, is determined in this way. The rent of a particular house, or a particular class of houses, may be affected very differently, or may not be affected at all, by taxation. Take, for example, a section of a city, once fine and prosperous, which has been thrown out of its original character by

[1] Of course the owner of house and land may himself be the occupant of it; in that case the whole tax falls upon him; but while the land part falls upon him as owner, the house part falls upon him not as owner but as occupant—he could shift it to a tenant if he did not occupy the house himself.

changes in business or fashion, and which is quite out of the current of building enterprise; in such a situation the owner has to take what he can get people to pay, and neither taxes nor any other element of cost has anything to do with the case. And there are many other peculiar situations or circumstances which may alter the result above indicated. But it is folly to let this stand in the way of our appreciation of the general principle; to ignore it because it does not take account of every case is as though one should refuse to think of the earth as a sphere because of the irregularities of its surface.[1]

Other Aspects of Taxation

Of course there is a vast amount to be said on other aspects of the question of taxation than those that have here been considered. The desirability of a tax often turns on such questions as the ease with which it can be collected; the expense of the collection itself; its accordance with the sentiments of the people, etc. Again, the incidental effect of a tax must be considered—consequences that were not contemplated in the levying of it as well as those that were. Of the former kind a classical instance is the window tax—a tax imposed in England a couple of centuries ago, which required a person to pay according to the number of windows in his house. This was supposed to be a fairly

[1] In connection with the single-tax doctrine, however, we shall take up some extremely important *general* considerations which bring out other aspects of the taxation of land and houses.

good measure of the scale on which he lived, and therefore of his ability to pay; but it had the consequence of leading people to have as few windows as possible in their houses, thus causing great injury by the cutting off of light and air. Of consequences directly intended by a tax, an important instance is that of a tax on liquor, which is made high for the express purpose of restricting the use of liquor. A notable case of an absolutely prohibitory tax is the Federal tax of ten per cent. on State bank-notes, the purpose of which was to have no notes circulating as money in the United States except those issued by the Federal Government and by the National Banks; a purpose which, of course, it completely accomplished.

But into these manifold aspects of taxation we cannot enter. All that has been attempted is to present some of those aspects of taxation which are most nearly related to broad economic principles; and even in regard to these, it has not been the purpose so much to discuss them with anything like completeness as to indicate and illustrate the way in which we must discuss them if we are to have clear views on the subject.

CHAPTER XXIII

THE SINGLE-TAX DOCTRINE: ITS BASIS

NEARLY fifty years ago, there appeared in our country a very remarkable book, which proposed what its author regarded as a remedy for all of the gravest economic ills under which the world suffers. Its title was *Progress and Poverty*. The subtitle indicated two purposes: first, to inquire into the cause of "the increase of want with the increase of wealth," and secondly to point out "the remedy." Its author, Henry George, had qualifications not usually possessed by persons who undertake ambitious projects of this kind; he was a writer of extraordinary lucidity as well as eloquence, and he had got a firm grip on a fundamental economic principle which furnished the backbone of his book. Add to this a genuine moral fervor which animates the most impressive passages of his book, and we have a combination not often met with. The book made a profound impression not only in this country, but throughout the world; and for a time many thought that its doctrine would steadily advance everywhere and would, before very long, find general acceptance.

This has not happened; but the doctrine still commands a devoted following, and from time to time comes into prominence as a public issue. Since this is so, and especially since there are few economic doctrines that it is more interesting or more instructive to examine, it seems desirable to devote a considerable amount of space to its discussion.

Progress and Poverty

Before entering upon that discussion, it will be well to say just a word about "the increase of want with the increase of wealth," to which Henry George devoted a large part of the space and of the eloquence of his book. He was firmly convinced that with the increase of wealth there went an actual "increase of want"; that as the rich grew richer the poor grew poorer, not only relatively but absolutely; that in spite of all the wonderful advances of modern science, invention, and industry, there was constantly more and more poverty and wretchedness. That he was wrong in this, hardly anybody today would dispute; and so, too, he was clearly wrong in some other things even more fundamental. But we are not examining the merits and defects of the book as a whole. We must limit ourselves to an attempt to understand the essentials of his doctrine, and of the arguments for and against it.

Henry George was not a Socialist; on the contrary, he was an ardent individualist and a thorough believer in the right of private property in general. But he held that private ownership of *land* is robbery; that the land justly belongs to all the people; and that by resuming possession of the land, the community would rid itself of the whole burden of taxation and would throw open to everybody such opportunities, now denied them, as would put an end, or almost put an end, to poverty.

Property in Land Unlike Property in the Products of Labor

Of course Henry George was not the first to point out the difference between property in land and property in other things. A house, a ship, a machine, a bale of cotton, a bushel of wheat, a barrel of flour, a coat, a table, a piano, is the result of human effort. Land, on the other hand, is provided by nature; the man who owns it cannot say that he made it.[1] All he can say is that he has got possession of it; nor can he, by taking thought, add a square yard to its area. Its *value* depends not upon its cost of production, for it cost nothing to produce,[2] but upon its desirability—the advan-

[1] It is true, as was pointed out in an early chapter of this book, that nothing is absolutely "made" by man; all he does is to take what nature provides, and, applying various processes to it, cause it to supply his uses. And it is also true that in a large proportion of cases the land, as used by man, is not simply the land as nature furnished it; there has been perhaps stumping and draining, perhaps road-building to make it accessible, perhaps cutting or filling to fit it for building; and it may be that the owner has paid for these things. But, after duly considering these points, the difference between property in land and other property remains essentially unimpaired.

[2] Again the reader is reminded that there may have been a great deal of cost in bringing the land to its present condition; some allowance

tage that its use offers to the user. And this desirability, this advantage to the user, depends in turn upon the gradual development of the community. An acre of rocky land on what is now Fifth Avenue, New York, was worth exactly nothing two hundred years ago, while today it is worth perhaps ten million dollars; and this increase of value has been quite independent of anything the owner has done to the land.[1] So far we can all go, so much as this the standard economists have always recognized. But Henry George goes a step farther. Human effort, he says, is the only just basis of the right of private property; no man is entitled to claim as his own what was a free gift of nature to all mankind. Accordingly, since land is not produced by human effort, and since its value is created by the development of the community as a whole, the private ownership of land is a robbery of the community as a whole; and, no matter how long that robbery has passed unchallenged, the rightful owner, the community, should assert its claim and resume that ownership which it never ought to have relinquished. If this were done the revenue derived from the land would be, he un-

---

must always be made mentally for this consideration, but it should not be allowed to interfere with our recognition of the fundamental fact in the case. Moreover, it should be noted that the *value* of the land, even when there has been such cost of improvement, is determined not by that cost but simply by the desirability of the land in its actual condition, as stated in the text.

[1] He has paid taxes, of course, and in the aggregate these (with interest) have amounted to more than most people realize; but after deducting what he has thus contributed to the public treasury, all the rest of the value has been created by the development of the community at large.

hesitatingly assumed, sufficient to pay the expenses of government, not only as they existed in his time but as they would become if the functions of government were vastly enlarged.[1]

Holding Land out of Use

In addition to thus relieving the community of the entire burden of taxation, Henry George and his followers have claimed another enormous benefit as sure to result from abolishing the private ownership of land. Under private ownership, they assert, vast quantities of land are held out of use, the owners speculating on the prospective rise of value; under public ownership, they say, this land would be thrown open to use and any person out of employment, or unable otherwise to earn his living, would have an opportunity to extract his living out of the soil. What with the extinction of taxes, and what with the benefits of this enlarged access to the land, poverty, they hold, would be almost completely abolished; for, according to their view, the main cause of the continuance of poverty—or, as Henry George put it, of the increase of poverty—with the increase of wealth is to be found in the enormous tribute which the community as a whole pays to the landowners.

[1] This estimate of the magnitude of the proceeds of land ownership has been sharply and, I think, successfully challenged; and very great difficulties are obviously connected with the question of a proper apportionment of those proceeds between the nation and its various subdivisions. But it is impossible here to go into these questions; for the sake of the argument we may admit Henry George's view of the amount, and overlook the difficulties of apportionment.

The Single Tax Equivalent to Confiscation

So much for the idea underlying Henry George's book, and the general argument by which it is supported; but it remains to mention one more cardinal point in his actual proposal. While he himself declared that confiscation of the land would be not only expedient but entirely just, he recognized that the idea of confiscation would be so shocking to most people that there would be little prospect of its obtaining general approval. Accordingly, he proposed to avoid confiscation in form while accomplishing it in substance. Abolish all taxes except a tax on land, he said; raise all public revenues by a *single tax*, namely a tax on land values. If that tax was so large as to absorb the *entire rental value* of the land—if, upon a piece of land that was worth to the occupant $1,000 a year was levied a tax of $1,000 a year—the land would be virtually confiscated, for it would be worth nothing to the owner; and if a tax of *very nearly* $1,000 was levied, the land would be worth *almost* nothing to the owner, and yet enough to cause him to hold on to it. Moreover, said Henry George in substance, it is not necessary to declare that the tax will take up the entire, or nearly the entire, rental value; all that we need do is to *abolish all other taxes*, and the rest will soon take care of itself. It is interesting to quote his own words on this subject:

> Let the individuals who now hold it still retain, if they want to, possession of what they are pleased to

call *their* land. Let them continue to call it *their* land. Let them buy and sell, and bequeath and devise it. We may safely leave them the shell, if we take the kernel. *It is not necessary to confiscate land; it is only necessary to confiscate rent.* . . . [The italics are Henry George's.]

By leaving to land owners a percentage of rent which would probably be much less than the cost and loss involved in attempting to rent lands through State agency, and by making use of this existing machinery, we may, without jar or shock, assert the common right to land by taking rent for public uses. We already take some rent in taxation. We have only to make some changes in our modes of taxation to take it all. . . .

It will be necessary, where rent exceeds the present governmental revenues, to commensurately increase the amount demanded in taxation, and to continue this increase as society progresses and rent advances. But this is so natural and easy a matter, that it may be considered as involved, or at least understood, in the proposition to put all taxes on the value of land. That is the first step, upon which the practical struggle must be made. When the hare is once caught and killed, cooking him will follow as a matter of course. When the common right to land is so far appreciated that all taxes are abolished save those which fall upon rent, there is no danger of much more than is necessary to induce them to collect the public revenues being left to individual landholders.

Having now got a general view of the nature of Henry George's doctrine, and of the grounds upon which it rests, we shall, in the next chapter, consider some of the chief objections to it, both ethical and economic.

CHAPTER XXIV

THE SINGLE-TAX DOCTRINE: OBJECTIONS

In the foregoing chapter, it was stated that the profound impression made by Henry George's famous book was due to a combination of two elements—the fervent eloquence with which he presented the moral or ethical aspect of his proposal and the firm grip that he had on the economic principle which furnished the backbone of his work.

It is frequently the case with any great proposal of change, whether meritorious or not, that its advocates are likely to know a great deal more about the subject than its opponents, since it is with them a central subject of thought while with others it is merely a matter occasionally thrust upon their attention. In the case of the single tax this is peculiarly true, because of the lucidity and the definiteness of Henry George's teaching. His disciples hold fast two central ideas. First, that the right to property in land rests upon no such basis as the right to other property, because land is not the product of human labor, but is a free gift of nature: whence they conclude that private ownership of land is robbery, and that it would be *just* to recover that property for the community, without compensation to those who now wrongfully possess it. Second, that if all taxes except those on land values are abolished, this *single tax* would be sure to attain, before very long, the height of the full rental value of the land, and would be equivalent to outright confiscation. And, having these things so clearly in mind, the single-taxers feel a sense of great superiority over "the man in the street" who brushes the whole thing aside by simply saying, as to its ethics, that all confiscation is robbery, and as to its economics, that all taxation is shifted.

But, plausible as is the single-tax doctrine, and resting, as it does, upon considerations that are entitled to weight, a fuller consideration shows it to be utterly wrong from the standpoint of ethics, and open to objections of the gravest kind from the standpoint of economics. We will take it up from these two standpoints successively.

The Ethics of Land Confiscation

First, then, as to the rightfulness of the confiscation of land. Let us consider who are the owners of land in a country like ours,[1] and how they have

[1] In such a country as the Russia of the time of the Tsars, or France before the great Revolution, the question of confiscating the land held by a privileged aristocracy merges with the general question of the abolition of hereditary privileges. Such a situation may justify revolution, and the confiscation of the land as a necessary part of the revolution. But the case is wholly different in a country like ours, or any country where land has for many generations been the subject of ordinary purchase and sale in which the whole people have freely participated.

come into possession of it. The persons who own land do not form a distinct class in the community; they are persons who (or perhaps their fathers or grandfathers; it seldom goes further back than that) have thought fit to invest their savings in the purchase of land, rather than in the purchase of ships, or houses, or railroad shares, or what not. It is true that the owner of land did not *create* the land; but there is every bit as much reason for supposing that the ownership of the land *represents* the fruit of his labor as there is in the case of the ownership of any other form of property. He made use of no special privilege to get possession of it; the purchase was equally open, and open on the same terms, to millions of other people who deliberately chose to invest their means in other ways. Before *Progress and Poverty* appeared, it never entered anybody's head in the United States to suppose, when he took the earnings of his labor, or of his professional skill, or of his business ability, and exchanged them for the title to a piece of land, that anybody would question that title; in his own mind, in that of the man who transferred it to him, and in that of the community at large, it stood upon precisely the same footing as any other form of property.

Granting for the sake of argument that it is both necessary and just that the community as a whole shall acquire possession of all the land, it is perfectly clear that in whatever loss may be entailed upon individuals in this process the owners of *all forms of property* should share alike. Granting for the sake of argument that the early settlers who took up the land which now forms our farms and villages, our towns and cities, were robbers, it is still evident that no moral distinction can be drawn between the individuals who today own city lots or farms and those who happen to have put their possessions into the shape of stocks or bonds or railroads or warehouses or manufacturing plants. It seems hardly possible that anything but wilful blindness could shut the eyes of anyone to the fact that if the private ownership of land is a great evil, the cost of remedying this evil cannot, without the grossest violation of equity, be assessed exclusively upon particular individuals unless they can be shown to have been guilty of some wrong in which the community at large did not share. Whatever may be the actual merits of the institution of private property in land, it is quite certain that the community as a whole is responsible for the existence of that institution. If the ethics of land confiscation be admitted to be sound, there is no security for any property right; and, what is even more important, the very idea of good faith dissolves into thin air. Suppose some brilliant successor of the author of *Progress and Poverty* should call the attention of the people of any country burdened with a great national debt to the startling fact that this vast indebtedness never would have been incurred but for the recognition of war, the greatest of all crimes, as a legitimate object of national expenditure. Would he not have every bit as good a reason for advocating repudiation of the debt as did Mr. George for justifying land confiscation? I do not assert positively that he would. What I say is that the answer to the question would depend, like the spelling of Sam Weller's name, on the taste and fancy of the answerer. If the preservation of good faith is to rest not on considerations either of equity or of honor, but on the view that people happen to take of the abstract justice of transactions in the remote past, good faith will cease to be a corner-stone of human society, and in its place will be substituted a mere juggling of academic subtleties. Mr. George has a great deal to say about justice, but I do not remember to have found the word "equity" anywhere in his discussion. And that sort of justice which ignores equity is either too high or too low—and really the two things come to the same thing—for the uses of man.

Having given to this question of the ethics of confiscation so much space because of the very great desirability of a thorough understanding of it, the remaining points, although highly important and interesting, must be discussed more briefly.

The "Unearned Increment"

A case much stronger ethically than that for outright confiscation can be made out for taking up by taxation not the *entire* value of the land, but only what has been called the *unearned increment* of that value. Indeed, long before Henry George's time, this was advocated by John Stuart Mill, not only a great economist but one of the greatest and noblest minds of the Nineteenth Century. Mill emphatically condemned confiscation as utterly indefensible; but he held it to be both just and expedient for the community to take possession of any future *increase in the value* of the land. This increase is caused, generally speaking, not by anything the owner of the land does, but by the general development of the community; let the owner, then, said Mill, be left in full possession of what he has now, but let any future addition to its value go to the people at large. Much can be said for this proposal, but the matter is by no means so clear as may at first sight appear. Everybody is familiar with striking cases of enormous increase of values in land specially favored by developments; but the cases in which no such increase takes place —cases in which the owner would be far better off if he had invested in something else instead of land —are incomparably more numerous than these brilliant examples of enormous gain. As nobody proposes to make good the losses of those whose investment in land turns out ill, it becomes at least questionable whether it is either right or wise to cut off the gains of those whose investment turns out well. But I cannot enter further into this question, though a great deal might profitably be said about it.

Land "Held out of Use"

Next to their fundamental doctrine that private ownership of land is robbery, what the single-taxers make most ado about is the injury that is done to the community by private owners "holding land out of use." This injury, though it looms into gigantic proportions in the minds of single-taxers, is almost entirely imaginary. Great quantities of rural land are, indeed, uncultivated; but the price that it would take to buy such land plays an extremely small part in the matter. It is left uncultivated not because it is in private ownership, but because even if it could be had for nothing, or next to nothing, it would not pay anybody, all things considered—remoteness, unfertility, expense of putting it into shape for use and of building the necessary houses, etc.—to cultivate it. But it is chiefly of city land that most people think who talk of "holding land out of use" as a terrible deprivation to the community.

And yet this is almost absolutely a pure delusion. These people talk as though, if the land in and around a great city like New York were not "held out of use" for speculative purposes, it would all be covered with houses; and yet a very little thought should suffice to show the absurdity of such a view. The land that is now occupied by houses in New York City, for example, was all there a hundred years ago, and hardly any of it was occupied. All of this unoccupied land was, if you please to say so, "held out of use" by its owners—that is, they would not give it away for nothing. But throughout nearly all of this area, a building lot could have been bought a hundred years ago for so little money that the purchase price would have been practically nothing in comparison with the cost of building a house on it; the real reason the houses weren't built was that even if the land had cost nothing, nobody could have been found to buy or rent the houses. During this hundred years the population of what is now Greater New York has been growing from about 150,000 to more than 6,000,000; and, whether the land had been owned by private individuals or by the community, its occupation would have had to be a gradual process, corresponding to the growth of the population. Throughout all this time, too, the owners of *all* the land have been paying taxes—the amount of which, at compound interest, is a tidy sum. The land was sure to *be* out of use, whether "*held* out of use" or not; and it is by no means clear that the community as a whole has suffered from its gradual occupation having been determined by the conditions of private ownership instead of by those of public ownership. Into this question, however, we cannot enter more particularly.

Single Tax and Building Enterprise

But there is one point about the *practical operation* of the single-tax plan in cities, which, though it has received little attention, is so vital that I shall endeavor to make it as clear as I can, though it will require some space to do so.

It is perfectly true, as the single-taxers charge, that the owner of vacant land in an urban area—that is, vacant land within a city or in its immediate neighborhood—does hold it as a "speculation." That is, he calculates that it will be to his advantage to wait until this land is in better demand, until it can be put to more profitable use; and in the meanwhile he pays taxes and loses interest on his investment, without getting any income from it. The ordinary real-estate tax does operate as an incentive to him to put his land to some use, but it does not subject him to the absolute necessity of doing so. He is not compelled to build at once; he balances the prospects of the future against the conditions of the present.

But under the single-tax system he could gain nothing by holding on to the land, since however much its value might increase the increase would be taken away from him by taxation. In the meanwhile he would be paying out in taxes every year the full rental value of the land, whether the land was occupied or not; and all of this would be a dead loss. Accordingly, he would find himself compelled to do one of two things—either throw up his ownership altogether, or build immediately the kind of house which fits the immediate situation, whatever the future uses of the land might be expected to be. And here comes in the point to which I have referred.

When a house has once been built on a lot, the whole thing—house and lot—becomes a unit; and the whole thing, lot and improvements, may increase or decrease in value. When the land becomes less valuable the whole thing is almost sure to fall in value, and the owner suffers the loss.

When the land becomes more valuable, the whole thing generally rises in value, and sometimes rises enormously in value; and, under the existing system, the owner gets the benefit of the gain. But under the single-tax system all the increase in the value of the *land* would be taken from him; and, so far from being compensated by any gain from the ownership of the house, he would actually, as a general rule, be a heavy *loser* whenever a great advance took place in the value of the land. If, for example, a man has built a modest residence, at a cost of $10,000, on a lot worth $5,000, and the site becomes worth $50,000 (either because the street becomes an important business street or because it becomes a splendid residential street), the *house and lot together* are worth no more than the lot alone, since the house is quite unsuited to the location; and therefore, as the whole of the value of the *lot* is, under the single-tax system, taken up by the tax-gatherer, the owner's investment of $10,000 in the house is a dead loss. It would be interesting to enter more fully into this matter; but if you will think it out, you will see clearly that under the single-tax system the only case in which (speaking generally) ownership of a house and lot would not mean a loss to the owner would be the case in which the character of the land, the uses to which it is best fitted, underwent no marked change, *either up or down*—or, for that matter, sideways, since a great change in the *kind* of building wanted on it would be as disastrous as a change in the *value* of the land. As soon as the building became a *misfit*, the owner would lose, so far as regards the building; and he would get no compensating advantage from any increase in the value of the land, since that would all be cancelled by the tax, which would be just as heavy as if the house were a perfect fit. In the case of a great rise in the value of the land, he would have to tear down the house and build another out of which he could get enough revenue to pay the tax, unless he threw up the investment altogether; and whichever he did, he would suffer a dead loss of the entire value of the house.

In view of this situation, the building of houses would evidently be an extra-hazardous business; there would be *no* chance of the investment increasing in value,[1] and a very great probability of its diminishing in value. As things are now, everybody knows that the house on a given lot is likely to be a misfit in the course of time, and may have even to be torn down; but the investor sets off against the prospect of this loss the probability of a compensating, and more than compensating, increase in the value of the land. Were this prospect taken away, one of two things would happen: either building enterprise would be paralyzed, or rents would have to be set high enough to cover not only a proper annual return on the capital invested in the house, but a very substantial additional sum to cover the great risk of the whole or a large part of

[1] I am ignoring here the changes in the *general level of prices*, which of course may affect houses as well as anything else; but this is a consideration which is irrelevant to the present question, since changes in the price-level may go down as well as up, and do not affect houses in any distinctive way as compared with other property.

the capital being lost in the course of time. And it is not at all unlikely—indeed I think it is highly probable—that the net result would be that rents would be higher under the single tax than under the existing system.

The Farmer and His Land

The case of agricultural land is in many respects different from that of city land; but I must dismiss it with a few brief remarks. First, as to the question of "robbery." Whatever may be said about city lots, hardly anybody can say with a straight face that the settlers who opened up the land were "robbers"; everybody must see that it was to the advantage of the whole community that it should be opened up, and certainly nobody had thought of any way of inducing men to do so except by making them feel that they owned the land and that any advance which might take place in its value would be to their individual benefit. Secondly, as to the use made of the land afterwards. Unlike city lots, the personal care and interest of the farmer is of constant importance to the proper utilization of the land; and this care and interest are inseparably connected with ownership. Thirdly, the distinction between what the land is by nature and what it has been made by the labor and expense bestowed upon it by those who have owned or occupied it—a difficulty which because of its comparative unimportance I have ignored in the case of city land—is a matter of first-rate importance in the case of farming land.

Finally, destruction of the sense of ownership would, in the case of the farmer, be profoundly injurious in its human, as distinguished from its merely economic, effects.[1]

Thus our conclusion is, that in spite of the strong *prima facie* case that can be made for it, the single-tax scheme is wrong from the standpoint of ethics and open to what it is hardly too much to call fatal objections from the standpoint of economics. Of the economic objections, I have confined myself to only a few—those which seemed to me most important. One more objection, however, should not be passed over without mention. Under the single tax, at least up to the time that it had actually absorbed the full rental value of the land, the great body of the population would feel no interest whatever in keeping taxes down; and therefore no interest in keeping government economical. When Henry George was candidate for Mayor of New York, one of the cries in his campaign was "No taxes at all, and a pension for everybody." With taxes levied on land-values only, that would be the feeling of the masses; they wouldn't be a bit afraid, as they are now, of any part of the heavy taxation falling upon their own shoulders. That this would be anything but a healthy condition for government and politics seems plain enough to require no argument.

[1] Into the case of mining land, though it is very important, I cannot enter. The single-tax idea is, in the nature of things, far more properly applicable to mining land than to either city land or farming land; but the subject is too special to permit of its satisfactory discussion here.

CHAPTER XXV

PROTECTION AND FREE TRADE. (*First Part*)

A PROTECTIVE duty laid upon any article is a charge made by the government for the privilege of importing it, and with the purpose of discouraging such importation and encouraging the production of the article at home; and a set of such duties covering various kinds of goods is called a *protective tariff*.

We saw, in the chapter on Foreign Trade, that any protective duty which accomplishes the object for which it is intended—a duty which causes people to purchase at home what they would purchase abroad if there were no duty—entails, *on its face*, an economic loss. This is, indeed, fairly evident from the simple consideration that the very reason for imposing the duty is that, in the absence of the duty, the article could be bought for less money from foreign producers than from home producers. But we went behind this obvious fact; we considered the question of *real cost*—the cost in human effort as distinguished from the cost in money—and saw the true nature of the gain which a country derives from its foreign trade. If we import cloth from England and export wheat to England, it is because with a given amount of human effort we can get a greater amount of cloth by producing wheat and exchanging it for cloth[1] than we could get by producing the cloth ourselves. A protective tariff, in so far as it is effectively protective, diverts production from those channels into which it would go if trade were left to take its own course; and if trade were left to take its own course production in any country would flow into those channels in which the productive advantages of that country were greatest.

The Tariff Controversy

But if the matter is so simple as all this, you may ask, how does it come that the question of protection remains, not only in our own country but throughout all the world, almost a perennial subject of controversy? How does it come that during a large part of our country's history the two great parties have been ranged against each other on this issue—the one often going so far as to declare that a protective tariff is sheer robbery, the other often going so far as to declare that it is the great source of the nation's unrivalled prosperity, and especially of the well-being of American workingmen? To answer this question anything like adequately would be impossible in a brief space; but we shall endeavor to get something like an intelligent understanding of the case.

[1] That is, by selling the wheat for money, and buying the cloth with that money.

To do this, it will be necessary, above all, to make two distinctions—the distinction between immediate and remote effects, and the distinction between strictly economic effects on the one hand and political and social effects on the other.

So far as regards immediate economic effects, the protectionist argument is almost wholly fallacious; but the two fallacies upon which it is chiefly based are of a peculiarly persistent kind. One of them is indeed essentially the same as that which was discussed in the chapter on Overproduction; the other is an old fallacy connected with "mercantilist" ideas on the subject of money. Let us take them up successively.

The Labor-employment Fallacy

The protectionist points to a large number of articles which are manufactured in this country but which could not be manufactured here if they had to meet the competition of other countries in which the rate of wages is far lower; and he says that the tariff which enables these industries to be carried on here benefits the country by the addition of these industries, and benefits the workingmen by making it possible for the manufacturers to pay the high wages. The argument is plausible; but it breaks down in exactly the same way as the overproduction argument—the argument illustrated by the case of the glazier and the broken window-pane—breaks down.

When a new industry is introduced in a country by a protective duty, it is a natural impression that the opportunity for employment is thereby enlarged—that work is found for the unemployed. But in reality the *opportunity* was there all the time; only it was not a sufficiently profitable opportunity to tempt people to make use of it. The tariff does not *create* the opportunity, but only causes it to be more profitable; and it causes it to be more profitable not through making it *less difficult* to produce the article at home but through making it *more difficult* to procure the article from abroad. And if we had got the article from abroad we should have had to pay for it by sending abroad something else that we had produced at home. The persons who are employed in the new industry are not persons who, if they were not engaged in it, would be do-nothings and a charge upon the public; they are persons who would be engaged in some other form of productive activity. Just so much effort as is put into the making of the protected article is withdrawn from the making of something else; there is not the slightest reason to suppose that, as a general proposition, there will be less unemployment because of the introduction of the protected industry; there will only be a change in the distribution of employments.[1]

So much for the creation of opportunities for the employment of labor. But how about the rate of wages? The protectionist says that without the protective tariff it would be impossible to pay the American scale of wages in competition with

[1] It might be well for the reader here to refresh his memory of the nature of the overproduction fallacy, as discussed in Chapter XVII.

the "pauper labor" of Europe. But how did the American scale of wages arise in the first place? Wasn't it precisely because wages were *already* high here that the claim was made, from the beginning, that higher prices were necessary to compensate the manufacturer for the greater expense to which he was put for his labor? Surely it was not for the purpose of making wages *higher than they already were*, but at best for the purpose of *maintaining them at the American level*, that any manufacturer asked for protection; it was to enable him to pay to the American workingman, in a particular enterprise, the wages which were *current* in America. The reason that wages *were* high in America was that American productiveness was great—this itself being due to many causes, not least among them the superior efficiency of the American workman. Finally, as an additional indication of the falsity of this "pauper labor" argument, it should be remarked that throughout decade after decade during which the well-paid labor of the United States was alleged to have required protection against the ill-paid labor of Europe, the workingmen of free-trade England were very much better paid than those of the protectionist countries of the Continent, whose products were allowed absolutely free entry into English territory.

The Money Fallacy

Of the other fallacy concerning the immediate economic effect of protection, one has heard less in recent times than formerly. It seems as though people in general had outgrown the notion that we must keep goods from coming into the country, in order to keep gold from going out of it. As was pointed out in the chapter on Foreign Trade, there is no ground for the fear that a country carrying on its business on a gold basis will not have, generally speaking, the amount of gold that it needs for that purpose; and the way in which this amount is determined, and is automatically provided by the ordinary processes of trade, was there briefly explained. This view, which economists have so long insisted upon, seems at last to have become pretty generally acquiesced in by the public. But so far is the general public from a real understanding of the subject that one still encounters, every now and then, not only the erroneous view that the country ought to avail itself of every means of holding on to gold, and of draining it from other countries, but even a much grosser error—a pure and unadulterated fallacy—as to the way in which imports affect the matter. This fallacy, gross as it is, has found acceptance in such apparently intelligent quarters that it will be instructive to examine it. A conspicuous instance of it is to be found in the following passage in a speech made some years ago by a prominent Southern Congressman at a meeting of the National Tariff Commission Convention:

> Being a citizen of Louisiana, which has so many protected industries—sugar, rice, lumber, etc.—I

> cannot help leaning somewhat to that side. and in my opinion the whole South is rapidly changing its ideas on this subject. Lincoln once said: "I don't know much about political economy, but I know that when we purchase a ton of steel rails from Great Britain for $100 we get the rails and Great Britain gets the money, and when we produce the rails from our own mines and in our own mills, we have both the money and the rails." Now, surely the latter condition is much better than the former, and it seems right and proper to assist in procuring and maintaining it by wise tariff enactments whenever possible.

There is no reason in the world to believe that Lincoln ever said anything of the kind; for though this Lincoln quotation with slight variations[1] has been used hundreds of times in protectionist speeches and editorials, there is never any reference to the place where it is to be found. However, that is not the question; the point is that this notion about having "both the money and the rails," though it seems to pass muster with many prominent Congressmen and editors, is a blunder of which a schoolboy should be ashamed.

The thing that is overlooked in the alleged Lincoln quotation is that when we buy an article abroad we do not also expend the labor and capital necessary for its production at home. When we pay $100 for steel rails to an English producer, we do indeed part with the $100,[2] but the labor and

[1] It may be observed that Congressman Ransdell has "steel rails" in his version of the quotation; but steel rails were hardly known in this country until some years after the Civil War.

[2] Or rather, for that is the truth, with $100 worth of other goods.

capital that would have been required for the production of the rails has been free to employ itself in other ways. It is true, to be sure, that when we make the rails at home "we have both the money and the rails," but then it must not be forgotten that we had to *make* the rails; when we buy the rails abroad, foreigners have had to go to the trouble and expense of making them for us, and we have presumably utilized for the making of something else the resources and the labor which we should otherwise have had to expend on making the rails.

It seems almost laughable that an error so obvious as this should need any elaborate disproof, and yet experience shows that this particular error —like many others, alas—has in an eminent degree the quality which the poet too optimistically ascribed to truth only: though crushed to earth a hundred times, it persistently rises again. So it will not be superfluous, perhaps, to give it one final thrust before we leave it. What, let us ask, would happen if instead of speaking of America and England somebody were to use the same argument in regard to two American cities? Suppose that some genius in Pittsburgh, say, were to startle the inhabitants one fine morning by the great discovery that whenever they buy cotton cloth at Fall River they get the cloth but the Fall River people get the money, while if they buy the same thing in Pittsburgh the Pittsburgh people have "both the cloth and the money." The announcement would certainly be most important if true; and the Pittsburgh people would doubtless appoint a committe at once to look into it. The committee, however, would not be long in reporting. They would report that, in the first place, they couldn't have "both the cloth and the money" unless they first *made* the cloth; that the capitalists of Pittsburgh had been perfectly well aware all along that it was physically possible for them to erect cotton mills instead of iron foundries, and to employ labor for the making of cotton cloth instead of the making of steel billets; that the business men of Pittsburgh had deliberately chosen to put all their energy into lines other than cotton manufacture, and that they could not put any of it into cotton cloth without taking some of it away from steel or something else; and the committee would doubtless wind up with the remark that the next time anybody asked them to investigate a proposition which contemplated the making of something out of nothing, they begged to be excused from wasting their time upon its consideration.

Thus we see that, so far as regards the direct and immediate economic effect of a protective tariff, the most familiar protectionist arguments are wholly fallacious; but we shall find a very different state of things when we come to consider the case of protection as related to more remote economic effects, and to political and social objects. This we shall endeavor to do in the next chapter.

CHAPTER XXVI

PROTECTION AND FREE TRADE (*Second Part*)

As was stated in the foregoing chapter, the case for protection does not by any means rest wholly on the crude fallacies we have been considering. Even on the strictly economic side, there are strong and valid arguments for protection; and there are also arguments based on political and social considerations which, if granted sufficient weight, might justify protection as a national policy, however clear might be the demonstration that it involved not only temporary but permanent economic loss.

The Infant Industries Argument

Of the strictly economic arguments for protection, incomparably the most important is what is known as the *infant industries* argument. Our reason for saying that protective duties entail an economic loss was that it diverts the country's production from the channels into which it would flow if trade were left to take its own course, and that if trade were left to take its own course production would flow into the channels in which it was most profitable—those in which the country had the greatest advantage. This argument is conclusive as regards the *immediate* effect of a protective duty; and it would be conclusive as regards the more remote effect also, if all the advantages and disadvantages which a country possesses at any given time in regard to various branches of production were inherent and permanent—if they were always the result of what may be called natural causes. But it is quite possible that a country is at a disadvantage in regard to a particular branch of production not because of natural causes, but because of want of familiarity with the business, lack of expert knowledge, or even of the trained workmen necessary to carry it on. Moreover, the risk attending the investment of capital in a new and untried line of production may be a great deterrent; especially as the foreign manufacturers have the inside track, and may even resort to selling at a loss for a while (a process known as *dumping*) in order to stifle the beginnings of the new competition. Thus the fear of loss in the initial period may prevent for a very long time the establishment of some line of production which, if once established, would show itself perfectly capable of holding its own without artificial support. In our own country, the majority of intelligent advocates of protection, during a long period, rested their case chiefly on this ground. We want a protective duty, they said, so as to give new industries a chance to live through those initial years in which they are not strong enough to hold their own against powerful competitors abroad who enjoy all the advantages of established position and long experience; though this will entail an economic loss for a limited number of years, it may in the end yield a great economic gain; for it will bring about the establishment of industries which we can carry on to full advantage once they are thoroughly established, but which will not be started unless they are given for a time the assurance of a home market from which foreign competition cannot dislodge them.

This "infant industries" argument is, in the abstract, perfectly sound; and its theoretical validity is admitted by fair-minded free-traders. Moreover, there are some important examples of its practical validity; there are important articles—such as steel rails, tin plate, etc.,—which it was vehemently asserted by many free-traders that we could never produce as cheaply as they were produced in Europe but which, after a number of years of protection, are made here at about the same prices as abroad. But these are the exception, not the rule; in the majority of protected industries a protective duty apparently continues to be necessary in order to keep them going. Moreover, whether the duty is necessary or not, the persons interested in the industry insist on its being retained; a protective duty, once established, has rarely been got rid of altogether. When the Republican party is in power, it is apt to be raised; when the Democratic party is in power, it is apt to be lowered; but it is only in comparatively few instances that it is entirely wiped out. Accordingly, though it may be true in a large number of cases that the infant industries theory has been justified, we can hardly ever be sure that it is so— for there appears to be no end to the period during which a protected industry is willing to be regarded as an infant.

One more remark, before we leave this phase of the subject. Sensible men, whether protectionists or free-traders, recognize that even if the maintenance of a protective duty for a given industry that has been established in the country does involve a continuing economic loss, the utmost care is necessary before deciding upon the abolition of any particular protective duty; for if removal of the duty should destroy the industry, the loss of capital and the dislocation caused by the change would be productive of serious distress to the persons immediately concerned, and might create grave disturbance in general business conditions. Thus we see that the question of how to deal with the tariff is not altogether simple, even from the strictly economic standpoint.

Social and Political Arguments

When we come to the arguments that are social or political rather than economic, it is of course impossible to dispose of them on the basis of any economic doctrine. They have to be judged from the standpoint of the general interests of society, and no numerical measure is possible of the advantages or disadvantages presented. First we have the argument for *diversity of employments:* if any nation devotes itself altogether to the occupations in which it has the greatest advantage, it may become very one-sided; thus England, under free trade, has become overwhelmingly industrial. It used to be said, half a century ago, that we didn't want the United States to remain a merely agricultural nation; development of manufactures was desirable to round out the national life. There can be no question that the protective system has actually accelerated this development. We are more of a manufacturing and less of an agricultural nation than we should have been under a policy of free trade. Whether this is a gain to the national well-being is a question on which every person may form his own judgment; though it is safe to say that there would be few who would hold the opinion that discrimination in favor of manufactures as against agriculture is any longer demanded in the interest of a healthy diversity of employments, whatever may have been the case in the past.

But even as to the past, a point of great importance must be made. It never was a question between exclusive devotion to agriculture and a development of manufactures. Manufactures would unquestionably have developed, and would long ago have reached vast dimensions in our country, even had there been no protection. They actually did develop with unprecedented rapidity in the decade from 1850 to 1860, when the tariff was so low as to approximate to a state of free trade. And one reason why this is so is of a simple theoretical kind. Conditions within a country are not uniform; neither are the dispositions and abilities of persons who command capital uniform. While some industries fostered by a protective tariff may be of such a character that they will not be carried on at all without its aid, most of them are such that they will be carried on under the most advantageous conditions which the country affords, but will not be carried on under less favorable conditions. The effect of the tariff in that case is not to *introduce* the industry, but to permit it to be carried on under less favorable circumstances and with less able management than was the case before. There is hardly a great branch of manufacturing fostered during the high-tariff régime that was not carried on to a considerable extent and with satisfactory returns during the low-tariff period from 1846 to 1861.

Economic Independence

Another important argument advanced by protectionists is the necessity of maintaining within a country all those branches of production which are essential to its safety and sustenance in time of war. This involves a large question of statesmanship, upon which it would be presumptuous to pass a general opinion. It is unquestionably a valid consideration; how important, and whether it outweighs other considerations of equally vital national concern, is a matter that demands the highest exercise of judgment in each case. A particularly instructive illustration of this is to be found in the case of England. Before she became a free trade country (about eighty years ago) she had a tariff system designed chiefly for the protection of the agricultural interests, the landowning class being dominant in English government. There was a heavy duty, especially, on the importation of wheat; and it was the repeal of the "corn laws" that introduced the free trade régime in England. Under that régime, England developed her manufactures enormously, but she became dependent on importations from the outside world for a very large part of her food supply. The consequence was that it became absolutely a matter of life or death for her to maintain command of the sea, since without it she might be starved out in a very short time in the event of war. How this situation will be affected in the future by the enormous development that is taking place in aerial navigation is a most interesting question; but as to the past it is plain that the abolition of the corn laws has made it necessary for England to devote unstinted energy and unstinted expense to maintaining command of the sea. On the other hand, had she stuck to the old policy of the corn laws, with a view to depending on her own soil for her food-supply, she could not possibly have maintained within her narrow limits the great population she now has. It seems plain, in spite of the need of securing essential food-supplies from abroad, therefore, that the free trade policy has thus far conduced more to the preservation of England's rank among the Powers of the world than the opposite policy would have done. What the future may bring forth, no man can say.

Actual Character of Tariff Legislation

Neither in this nor in the preceding chapter has any attempt been made to go into the numberless complexities of the protective tariff question; only its most salient aspects have been treated, and these only on the broadest lines. But we must not leave it without a brief reference to the actual processes of tariff legislation. Every intelligent citizen ought to have a fair understanding of the intrinsic merits of the chief arguments on the subject, and it is with these that we have here been concerned. But all experience—not only in our own country, but wherever there is a protective tariff—shows that the actual making of a tariff is in very large measure determined not by the merits of any abstract argument or even of any general public policy, but by the insistence of the interests immediately concerned. Both in the original establishment of a protective duty upon any particular article, and in its retention afterwards, those engaged in producing the article are so intensely interested in the advantage it gives them, and exert so great a pressure upon legislation, that the chance of a protective tariff being instituted on any clear principle of benefit to the whole people is very small. Sometimes this pressure is justified; particularly is this so when (as has been indicated above) the taking away of protection from an industry which was built up on the strength of it would cause disastrous loss of capital and disturbance of labor conditions. But the pressure is sure to be there, whether justified or not; and to *any* argument in favor of a protective tariff one of the chief counter-arguments is that in practice the tariff will not conform to the requirements of the argument, and moreover that pressure for legislation favoring any particular interest is a highly corrupting influence in politics. How much weight is to be attached to this consideration, and in what degree it ought to be regarded as outweighing the valid considerations by which a protective tariff policy is supported, is a question of political wisdom to which the economist can give no authoritative answer. His distinctive function is to set forth the elements upon which a sound opinion must be based, and to clear the air of fallacies; this done, he must leave the question of whether, upon the whole, protection is a good policy to be decided by the exercise of sound judgment on the case as a whole.

CHAPTER XXVII

CHANGES IN THE VALUE OF MONEY

THE use of gold[1] as the basis of all money has been of incalculable service to the world. It has furnished a simple and solid foundation for the transaction of all business, and for the measurement and payment of all financial obligations, between man and man and between individuals and governments. It is not necessary to repeat here what was said in Part I about the way in which money serves not only as a medium of exchange but also as a measure of value. But we must now fix our attention more fully on the *imperfection* of money—money based upon gold—as a measure of value. It serves perfectly to measure the relative value of any two things *at a given time;* if at a given time a yard of cloth sells for four dollars and a barrel of flour for eight, we say, and it is evidently right to say, that the value of the flour is twice

[1] Or, in former times, gold and silver. In the great commercial nations of the world, silver ceased to play the part of fundamental money about half a century ago. For the sake of simplicity, little or no reference will be made in our discussion to the use of either silver alone or both silver and gold as fundamental money; the discussion would, however, be essentially the same if those possibilities were taken into account.

that of the cloth; and so with any two things of which we know the price. But if *the cloth, and the flour, and everything else*, sells for twice as many dollars today as it did ten years ago it would be silly to say that the value of everything is twice what it was; what we *do* say, and what is the only sensible thing to say, is that the value of the dollar is half what it was.

Economists have always been fully aware that gold (or money based on gold) is not a perfect measure of value; that while it serves very well to measure the value *of any one thing in comparison with any other* at a given time, its own value is by no means constant; that a gold dollar may be worth much more, or much less, *in comparison with things in general*, at one time than at another. In spite of this, however, economists have prized the gold standard and stuck to it, because although it was not a perfectly stable measure of value it was far more stable than anything else that could be practically substituted for it. But we must clearly recognize that any serious change in the value of the monetary unit—any serious alteration, up or down, in the purchasing power of the dollar—is a grave evil; and accordingly that any well-thought out plan for *stabilizing the dollar*—for keeping its purchasing power as nearly constant as possible—is worthy of most earnest attention.

Debtors and Creditors

The most obvious evil of a serious change in the value of the dollar is that it brings about grave injustice as between debtors and creditors. And we must not think of debtors as poor and creditors as rich; in modern times, it is fully as likely to be the other way. If I have saved, perhaps by hard labor and strict frugality, ten thousand dollars and with that ten thousand dollars have bought five per cent. bonds of some great corporation, that corporation is my debtor and I am its creditor. If the bond has thirty years to run, the corporation is obliged to pay me five hundred dollars a year for thirty years and at the end of the time to return my ten thousand dollars. And if we had a perfect monetary standard—if the dollar were a perfectly stable measure of value—the $500 ought each year to have the same purchasing power as it did at the beginning, and the $10,000 likewise. If the $10,000 that I lent the corporation could buy so and so much of things in general, the $10,000 that the corporation returns to me ought to do the same, neither more nor less. For it is not the money itself, but what can be bought with the money, that men care for; and if I can get only half as much with the $10,000 at the end of the thirty years as I could have got with the $10,000 at the time I lent it, I am really getting back only half what I lent; and of course in like manner as to the annual interest—if $500 will buy only half as much as it used to buy, I am really getting only 2½ per cent. interest instead of 5 per cent. A fall in the value of the dollar—that is, a general rise of prices, a rise of the price-level—helps the debtor at the expense of the creditor; a rise in the value of the dollar—

that is, a general fall of prices, a fall of the price-level—helps the creditor at the expense of the debtor. The time of the great free-silver agitation, culminating in the Bryan campaign of 1896, was a time of low prices; the dollar had risen in value, and farmers were suffering as debtors because they had to pay off their mortgages in dollars that were worth much more than were the dollars they had borrowed. In this present period of high prices, millions of persons who have fixed incomes derived from bonds, annuities, etc., are suffering as creditors, because the dollars in which they receive their income are worth much less than were the dollars which they invested.

Salaries and Wages

And it is not only in the matter of actual debts that the instability of the dollar works great injustice and hardship. Prices of *commodities* can be adjusted pretty quickly to a change in the general price-level; but there are many things which necessarily take a very long time to adjust to it. *Salaries* are very slow to respond, because these are a matter of personal arrangement. When a salary is once raised, it is an unpleasant and difficult matter to put it down again; when it is once lowered, it is an unpleasant and difficult matter to get it put up again. The dollar will be a very long time down before salaries are put up to correspond; and it may be quite a long time up before salaries are put down to correspond. In the case of government employees, legislation is necessary to effect the change; and of course that is very slow work. *Wages* respond more rapidly than salaries; but in the case of wages also there is much difficulty and delay; you can't put wages up and down with the ease and promptness with which you can change your price-labels in a retail store, or your price-lists in a manufacturer's catalogue. So changes in the purchasing power of the dollar are capable of doing a vast amount of injustice and injury, and creating a vast amount of discontent, owing to the *slowness* of adjustment in such matters as salaries and wages, and the *impossibility* of adjustment in such matters as debts and fixed incomes.

The Business Cycle

In recent years attention has been directed more than ever before to still another evil caused by a fluctuating standard of value. We are all familiar with the fact that business seems to be subject to recurring waves of exaltation and depression—"boom" times and hard times following each other in something like regular succession. These recurrences of expansion and depression—these *business cycles*, as they have come to be called—have in recent years been made the subject of profound and extensive study. Many causes contribute toward bringing about these changes in the condition of the business world; the most striking thing about them is the way in which a business "boom," once started, feeds upon itself, and spreads into almost every branch of production and trade; and in like manner business depression, once started, spreads from business to business and keeps growing worse and worse. The thing is not altogether mysterious, however. When, no matter for what reason, everybody feels that times are good, everybody is encouraged to push any enterprise he is engaged in to the limit of his possibilities, for he feels confident that there will be a good demand for what he produces; and when every enterprise *is* pushed to the utmost, there is little or no unemployment, and the general prosperity, or even the general feeling of prosperity, actually makes a good demand for nearly everything. But in the sanguine business temper thus arising, many people will go beyond what is warranted by the facts; they will produce perhaps more than they can dispose of, and almost certainly stretch their credit beyond the limit of safety. Thus at some point or other—perhaps at many points at once—the "boom" will be overdone; people will begin to realize that everything is not as rosy as they thought; some factories will slow down, or perhaps close altogether; there will be unemployment on a serious scale, and a general feeling of doubt and caution will begin to take the place of the former general feeling of sanguine confidence. And this depression tends to feed on itself, just as the "boom" did. Thus it takes a considerable time, perhaps a long time, to get back to normal; and then after a while some favorable turn of circumstances starts a "boom" again. And so the cycle repeats itself.

Attention has recently been very strongly directed to the part that changes in the value of money—changes in the general price-level—play in all this. While all sorts of circumstances may contribute to the making of a business boom or a business depression, there is one cause that is sure to have a powerful influence in doing so. When all prices are rising, people engaged in business enterprise make big profits. The merchant's stock of goods is worth more dollars than he paid for them, and the difference is an addition to his profits. The manufacturer's stock of raw materials would cost more money to buy now than they actually did cost him; he gets for his finished product a price based not on the former price but on the present price of the raw materials, and the difference is an addition to his usual rate of profit. Moreover, wages and salaries are slower to rise than the prices of commodities; and here again the merchant or the manufacturer gets an advantage out of rising prices—his income increasing without a corresponding increase of outgo. Besides all this we must remember that business enterprise is carried on in large part upon credit—it is the great entrepreneurs who are the great borrowers; and when prices are rising, the money they pay back is worth less than the money they borrowed. Thus a time of rising prices is a time of big business profits; and hence rising prices tend very powerfully to boom business. Of course, exactly the reverse is the case with falling prices—they tend very powerfully to depress business. And it hardly needs any argument to show that we should be better off if, instead of these periods of over-sanguine business followed by business depression with its widespread unemployment and suffering, we kept business sailing on a fairly even keel.

CHAPTER XXVIII

THE INDEX-NUMBER AND "THE STABILIZED DOLLAR"

We have seen that besides the clearest and greatest evil of a change in the value of money—the injustice and injury which it inflicts upon debtors or creditors—it has many other evil consequences. Accordingly any well-thought out plan to provide a measure of value more stable than gold, or money based on gold, is worthy of our most serious attention. The plan proposed, and very ably advocated, by Professor Irving Fisher of Yale, I will attempt briefly to explain.

What we mean by a dollar is a certain fixed amount of gold—25.8 grains of gold, nine-tenths fine—or something which can, with little trouble, be exchanged for that amount of gold. We all know that, whether the money we have is in the form of gold, or notes, or a balance to our credit at the bank, every dollar of it is just as good as a gold dollar containing that fixed amount of the precious metal, neither more nor less. Our banking and currency laws are designed to assure this, and they do assure it. It is a great thing to have the meaning of every dollar perfectly certain in terms of gold; we should be exposed to all sorts of confusion and disaster if there were any doubt about it. But while every dollar represents a fixed amount of *gold*, it does not by any means represent a fixed amount of *general purchasing power;* and Professor Fisher's proposal is, in a word, that the dollar, instead of being defined as a fixed amount of gold, should be defined as a fixed amount of purchasing power; so defined that if a ten-dollar note today will buy a certain quantity of each of a long list of representative commodities, it shall buy the same quantity of those things a year from now, and ten years from now. But of course it would be quite out of the question actually to *redeem* the dollars in a long list of miscellaneous articles—to arrange that any one presenting a hundred dollars in notes or certificates shall receive so and so much wheat and flour and beef and steel and oil and what not. The Government couldn't undertake to give this *omnium gatherum* for the notes, and nobody would want to take it. What Professor Fisher proposes is that every dollar shall still be *redeemed in gold* on demand; but instead of a *fixed amount of gold* the dollar shall mean *so much gold as will buy a fixed amount of a representative list of commodities.*

Meaning of the "Price Level"

The means by which it is proposed to accomplish this is, in principle, simple enough. We have had occasion, more than once, to refer to the *price-*

level; let us now look a little more closely into the meaning of that expression. Prices change in a very irregular way. It often happens that the price of some things rises, and even rises very much, at the same time that the price of other things falls. It may happen, therefore, that very great changes of price take place without any change in the *average of prices;* and then we say that the *price-level* has not changed. When, however, the average of prices has risen or fallen by a certain percentage, we say that the price-level has risen or fallen by that same percentage.

But what do we mean by the average of prices? It won't do to set down a list of articles at random, or even a list of important articles, add up their prices and divide by the number of articles; an average obtained in this way would mean nothing of any consequence. In order to get an average which shall be really significant, we must first select, out of the endless multitude of things that are bought and sold, a set that is fairly representative of the great bulk of human demands; and then we must endeavor to attach to each a weight that corresponds to the part that it plays in the general expenditure. If our list contains fifty things, we take such a quantity of each as corresponds (roughly, of course) to the amount of that thing actually demanded by the community; the average price of all these fifty things, each taken in the amount that fits its actual importance, may be regarded as representing the general price-level. Of course, instead of taking the *average* of these fifty prices it is just as well to take the *total* of all the fifty, since when the total increases or decreases by twenty per cent., say, so also does the average.

The Index-number

When a list of things nas been chosen which is regarded as fairly representative of things in general, and the proper amount of each thing has been fixed upon so as to correspond to its actual importance, the sum of the prices of all these things is called an *index-number*[1]; meaning a number which is a fair index, or indication, of prices in general. Suppose that upon a given day the sum of all these prices is $1000, so that the index-number at that time is 1000, and that a year later the sum of the prices of these same things, taken in the same quantities, is $1250, so that the index-number is 1250: then we say that prices in general have risen by 25 per cent.; or, what is the same thing, that the purchasing power of the dollar has fallen by 20 per cent.

"*The Stabilized Dollar*"

Now in order to prevent this kind of thing from happening, or to keep it from going far when it has

[1] There are many other ways of defining and computing index-numbers; the one given in the text is the simplest, but not the best. It serves, however, to bring out the essential idea of the index-number; and it is quite out of the question for us to go into the refinements of the subject.

happened, Professor Fisher proposes that instead of having the dollar always mean the same amount of gold, the amount of gold it means shall be varied at regular and frequent intervals to correspond with the index-number; and the dollar so defined he calls the "stabilized dollar." If, at the time this scheme was first put into operation the index-number was 1000 and three months later it was found to be 1050, that would mean that it would take 1050 of our present gold dollars to buy what 1000 dollars had bought three months before; he would therefore increase the weight of the dollars to correspond, he would make them contain five per cent. more gold than they do now. This would tend to bring down the index-number correspondingly; for, of course, whatever a given amount of gold can buy of things in general, five per cent. more gold may be expected to buy five per cent. more of things in general.

For the actual working of the plan it would be necessary (or at least highly desirable) to have no actual gold coins in circulation at all; but there is no great difficulty about this. In fact in this country there is very little actual gold in circulation; it is represented by gold certificates[1] which are redeemable at the Treasury in gold coin on demand. Under Professor Fisher's plan there would be no gold coins at all; the gold certificates would be redeemable on demand in gold bullion, and the

[1] Besides the gold certificates, the whole mass of our paper money (bank notes, silver certificates, etc.) is practically redeemable in gold on demand, and of course all these forms of money would be affected alike by the Fisher plan.

amount of that gold bullion which would be given for every dollar of gold certificates would go up and down with the index-number. Thus the index-number, it is thought—and I believe justly thought—would vary very little: every variation up or down would be checked by correspondingly varying the weight of gold in the dollar—or rather, since there would be no actual gold dollars, the weight of gold that could be got for a paper dollar on demand. And to say that the index-number did not vary, or varied very little, is the same as to say that the general price-level, the general purchasing power of the dollar, did not vary or varied very little.

I have, of course, reduced all this to its simplest form, and taken no account of any of the finer points connected with the plan. But enough has been said to show that the plan aims at a very important object, and that it rests on a clear and reasonable foundation. Many able economists approve it; others point out what they regard as very serious objections to it. To enter into any of the complexities of the question is impracticable here.

A Legislative Danger

There is, however, one objection to the plan which I consider of so important a character that I cannot omit mention of it. With all its faults, there is one merit about the simple gold dollar—the dollar which means simply a fixed weight of gold—which the index-number dollar would not have. However fair, however scientific, the index-number method might be, it would be a method adopted by legislation in order to bring about just relations between debtors and creditors, and that steadiness in the price-level which is thought desirable for the general welfare. The simple gold dollar, on the other hand, is a fixed material thing which the lawmakers don't feel that it is their business to do anything about. We all take chances as to its ups and downs; some of us suffer by them, some of us profit by them, without any demerit or merit of our own. A lot of harm and a lot of injustice is unquestionably caused by all this. But we don't run to Congress to deliver us from these evils; we all accept as an ultimate fact the definition of a dollar as so much gold. But as soon as the definition of the dollar becomes a matter of Congressional determination, no matter how sound and just the principle on which that determination was based, you cannot tell what clamor may arise, in time of widespread discontent, to get Congress to adopt some other principle; and it is impossible to say whether more harm might not come from the uncertainties to which proposals of political interference with the basis of the monetary system might give rise than comes now from the imperfections of a rigid basis, serious as those imperfections unquestionably are.

It happens that at this very time—I mean in the past year or more—a very striking situation has been presented in our own country which illustrates the possibility I have in mind. The prices of certain farm products, especially wheat, have been abnormally low in comparison with other things. Prices in general are high—the index-number is high; the price of wheat is *relatively* very low. Now suppose that at a given time the price of things in general is rising, so that the index-number is rising, but the price of wheat, already low, is falling still farther. Under the plan of the index-number dollar, the dollar would then have to be made bigger so as to bring down the general level of prices, which was rising; but this would mean that the price of wheat, which was already *falling*, and which had already been low, would also be brought down. Would not the wheat farmers raise a tremendous outcry? Would they not demand that Congress should abandon a plan which causes a bushel of wheat to fetch even less than the low price that it would fetch if the dollar were kept at a fixed weight? Would they not insist that since Congress has undertaken to define a dollar so as to mean what it thinks is right and just, it must revise its judgment when the definition does not work out so as to be right and just to the farmers?

I do not say that the consideration of the possibilities of political interference with the monetary unit outweighs the argument for the index-number dollar; I only say that it is something that should be very seriously weighed.

Finally, it should be remarked that *some* of the benefits—though by no means all—that are aimed at in the index-number dollar can be obtained by voluntary agreements without changing the meaning of the dollar at all. While still keeping firmly to the simple gold standard—while continuing to mean by the word "dollar" simply 25.8 grains of gold, nine-tenths fine—it is perfectly possible to make contractual and other engagements upon an index-number basis. There are, indeed, objections to this also; but the objections can be weighed against the advantages in each particular case, and the plan adopted or rejected as the parties immediately concerned may think best. It is highly desirable that the practice should become familiar of long-term obligations being made in index-number terms when that course seems advisable under all the circumstances; that is, of having such obligations call for the payment not of a stated number of dollars but of a number of dollars greater or less than the stated number according as the price level has risen or fallen, and in the degree in which it has risen or fallen as shown by the index-number. As is well known, this plan serves as the basis of a sliding scale of wages which is widely used in Great Britain, where about three million laborers have their wages regulated annually by an index-number of retail prices.

There is nothing to prevent the application of the scheme, by voluntary arrangement, to any class of contracts or understandings in which it may seem desirable to resort to it. It is true that this kind of adjustment cannot accomplish all that is claimed for the plan of automatic enlargement and diminution of the monetary unit itself; but while it is less comprehensive in its scope, it has the inestimable advantage of leaving wholly undisturbed the bed-rock foundation of the monetary standard.

CHAPTER XXIX

FOREIGN EXCHANGE

In the latter part of the year 1919 and the early months of 1920, the pound sterling, which everybody was accustomed to think of as worth \$4.86, rapidly fell to about \$3.30. During the war, and for some time after its close, the British Government had artificially (it matters not by just what means) "pegged" the pound at nearly its usual exchange value of \$4.86; when it took its hands off, that big drop took place. Most people were not only startled but puzzled by this; they wondered why the pound should be worth only \$3.30 in 1920 when it had never varied by more than the merest trifle from \$4.86 during decade after decade preceding the war.

Exchange and the Gold Standard

But there is not much sense in wondering at the pound sterling falling so low after the war, unless you have clearly in mind the reason why it stood so steady at almost exactly \$4.86 before the war. This reason is, of course, extremely simple: Every dollar meant a definite amount of gold, 23.22

grains of pure gold—if the money was not in the shape of gold coin but of bank notes or government notes or certificates, the banks and the government stood ready to give that amount of gold for every dollar of the notes; and in like manner every pound sterling meant a definite amount of gold. Thus the pound sterling exchanged for $4.86 (strictly 4.8665) simply because it contained 4.86 times as much pure gold as the dollar did.

But when the war came on, Great Britain found it necessary to issue a far greater amount of paper money than it could undertake to redeem in gold, while the United States did not; every United States dollar continued to mean the same amount of gold as before, but the pound sterling ceased to mean any definite amount of gold. Of course actual British gold *coins* were worth as many dollars as they had ever been; but gold coins had ceased to circulate in England, and when one spoke of a pound one meant a pound in paper money: a thing still *called* a pound sterling but no longer meaning *any* definite amount of gold, since the paper was no longer redeemed in gold by the banks or the government. We thus see that neither in the steadiness of the pound before the war, nor in its big fall after the war, is there any occasion for wonder. The pound sterling had been *worth* $4.86 because to all intents and purposes the pound was *the same thing* as the $4.86; when they no longer meant the same thing, there is no reason why they should not mean things as different from each other as you please.

Of course what has been said about the pound sterling applies likewise to the franc, the mark, the lira, or any monetary unit based on the gold standard. The franc used to *mean* .193 times as much gold as is in a dollar; accordingly the franc used always to exchange for almost exactly 19.3 cents; but when an enormous quantity of paper francs was issued, and you could not get them redeemed in gold, there was no reason in the world why the franc should continue to exchange for 19.3 cents; and in fact it exchanges nowadays for about 5 cents. As for the mark, which used to be worth 23 cents, it has been issued in such preposterous quantities that the wonder is that anybody will give a dollar for seven thousand billions of them, which is about the present quotation. We shall look into this matter of irredeemable paper money a little more closely in the next chapter; here it is brought in only incidentally, and because the contrast between its behavior and that of normal money—money that is either gold itself or redeemable in gold on demand—forms a good background for the discussion.

Normal Fluctuations of the Rate of Exchange

Let us go back then to a normal state of things—when the dollar, the pound sterling, the franc, etc., each means a definite quantity of gold. In that case, as has been said already, the pound sterling always exchanges for almost exactly $4.86, the franc for almost exactly 19.3 cents, etc. But why not *exactly*, instead of *almost* exactly? The question of the course of *foreign exchange*—of the variation of the price in dollars that a pound sterling (and likewise a franc, a mark, a lira, or what not) commands at different times—involves many complexities; but the essence of the matter is fairly simple. Since the pound sterling is at bottom the same thing as $4.86, that price is called the *par of exchange* between the pound sterling and the dollar; and what puts the pound above par at some times and below it at others is the situation at the time, as regards the need on the one hand for pounds sterling wherewith Americans may settle their immediate obligations to Englishmen and on the other hand for dollars wherewith Englishmen may settle their immediate obligations to Americans. If, at a given time, payments due from New York to London exceed those due from London to New York, the pound goes above par; in the reverse case it goes below par. And the reason is plain, as we shall see.

To make these international payments, it is not necessary to go to the trouble, expense, and risk of shipping gold from the one country to the other; the payments are made by drafts which are called *bills of exchange*. The American creditor *draws upon* his English debtor for so many dollars; the English creditor draws upon his American debtor for so many pounds. And in what is called *the exchange market* these opposing credits and debits are exchanged against each other, so far as may be. It is possible that these credits and debits exactly balance each other in amount. In that case there is no occasion to ship gold either way; and in that case, therefore, there is no reason why the pound sterling and the dollar should not exchange for each other at just what they are intrinsically worth in gold—no reason why the pound sterling should be quoted at either above par or below par. But if the total of payments due in London exceeds the total of payments due in New York—if the bills drawn on London do not suffice to balance the bills drawn on New York—some portion of the total due in London will (at least on the face of things) have to be shipped there in the shape of actual gold. But this involves a quite appreciable amount of expense and inconvenience. Rather than incur that expense and inconvenience, people are willing to pay for a pound sterling more than the $4.86 which it is intrinsically worth in gold, and so the pound sterling goes above par. When this higher price is bid for sterling, various things are set in motion which we cannot here go into; arrangements of credit, sales of securities, etc., are made which that little extra price for the pound sterling renders profitable (so sensitive is the apparatus of finance) when without that extra price they would not be. In this way, the actual shipment of gold may be rendered unnecessary, the premium on the pound (its excess over par value) having the effect of restoring the balance. But whether this happens or not, we see that the pound can go but a very little above par—not more than enough to cover the expense and inconvenience of *shipping the gold to London.* Of course in the opposite case the pound goes below par, but not more than enough to cover the expense and inconvenience of *shipping the gold from London.* The extreme quotations thus possible for the pound sterling are known as the gold-export point and the gold-import point; they vary from par by less than one per cent., up or down.

Exports and Imports and the Rate of Exchange

Normally, the chief factor which determines the fluctuations of exchange is the export and import of commodities. The more goods we import from Great Britain, the greater is the volume of American obligations due in pounds sterling; the more goods we export to Great Britain the greater is the volume of British obligations due in dollars. Besides these current transactions in merchandise, there may be any amount of obligations of a more constant character—interest or dividends due to British investors in American securities, or to American investors in British securities. But these do not usually fluctuate greatly in amount during any short period of time; what does vary very much is the exports and imports of merchandise. The difference between the value of the exports and the value of the imports is called the *balance of trade.* When exports exceed imports, our balance of trade is said to be "favorable"; when imports exceed exports, our balance of trade is said to be "unfavorable."

But it is entirely erroneous to suppose—as so

many do, and as nearly everybody used to do before the principles of Economics were generally understood—that there is necessarily anything really favorable about an excess of exports, or unfavorable about an excess of imports. If other countries owe us, in a permanent way, much more than we owe them—if we have invested a much greater amount of remunerative capital in foreign countries than foreigners have invested in our country—then it will be necessary for them, as a steady thing, to send us more goods than we send them: for if they did not, they would have to send us the income on our investments in the shape of gold; a process which could not be kept up very long, since it would drain other countries of the gold necessary as the basis of *their* currency, and would send us more gold than we have any use for as the basis of *our* currency. Moreover, this drain of gold would be automatically checked; for the diminution of the stock of gold in the foreign country would tend to make prices there so low, and the increase of the stock of gold in our country would tend to make prices here so high, that our export of goods would be checked and our import of goods would be stimulated, until the balance of trade once more became what it ought to be. Before the war, England, which was a great creditor nation, regularly imported year after year something like a billion dollars' worth more of goods than she exported; but there was nothing in the least degree really unfavorable about this; she was simply being paid in goods what other countries owed her in the shape of interest, dividends, and ocean freight charges. She would not have been better off if she had taken her pay in gold, even supposing that such a thing had been possible; for she had all the gold she needed for currency purposes, and the only effect of getting more would have been either the hoarding of the gold as so much useless metal or the raising of prices.

These general remarks about the balance of trade have been something of a digression from our present subject; what we are here concerned with is the effect of an increase or decrease of exports or imports upon the *rate of exchange*, the price of a pound sterling in dollars. If at a given time, a certain state of the balance of trade will keep the pound sterling at par, anything that makes the balance more "favorable" (or less "unfavorable") to us will send the pound sterling below par. That is, an increase of our exports or a diminution of our imports tends to lower the market price of the pound sterling, because it increases England's current obligation to us or diminishes our current obligation to England. And of course in the opposite event the opposite effect will take place.

The foregoing will, I think, suffice to explain the essentials of foreign exchange—why the exchange value of a unit of foreign money does not suffer much fluctuation; between what limits its fluctuation is confined; and what causes such fluctuations as do occur;—always supposing that the money we are talking about, both the foreign and the home money, rests solidly on the gold standard.

"*Triangular*" *Exchange*

But while we have obtained, I think, a fair understanding of the essentials of the matter, it has been reduced to a simplicity which is far from being realized in the actual transactions of exchange. We have been treating the matter as though the transactions between two countries[1] were something entirely independent of the transactions of these two countries with other countries. This, however, is by no means the case. The obligations of an American to an Englishman may be balanced indirectly as well as directly; if Americans have sold goods to Frenchmen and bought goods from Englishmen, American bills drawn upon Frenchmen may be used to balance English bills drawn upon Americans. Thus there is set up a *triangular exchange;* and likewise with more than three nations. Thus the actual rate of sterling exchange will turn not only on the relation between our current obligations to England and England's current obligations to us, but on a whole network of similar relations between America and all other nations on the one hand, and between England and all other nations on the other.

It is, of course, out of the question for us to go into this matter more fully; but a little reflection should suffice to show that the essence of the case is unaffected. The greater the whole mass of payments *currently due* by other countries to us, the

[1] Whether it be America and England, or America and France, or England and France, etc., of course makes no difference.

higher does the dollar tend to be in terms of foreign moneys; the greater the whole mass of payments currently due by us to foreign countries, the lower does the dollar tend to be in terms of foreign moneys. But in no case can the exchange vary from its par—the pound sterling from $4.86, the franc from $0.193, etc.,—by more than a small percentage; namely, the amount necessary to cover the expense and inconvenience of shipping actual gold.

Once more, the reader is reminded that all this is on the supposition that the moneys concerned rest solidly on the gold standard. What happens when that standard is abandoned, or not strictly lived up to, we shall to some extent consider in the next chapter, which relates to "Fiat Money."

CHAPTER XXX

FIAT MONEY

A PIECE of paper with the words "One Dollar" printed on it has of course no intrinsic value; nobody would care to have it for any other purpose than to pay for other things with it. If, however, the printed piece of paper can be exchanged at will for a gold dollar, it becomes at once worth as much as the gold in a gold dollar—worth as much as 25.8 grains of gold, nine-tenths fine. And the gold *has* intrinsic value, in just the same way as platinum, or diamonds, or radium, or anything else that people prize for utility or ornament, has intrinsic value. If the issuer of the paper money—the government, let us say—stands ready to give for it its face value in gold, it is called *redeemable* or *convertible* paper money; if not, it is called *irredeemable* or *inconvertible* paper money. And instead of calling it *irredeemable paper money*, it has become quite customary to speak of it as *fiat money*, in order to point sharply to the fact that a scrap of paper which is not convertible into any definite thing having intrinsic value has no value except that which it derives from the *fiat*, or decree, of the government.

What Governments Can and Cannot Do About Fiat Money

Now the first thing to be noted about fiat money is that the power of the government to confer value upon a scrap of paper by its fiat is strictly limited. The government can, indeed, compel people to take a fiat paper dollar in settlement of every dollar of obligation it owes to its own citizens—whether it be payment for goods bought by it, interest or principal of money loaned to it, salaries it has agreed to pay, or what not. It can also decree that creditors in general[1] shall accept the paper dollars, just as though they were real dollars, in payment of debts due them; this is called making the paper money *legal tender*. And, easiest of all, it can itself accept its own fiat money in payment of taxes.

Thus a government that wishes to issue fiat money has no difficulty in *putting it into circulation* by using it in payment of its own current expenses and maturing obligations; and it has no difficulty in *keeping it in circulation*, because everybody knows that it can be used in payment of all taxes and in payment of at least a large proportion of all debts. Being worth something *for these purposes* it is bound to be worth something *for all purposes;*

[1] I say "creditors in general," instead of "all creditors," because unless the Government goes to a most violent extreme, it will not decree that a contract *expressly* calling for *gold dollars of a certain weight and fineness* shall be regarded as fulfilled when scraps of paper having no adequate relation to gold dollars are offered instead. Moreover, any Government that *did* attempt this would find that it could not put its decree into practical effect.

you will be able to buy something for your paper dollar, because even though the seller may not himself have debts or taxes to pay, he can pass it along to people who have.

But while the government thus has the power to get its paper money into circulation, and to make it *worth something*, it is utterly powerless *by its mere fiat* to make it worth what a gold dollar is worth, or half what a gold dollar is worth, or one-thousandth of what a gold dollar is worth. For though the government can pay its own expenses with it, can accept it in payment of taxes, and can require creditors to accept it in payment of debts, it cannot compel people to sell things at the same prices in scraps of paper called dollars that they would sell them for in real dollars; still less to keep on producing things to sell at those prices. If it wants to achieve this result, it must do something quite different from issuing a *fiat* to that effect; it must *keep the issue of paper dollars* down so that the total circulation shall not exceed what it would naturally be if *all the dollars were gold or as good as gold.* At a given scale of prices, a certain number of dollars is required to carry on the country's business; if twice that number of dollars is put into circulation and *you can't send it out of the country*, prices will, broadly speaking,[1] go twice as high. And to say that prices go twice as high is the same as to say that the dollar is worth half as much.

In ordinary times, it might be a little difficult

[1] The thing is not quite so simple as this; the modification that this proposition requires was in some degree indicated in Chapter X.

for some people to *feel* that this is true, even though they could see no flaw in the argument; nowadays the lesson is writ so large in the monetary condition of Europe that "the wayfaring man, though a fool" can hardly fail to read it: if you keep on issuing paper money there is no depth of worthlessness to which it will not fall. We had the same experience in the early days of our own country, when the Continental money fell so low that the phrase "not worth a Continental" became the popular term for utter worthlessness; in the Civil War we had an incomparably milder case, yet still a case, of depreciation of fiat money. But the public memory is short; and were it not for the colossal object lesson of Europe there would doubtless be far more readiness than there is today to accept wild notions like those of Mr. Ford or Mr. Edison in regard to the possibilities of Government-made money.

A limited amount of inconvertible paper dollars may be issued without causing their value to fall below that of the gold dollar. It is true that from the very beginning the issue of the inconvertible paper dollars *tends* to raise prices—that is, to lower the value, the purchasing power, of the dollar; because, as we have seen in the early chapters of this book, the greater the number of dollars in circulation the less is the purchasing power of each dollar. But the issue of the paper dollars at home does not affect the purchasing power of a *gold* dollar abroad, for this is simply the purchasing power of a certain quantity of gold, irrespective of the name that is stamped on it. And if the purchasing power of the gold dollar were to fall at home, while abroad it remained just what it had been, the gold in the gold dollars could be used to better advantage in paying for imports from abroad than in making purchases at home. Accordingly some of the gold dollars would go out of the country; this would check the rise of prices at home, and would also tend to raise prices abroad. By this process, the total number of dollars in circulation may be kept down to what it would be if all the dollars were gold or convertible into gold. But if, after you have by this process driven all the gold out of the country,[1] you still keep on issuing your inconvertible paper money, prices will rise indefinitely. The value of the paper dollar will have no assignable relation whatever to that of the gold dollar. For the word "dollar" will have become a mere name with nothing behind it; nor will there be in circulation any real dollars whose purchasing power is on a parity with that of the fiat dollars.

"Basing" of no Avail without Convertibility

A curious notion crops up every now and then, that paper dollars would not depreciate if only they

[1] Or even not out of the country but out of the monetary circulation of the country. Of course there may be hoards of gold, held by the government, by the banks, or even by private individuals, which are not used as money at all, nor as the basis of any money in circulation, but as a store of gold kept for use in the future. This may serve a very important purpose as giving promise of a return to the gold standard some time or other; but it has no direct and immediate influence on current prices.

were "based" on something or other—on real estate, or wheat, or cotton, or what not. But merely saying that the paper dollar is *based* on something substantial is entirely futile; the thing that keeps it *worth* something substantial is its actual convertibility into that thing. You might issue twenty billions of paper dollars "based" on all the land of the country, and imagine you were on solid ground because the land of the country was worth forty billions; but since there is no way of giving a man a hundred dollars' worth of land in exchange for his hundred-dollar bill, and furthermore he wouldn't know what to do with it if he got it, the "basing" does him no good whatsoever.

One of the most famous cases of the creation of fiat money was an instance of this delusion: the "assignats" which were issued in the time of the great French Revolution, and which were "based" on the vast amount of land that had come into possession of the Revolutionary Government by confiscation. The more assignats were issued, the less they were worth; the less they were worth, the more of them had to be issued in order to cover the needs of the Government. This process went on until they were worth practically nothing; the land was there all the time, but had no more to do with the case than if it had been at the bottom of the sea. It is the possibility of *actual redemption in gold*, and not the mere fact that it is "based" on gold, that keeps the amount of *redeemable* paper money within bounds and prevents its indefinite depreciation.

Why Bad Money Drives out Good

We have seen how paper money tends to drive gold out of circulation; and it will be well here to say a word about a more general proposition, known as "Gresham's Law"—namely, that when moneys of different intrinsic value circulate alongside each other, the worse money tends to drive the better out of circulation.

Suppose you have gold dollars and silver dollars circulating together, and that either can be used just as freely as the other in the payment of debts, taxes, etc.; and suppose that the gold in the gold dollar is worth, *as a commodity*,—as a lump of metal—twice as much as the silver in the silver dollar. Then a person who wants to use *either gold or silver* as a commodity, or to export *either gold or silver*, will never take silver dollars for the purpose, but will always take gold dollars. For if he melts or exports 100 gold dollars, he can get for them as much silver as there is in 200 silver dollars: the silver dollars are worth just as much as the gold dollars so long as they are used as money, but become worth only half as much as the gold dollars when they are melted down or exported. The silver dollars, therefore, will remain in circulation, while the gold dollars will *tend* to go out of circulation.

Nevertheless, if there are not *too many* silver dollars, they will keep on circulating alongside the gold dollars and on a parity with them; provided people have perfect confidence that the Government will not *increase the number* of the silver dollars to such a point that they will actually drive the gold out of circulation altogether. The case is essentially the same as that of inconvertible paper dollars issued in limited quantity. In both cases, however,—though for the sake of simplicity I have not mentioned it above—it is of great importance not only that the quantity be not excessive *at the time*, but that people shall have confidence in the Government's purpose to keep it within bounds *in the future*. For when that confidence is impaired, people will begin to discriminate in favor of the better money and withdraw it from circulation, not because it is *already* worth more than the other kind, but because they suspect that it may become so in the future.[1]

The Fiat-Money Plague in Europe

After this digression, let us go back to the subject of fiat money, and especially to the aspects of that subject which have been prominent in the post-war history of Europe. In all of the European countries that took part in the war, the enormous cost of carrying it on drove the governments to the issue of paper money beyond the point at which

[1] A very interesting case of money of small intrinsic value circulating on a parity with standard money is that of the coins that are used for small change. Nobody thinks of questioning the value of a silver quarter or dime, or of a nickel five-cent piece; such coins are called *token money*, because their intrinsic value has little or no relation to their value as money. And nobody questions their value as money because the idea of issuing them in vast quantities—indeed of issuing them in any quantity above what is needed for their use as small change—is never entertained by the government or anybody else.

they could undertake to keep it redeemable in gold. Whether that method of financing the war could in any of these countries have been avoided is a matter on which there is room for difference of opinion; certainly there was very strong temptation to resort to it. When the war ended, with all the countries loaded down with enormous debts upon which interest had to be paid, the difficulty of getting back to the gold standard was extremely great; and none of them have done so. But while Great Britain and France and Italy have, by strenuous efforts, kept the inflation of the currency within bounds, some of the other countries have not done, nor even attempted, anything of the kind. The two most conspicuous instances of inflation of the currency carried to preposterous extremes have been furnished by Russia and Germany; and a brief consideration of these will suffice for our purpose.

The case of Russia is peculiar; differing not only from that of the general run of countries, but even from that of Revolutionary France 130 years ago. The Continental currency issued in the early history of this country, the "greenbacks" of our Civil War period, and even the assignats of the French Revolution, were not issued with the express purpose of making them worthless; the issue was in no way inspired by a hostility to the very idea of sound money, but solely by real or supposed necessity. The Bolshevik Government of Russia, on the other hand, was animated by a desire to break down everything that formed part of the existing economic order, based upon private property, and substitute for it a thorough-going system of Communism. The prospect that the paper ruble would become worthless was probably, therefore, welcome to the Bolshevik chiefs rather than otherwise; they had abolished private property or gone as near to that as they could; and they seemed to think that in this state of things they could get on without money altogether, or at all events with money that meant nothing in the way of intrinsic value. The frightful collapse of industry in Russia has caused the Bolsheviks to abandon a large part of the Communist programme, and also to try to get back to something like real money; but while the ridiculous ruble contributed very much towards bringing about the collapse, the primary cause was the Communism itself—the Bolshevik régime had destroyed all the ordinary incentives of industry and had not provided for these incentives anything like an adequate substitute.

The spectacle presented by Germany's debauch of fiat money is of a wholly different character. There we see a country of enormous industrial capabilities, a highly trained and formerly thrifty people, carrying on multitudes of great enterprises under private ownership, and yet presenting a picture of impoverishment and destitution literally without parallel in history in any like circumstances. And the prime cause of this impoverishment and destitution is the progressive worthlessness of the German mark. Long before the paper mark had come down to its present ridiculous state, it had laid low the whole of the solid middle class, the backbone of the country, and had paralyzed business and enterprise in a thousand directions. The most remarkable thing about the story is that against this process of robbery and impoverishment no important and substantial protest has at any time been raised in Germany. People who had deposits in savings banks, who owned bonds of the government or of corporations, found what they called ten thousand marks became worth only a thousand real marks, a hundred real marks, one real mark, a hundredth of a real mark, and less than that; in other words they were absolutely robbed of all that they had acquired by years of industry and frugality. Salaries, though of course raised (in paper marks) from time to time, did not come anywhere near keeping pace with the abysmal fall of the mark; accordingly professors, teachers, clerks, salaried people of all kinds, were reduced to the direst straits. Wages, though adjusted more frequently, still were far from rising as fast as the mark sank. Farmers were naturally shy of parting with their produce when they didn't know whether the money they got for it would be worth half as much next week as it was today. And of course the bottom fell out of business in every direction; for how could business be conducted with any order, or any vigor, when the money you got for your goods would shrink in value almost before you had put it in the till?

An insane condition of things; and as dishonest as it is insane. That it could have been avoided if the nation and its leaders had been determined to avoid it, there is not the slightest reason for doubting; and if anyone disputes this proposition, he ought at least to be able to point to some substantial endeavor that was made to prevent the calamity. In the absence of such endeavor it is absurd to declare that the thing was impossible. What was actually done can be described in a very few words. The taxes collected by the government fell far short of its expenses, and it kept issuing paper marks to cover the difference. This constant flood of paper marks caused them to become more worthless every month; and hence the government revenue, received as it was in these more and more worthless marks, fell more and more short of meeting the government expenditures; hence the flood of marks issued to cover the deficiency became more and more enormous in volume; and so on indefinitely, until now it takes about seventy billion marks to be worth a cent. It is absurd to say that nothing could have been done to place the finances of the country on a basis less childish, less ridiculous, less dishonest; in fact proposals for a more decent system have been made by German experts, but they have never (at least until very lately) got beyond the stage of mere suggestion.[1]

[1]Since this was written (towards the end of 1923) and especially since the formation of what is generally known as the Dawes committee of experts, a much more serious effort has been made to put the German currency upon a more stable basis, and it has resulted in checking the fall of the mark. But this only confirms the justice of the criticism in the text.

Inconvertible Paper Money and the Rate of Exchange

The behaviour of the "rate of exchange" when the currency of one or both the countries concerned is inconvertible paper money demands a little attention. The fact is that under these circumstances, the "rate of exchange," while going by the same name, is of a wholly different nature from what it is when the countries in question are both on the gold standard. In that case the rate of exchange is simply the ratio of two fixed quantities of gold, or at most deviates from that ratio by the small percentage which covers the cost or inconvenience of actual transfer of the gold from one country to the other. Of course there is nothing of this kind when one (or both) of the monetary units has no fixed relation to gold. What is it, then, which does in that case determine the rate of exchange? The answer is, in its essentials, not far to seek.

Let us, for example, take the pound sterling and the dollar at the beginning of 1920, when the pound was at about $3.50 instead of its old value of $4.86. With a given volume of currency in England, the pound sterling had a certain general purchasing power in England; and at first blush one might be inclined to suppose that if the pound sterling was worth about $3.50 it was because its general purchasing power in England was about the same as that of $3.50 in the United States. This, however, would not be quite correct; what determines the matter is not *general* purchasing power but purchasing power as to commodities that can be exported or imported on a large scale. If *of these commodities* you can get just about as much by spending a pound sterling in England (allowance made for tariff and freight) as by spending a dollar in this country, then a pound sterling will exchange for about $3.50. But the rate of exchange from day to day will, of course, not exactly correspond to this ratio of purchasing power; it will be determined by the immediate pressure of need for payments to be made by Americans to Englishmen on the one hand and by Englishmen to Americans on the other. But the rate of exchange will not deviate enormously from the ratio of purchasing power; in the case supposed above, the pound will not deviate enormously from $3.50. The deviation will not be checked as simply or as promptly as when both the moneys were on the gold standard; yet it will be checked in somewhat the same way. If, in the case supposed, the rate of exchange fell to $3.00, for example, Englishmen could get a much greater number of dollars by shipping goods to America than by exchanging pounds sterling for dollars; and this exportation, by reducing the Englishmen's need of dollars, and increasing the American's need of pounds, would continue until the exchange was restored to pretty near its proper level of $3.50. But of course this adjustment is nothing like so fine as that which takes place when both the moneys mean definite weights of gold; the deviations may accordingly be far greater than the small percentage we spoke of in the preceding chapter.

Essential Vice of Fiat Money

A final word, by way of reminder of the essential vice of inconvertible paper money. If Governments could be trusted to regulate the issue in such a way that the purchasing power of the money should remain unaltered, and if *everybody knew* that the Government would do this, paper would serve the purposes of money (except for international transactions) as well as gold.[1] But it is idle to suppose that anything of the kind would happen. When the Government was in a tight place, it would be tempted to issue more money in order to meet its own expenses; and whenever people in general, or some important section of the people, felt that a more abundant supply of money would stimulate business or otherwise promote prosperity, the pressure for more money to be put into circulation would be very hard to resist. The thing would not, in normal times, go to a preposterous extreme such as that described above in the case of Germany; but the *kind* would be the same though the *degree* was very different. As soon as you get away from the anchor of redeemability, there is nothing to stop you; the more money you issue, the more you find you need. It is conceivable that a time will come when the principle of a paper money regulated in quantity so as to keep prices stable will become accepted as a fundamental rule, from which any departure would be branded by all

[1] Indeed if the rule were *literally* lived up to, it would serve *better;* for it would be a more stable measure of value.

men as dishonest; but that time seems very far off. And until that time comes, the issuing of irredeemable paper money is an invitation to evils, injustices, and dangers whose extent no man can foretell.

CHAPTER XXXI

LAISSEZ FAIRE

THIS famous phrase has had a very conspicuous place in the history of economic controversy. It first came into prominence long before Political Economy became a great subject of systematic thought; for it is generally regarded as having originated in the reply made to Colbert, the great minister of Louis XIV, when he asked a representative of French business what the government could do to increase general prosperity. "*Laissez-nous faire*," let us do, was the reply; in other words, let us manage our own affairs without government interference. There were in those days, and for a long time before and after, numberless regulations of business matters based on the supposition that governments could divert business enterprise into forms more beneficent than it would assume under the unrestricted operation of the desire for individual profit. And that many—perhaps all—of these interferences were not only unnecessary but harmful, it required only the insight of any shrewd practical thinker to see.

But it was not until about a hundred years after

this celebrated reply that *laissez faire* assumed something like the character of a fundamental doctrine. The teachings of the Physiocrats—the French forerunners of Adam Smith, the founder of the modern science of Political Economy or Economics—did much towards elevating it to this position; but it was Adam Smith's epoch-making work *The Wealth of Nations* (published in 1776) which gave to the doctrine of *laissez faire* a broad foundation in economic theory. It was the general tendency of his work to show that the free competition of business enterprise was better calculated than government control to promote the economic welfare of the community; and the development of economic theory in the hands of his successors—in England, France, and elsewhere—strongly confirmed this tendency.

A Practical Maxim, not a Scientific Doctrine

Nevertheless, it is a great mistake to suppose that the principle of *laissez faire*—the principle of non-interference of government in matters pertaining to industry and trade—is a doctrine of scientific Economics. Many economists have inclined towards the advocacy of that principle; and some have gone to extremes in dogmatic teaching of it. It is not surprising, therefore, that Economics has, on the one hand, been appealed to by opponents of government interference as incontrovertible authority for their position, and on the other hand has been condemned by advocates of government interference as being the sponsor of an unsound and mischievous dogma. Yet, as has been said above, the principle of *laissez faire*, while it has derived much support from the teachings of Economics, is not a doctrine of Economics at all.

And this for two reasons. In the first place, it is not a *scientific doctrine* at all, but a *practical maxim*. No science can tell men what they had better do, or leave undone; it can only tell them (at most) what will be the consequence of their adopting one course or another. Thus, while Economics[1] can say—or at least attempt to say—what will be the economic effect of a given course of action or non-action, it must leave the question of what course is most desirable to be decided by a consideration of *all* its effects, social and political as well as economic. But there is another reason, more specific than this, why the principle of *laissez faire* cannot be a doctrine of Economics. While in many large and important classes of cases it may be demonstrated—and indeed has been demonstrated—that government interference is calculated to be economically harmful instead of helpful, yet it is inconceivable that there can be any demonstration of the principle as covering all possible cases or even all possible cases of the highest importance. And certainly no such demonstration, nor any approach to it, has been forthcoming.

Let us turn away now from these generalities,

[1] As we saw, for example, in the chapters on Protection and Free Trade.

and look at a few specific instances of the question of *laissez faire;* we shall thus perhaps get something like a true perception of the relation of Economics to that policy—the policy of non-interference by government in the conduct of industry and trade.

Protection, *Usury Laws*, "*Speculation*"

One such instance, the question of Protection and Free Trade, has been treated at some length in previous chapters; at this point, therefore, we need only take notice of the *nature* of the light which Economics throws upon that question. What it does is to draw attention to the way in which economic forces, uncontrolled by government, actually operate; it shows that certain benefits supposed to be conferred by government restraints are not in reality so conferred, and that other benefits, overlooked by those who have not given proper thought to the subject, are conferred by the free play of economic forces. The consequence is that in this matter the policy of *laissez faire* is enormously favored by the considerations which Political Economy adduces; but this is because of the definite bearing of these specific considerations on this specific question, and not because of any supreme authority claimed for the general doctrine of *laissez faire.*

And the same kind of thing is true in every instance in which economic reasoning results in a recommendation of the principle of *laissez faire.* A notable example is the question of usury laws. In former times, it was the almost universal opinion—and probably even today it is the opinion of the great majority of people—that it is a good thing to forbid by law the taking of interest on borrowed money at a rate above some figure which, by a sort of common consent, is regarded as "reasonable"—say 7 per cent. Many loans, people say, are made at 6 per cent., some at 5 per cent. or less; anything above 7 per cent., therefore, must be extortion, and the law should step in to prevent the rich lender from fleecing the poor borrower. But, says the economist, your usury law will not have the effect you intend; it may *prevent the lender* from getting ten per cent. from the man in straits for money, but it will not *enable the borrower* in straits for money to get it at seven per cent.—he will either pay a higher rate in spite of the law or not get it at all. For if six per cent. is the usual rate, and if many loans are made even at five, poor Jones, who is in straits for money, could easily enough find people to lend him at seven if they were sure that he could pay the interest, and repay the principal, when due; they do not refuse the loan out of pure malice, but because the temptation of seven per cent. interest (as compared with six or five) is not sufficient to cover what they regard as the risk of loss through Jones's inability to pay. Accordingly, the very law that is designed to help Jones to get his loan at a moderate rate has precisely the opposite effect. He either doesn't get the loan at all, or has to deal with unscrupulous people who will find ways of circumventing the law. And in the latter case he is almost sure to pay a much higher rate of interest than he would if there were no usury law; because, instead of going out into a large market and openly getting the most favorable terms he can, he has to do the best he can with the special class of people who make it a business to lend at usurious rates. Thus we see that there is a tremendously strong case in favor of *laissez faire* in the matter of interest rates; and if any argument can be made for usury laws, it must be some special argument which seeks to justify them in spite of the overwhelming weight of the general argument against them.

Thus a clear perception of the consequences of interference with the free course of business transactions very often shows that those consequences are injurious—that indeed they bring about effects precisely the opposite of what is intended; and it is largely for this reason that *laissez faire* has come to be regarded as an actual principle of Economics. One more illustration of this will not be amiss. When the price of some necessary article, especially an article of food, is abnormally high owing to scarcity, a cry is always raised against the "speculators" who withhold it—or are supposed to withhold it—from market; but, as we saw in an early chapter,[1] the operations of professional dealers, even though they may withhold some of the supply from the market, are calculated to benefit and not to injure the public—unless these operations assume the character of a "corner," a monopolistic control of the market. A law compelling dealers

[1] Chapter V, Illustrations of Demand and Supply.

to sell at a time of scarcity would be calculated to intensify the scarcity; for the only reason the dealer can have for holding back the supply is that he thinks the scarcity will be still greater later on. He does not make his profit by *holding* now, but by *selling* later on. He may make a mistake of judgment; but if his judgment is correct he sells at the very time when the scarcity is greatest, and if he had been compelled to sell earlier the scarcity at that time would be even greater. And the chances are that his judgment is correct; for if he makes a mistake he will suffer serious loss, instead of making a gain, by his operation. And this is but one of innumerable instances in which it is seen that the motive of private gain directs business into the course that gives the best assurance of public benefit.

But to suppose that this is always the case is to make a wholly unwarranted assumption. Unfortunately, the assumption has been made by some economists, and by a far greater number of persons who, without being economists, have undertaken to speak in their name, with the result that Economics has suffered much disrepute.

Mistaken Opposition to Factory Laws

The most conspicuous instance of this is furnished by the early history of factory legislation, especially in England, the country in which the modern factory system was first developed on a large scale. It is difficult to believe that men of high character and humane ideals opposed legislation designed to remedy appallingly bad conditions in factory and mine labor—such as children under nine years of age working twelve hours and more a day, shocking sanitary conditions, absence of protection against dangerous machinery and the perils of mining. Yet some of the very best and most humane of British statesmen long opposed any interference by law with the conduct of industrial enterprises; and they did this largely because of a sincere belief that, whatever might be the immediate and direct effect of government interference, it would, on the whole and in the long run, do more harm than good through diminishing the productiveness of industry. This belief was in great measure due to the dominating position which the principle of *laissez faire* had acquired in their minds. It cannot be too strongly insisted on that to erect this principle into a general or absolute doctrine is to commit a gross error; and in this instance, among others, it was an error that had most deplorable practical consequences.

One more word about labor legislation will be instructive here. Opposition to labor legislation, at least in the early part of the Nineteenth Century, was due not only to a blind belief in *laissez faire*, but also in large measure to a mistaken view of the "principle of population." It was thought by many of the followers of Malthus that no permanent improvement in the condition of the masses could arise except through their keeping down their own numbers by their own insistence on a higher standard of living; a view which overlooked the possibility that a higher standard, once introduced by governmental measures or by any other means, might become fixed in the habits of the masses and in the established notions of the community at large. The progress of child-labor legislation, of compulsory education, and of legal requirements in regard to sanitary housing, which has been so marked a feature of the history of the past three-quarters of a century, has all turned upon the possibility of this kind of improvement of the standard of living.

Anti-Trust Laws

Another instance of unwarranted appeal to the principle of *laissez faire* was furnished when the great capitalistic combinations and consolidations known as Trusts first became the subject of serious concern in this country. Anti-Trust legislation was opposed by many economists, public men, and journalists on the ground that to obstruct this tendency was to interfere with the natural course of business, and that any such interference is sure to fail in the end and to be injurious while it lasts. But not only is this absolute doctrine of non-interference unwarranted, as we have seen; something more is to be said against the invocation of it in this case. In so far as the doctrine has any foundation in the principles of Economics, it rests on the conviction that *competition* will work for the best in the end; but in this matter of the Trusts the very trouble was that they stifled competition. Even upon the ordinary assumption of the *laissez faire* doctrine, therefore, here was a matter that would not come under its rule; to invoke the doctrine of free competition as a reason for not interfering with monopoly is to carry that doctrine to the point of absurdity. Many of the opponents of the anti-Trust laws did not, indeed, quite commit this absurdity; their point was not so much that the tendency towards monopoly in the great fields covered by the Trusts *ought* not to be interfered with, but that legislation could not successfully cope with it. And even at this day, many maintain that the anti-Trust laws have accomplished nothing to check that tendency. This, in my judgment, is an error; there is abundant reason to believe that, while not accomplishing all that they aimed at, the anti-Trust laws have prevented monopoly from attaining anything like the hold on the country's industry and trade which it would otherwise have acquired. Any one who compares the actual scope and strength of competition today with what believers in the "manifest destiny" of the Trusts twenty or thirty years ago expected it would be reduced to by this time must, I think, conclude that the anti-Trust laws have had a powerful influence in stemming that tide towards monopoly which so many thought irresistible.

Strong Presumption in Favor of Laissez Faire

Other important examples might be given of the error of looking upon *laissez faire* as an absolute principle; these two, however, will perhaps suffice as a warning. The warning is particularly necessary in regard to matters relating to the largest concerns of mankind—labor conditions, monopoly, the fundamentals of taxation, etc. But while avoiding this error, it is important that we should recognize that in almost all of the ordinary economic relations among men there is a strong presumption in favor of *laissez faire*. In instance after instance this presumption is found to be justified; and accordingly, when a new proposal of government interference presents itself, we shall do well to adopt a critical, though not a dogmatic, attitude towards it. Illustrations of the matter are scattered throughout this little book; one of them, for instance, was given in the very first chapter, in connection with the price of wheat during the Great War. Failure to look into proposals of government interference in this critical—or, if the word does not seem too pretentious, this scientific—spirit has often caused serious evil. One conspicuous and highly important illustration was that of the agitation for emergency rent laws—laws restricting the rents which landlords could demand of tenants—after the close of the war. These laws may, on the whole, have been wise; but if the people at large had realized that the laws were sure seriously to *hinder* the building of the needed houses, and thus prolong the period of shortage, the laws, if passed, would have been accompanied by other measures designed to *promote* the building of houses. The trouble with the "man in the street" is that when he sees an economic evil, he thinks the thing to do is to pass a law forbidding it; and one of the chief merits of Economics is that by pointing out the actual operation of cause and effect in such a case, it can warn against the adoption of futile or mischievous legislation.

CHAPTER XXXII

SOCIAL JUSTICE

WHATEVER objections there may be to Socialism, either from the standpoint of its practicability or of its desirability, it must be admitted that one of the chief motives which animate all high-minded Socialists is the desire to bring about what they regard as social justice.[1] And whether the Socialist's conception of social justice is well or ill founded, it is at all events a large and coherent conception, not a happy-go-lucky collection of shreds and patches.

Vagueness of the Term

But among persons who are not Socialists, even persons who are emphatically opposed to Socialism, the phrase "social justice" is very frequently used without any clear meaning, or any approach to a clear meaning. Many particular proposals

[1] I say "one of the chief motives," because an equally strong motive, quite irrespective of any question of justice, is the desire to increase the comfort and happiness of the masses, and especially to extirpate poverty.

that are urged on the score of social justice are inherently meritorious; many of them are entirely practicable as well as inherently meritorious; but the use of the phrase is nevertheless misleading. If we are to think straight about these things, we must distinguish between the claims of the proposal to acceptance on its specific merits and the claim that rests upon the catchword of social justice. In accepting such a proposal on its specific merits we may, it is true, be making just as much of a step towards a Socialist ideal of social justice as if we expressly accepted it upon the principle of social justice; but in the one case we should be thinking clearly, and not committing ourselves to a vague doctrine which, from the individualist standpoint, is full of danger; while in the other case we should be committing ourselves to that doctrine, though we had no intention of abiding by it, and indeed were quite in the dark as to what it was that we were committing ourselves to.

Workmen's Compensation Laws

I will try to make the importance of this distinction clear by one or two illustrations. One of the most interesting and most instructive is furnished by the history of the Workmen's Compensation laws in this country. The enactment of these laws has accomplished a vast amount of good, with a minimum of evil; and it is matter for genuine satisfaction to reflect that they were adopted without much delay, and without formidable resistance, when once the merits of the case in their favor came to be generally understood.

Under the common law—the law as it stood before these statutes were enacted—when a workman suffered an injury through an accident that occurred in the course of his employment, the only way in which he could compel his employer to compensate him for the injury was by a suit for damages. Now to any one who seriously considers the matter it is perfectly plain that in the carrying on of modern industry—with its complex, and often dangerous, machinery, and with the intricate relations between an employee and his fellow employees—the perils of accident to which a workman is exposed should be regarded as part of the very nature of the business; and that it is perfectly practicable for employers to make systematic provision for indemnifying *their employees* in case of injury to their bodies just as they make systematic provision for indemnifying *themselves* in case of injury to their property by fire or burglary. And not only is this practicable, but it does away with terrible hardships and a great deal of legal trickery and extortion, at practically no expense to anybody in the long run.

Under the old law, the poor and perhaps ignorant laborer was at the mercy of any low-class lawyer who might be on the lookout for cases of the kind, and was required to prove the exact facts of the particular instance; under these new and excellent laws, he receives as a matter of course that compensation to which, in perhaps ninety-nine cases out of a hundred, he is, from the general nature of the case, entitled. The law makes simple, inexpensive, and sure what had been complex, costly, and uncertain; it assures a great benefit to thousands without placing upon anybody any serious burden, without interfering in any serious way with anybody's liberty, and without putting any obstacle in the way of individual enterprise. To secure the adoption of such a law it was not necessary (although some did it) to appeal to any grand ideal of Social Justice, but merely to insist upon the unmistakable merits of the particular proposal.

Minimum-Wage Laws

Of a very different character is the movement for the minimum wage. In this country, the agitation for fixing a minimum wage by law has been in the main confined to the case of women; and in their case it has been advocated chiefly on the ground of social *expediency*, not social *justice*. It has been urged that if women are underpaid they will be undernourished or ill-housed, and consequently lacking in the health and strength that the mothers of the coming generation must have if the vigor of the nation is to be maintained. This is a special argument that has little relation to the subject we are discussing. But there may, at any moment, arise in this country, as there has in others, a strong movement for the enactment of minimum-wage laws for men as well as women;

and it is this proposal that I wish briefly to examine in its relation to the subject of the present chapter.

It would be going beyond the province of this book to undertake to pass judgment on the desirability or undesirability of a minimum-wage law —a law forbidding employers to pay less than a certain sum per day, or per week, to their employees. All that I can undertake to do—and even that imperfectly—is to point out the relation of such a proposal to certain broad principles and general ideas. The object of a minimum-wage law is to assure to every person who is employed in industrial or commercial work an income sufficient to provide him—or him and his family—with what, according to the existing standards of the community, are regarded as the necessaries of life. Every decent person wishes, of course, that every honest worker should receive a wage sufficient for this purpose; the question, therefore, is solely as to the desirability of endeavoring to assure this result by governmental compulsion.

If the government itself were carrying on the industrial and commercial activities of the country, there could be no question about the propriety of a minimum-wage rule. But what we have to consider is the effect such a rule is likely to have under a régime of private enterprise. Obviously, it is an interference with the free play of such enterprise; unlike the workmen's compensation law, it alters in a radical way the relation between employer and employed. In the absence of such a law, employer and employed may make any bargain they think proper as to rates of wages; and there are times when, owing to slackness of business, to uncertainty regarding the future, or to any other cause which tends to diminish the opportunities of employment, a large number of workers could be kept employed at wages less than the normal, but would be thrown out of employment if the normal wage was insisted upon. A rigid minimum-wage law might thus work immediate injury upon large numbers of workers by throwing them out of employment, and more remote but far more serious injury by hindering the restoration of good times; for, as was pointed out in the chapter on Overproduction, not only do hard times produce unemployment but unemployment produces hard times. Whether this objection, and others that might be adduced, outweigh the arguments in favor of a minimum-wage law, I shall not undertake to discuss; it is sufficient for the present purpose to note that the objections exist.

Specific Merits versus Abstract Doctrine

And now as to the bearing of all this on the question of "social justice." Whatever the specific arguments may be in favor of a minimum-wage law and against a minimum-wage law, the decision we arrive at in regard to it will be of a wholly different nature if our judgment is based on those specific arguments from what it would be if it were based upon any abstract doctrine of social justice.

In the first case, we shall be making a relatively minor (though, to be sure, an important) practical adjustment, and shall be careful to keep things fairly close to what they would be if there were no law at all; and this is in fact what is done in England, for example, where minimum-wage laws have been in operation for some time. The minimum wage is fixed by local wage-boards at a point fairly near to the lowest wages that are actually paid in normal circumstances without the interposition of any law at all; and accordingly the evils indicated above as likely to spring from an arbitrary rule are reduced to comparatively small dimensions. But if we acted, and sincerely acted, upon an abstract principle of social justice, we should be completely at sea. The minimum wage would have no relation to trade conditions, but only to the deserts—and who shall say what they are?—of the workers; and the consequence of this would be such a strain upon the existing order as it could not possibly stand. Private undertakings would go to the wall by the hundred; the government, having undertaken to improve conditions which private enterprise could not meet would find itself compelled either to abandon this effort at social justice altogether, or itself to take over the task of providing employment and carrying on a large part, or perhaps all, of the industries of the country.

I hope that these examples will help to make clear the cardinal point which it is the object of this chapter to bring out. Under the existing order of society, the economic condition of individuals is not determined upon any abstract principle of social justice; and, so long as we retain the essentials of that order, when social justice is appealed to as the basis of any specific proposal the appeal is almost sure to be based either upon confused thought or insincere purpose. As has been pointed out in previous chapters, it is not by virtue of any consideration of abstract justice that an eminent lawyer receives for his interesting and stimulating work a thousand times as much as does a stevedore or a coal-miner for his exhausting and uninviting labor; nor is there any correspondence in point of human desert between the splendid profits of a successful merchant and the modest income of a competent civil engineer or physician.

The benefits of the existing system, with its freedom of initiative, its variety of opportunity, its very vicissitudes of fortune and inequalities of reward, are, in the opinion of many of the best thinkers in the world, far greater than those that would result from an attempt to organize society upon a basis of social justice; but whether their opinion of the *desirability* of the existing system be right or wrong, there is no question as to the *nature* of the system. The benefits of competition, of individual responsibility, of the relations between man and man that arise from the free play of economic forces, may not be so great as these people think; but so long as we accept the system we must not pretend to regulate our affairs upon a principle to which the system is not adapted, and is not adaptable.

This does not mean that there shall be no regulations that interfere with the free play of competition, the free action of supply and demand, the placing upon every individual of the responsibility for his own welfare; there are, and always have been, scores of matters in which we deviate, and deliberately deviate, from the general rule. But when we do so in any instance, let us do it as practical men dealing with the pros and cons of a specific question, and not pretend that our verdict upon it is a fulfilment of social justice.

Self-Delusion or False Pretence

Once raise the cry of Social Justice—if you raise it in a sincere spirit, and understand what you are doing—and you cannot stop with seeing that no workman's wage shall be less than three dollars a day, or that every disabled workman shall get two-thirds of his pay during his disability. The latter of these is evidently a sound practical measure; for the former there may also be much to be said. But if you are really going in for Social Justice, why should not the poor devil who is disabled for life get *three halves* of his old pay, instead of *two thirds*, to compensate him for his crippled condition; and why should not the man that does the most exhausting and repulsive work get thirty dollars a day instead of three?

An unusually instructive illustration of the importance of seeing clearly in this matter is furnished by the story of the Kansas Court of Industrial Relations. This was established by a law passed a few years ago at the instance of Governor Henry J. Allen, a man of unquestioned public spirit and high purpose, as well as intelligence. It grew out of the extensive public inconvenience and hardship caused by one of those stoppages of coal mining which so frequently spring from a dispute between mine-owners and mine-workers. The particular point Governor Allen insisted upon was that the law should establish a real court, a court of *justice*, and not a tribunal of *arbitration*. Compulsory arbitration, he pointed out, had proved a failure in Australia; and he ascribed the failure to the fact that in an *arbitration* tribunal both sides are represented, and the object is to arrive at some settlement with which both will be pretty well satisfied—a compromise based on no principle, but upon give-and-take, pulling and hauling. In a court, on the other hand, neither side is represented; the object is to decree what is just, whether the parties like it or not. But it was pointed out by a perfectly friendly critic, when the court was first instituted, that if the court was to have any chance of success it would have to confine itself—in spite of its name of "court"—to the more modest function of an arbitration tribunal, since there was no rule of justice, but only of reasonable accommodation, by which it could govern its decision in a labor dispute. And the history not only of the court, but also of the administrative acts of the Kansas government under the law which established the court, have amply shown how unfortunate was the assumption upon which the law was based. At the present moment there are strong indications that the experiment may soon be abandoned altogether.

CHAPTER XXXIII

EQUALITY OF OPPORTUNITY

THE foregoing chapter, on Social Justice, had for its object the clearing up of certain misty notions. It pointed out that Socialists, whether right or wrong in their conception of social justice, and whether mistaken or not as to the practicability or the desirability of their programme, may rightly claim that social justice, in some genuine and definite form, is one of the chief objects which they propose to accomplish; while, on the other hand, persons who are not Socialists, persons who believe in the maintenance of the fundamentals of the existing order—the essentials of private property, individual initiative, and individual self-dependence—must abstain from professing to base any particular economic arrangement or proposal upon an abstract theory of social justice. From the standpoint of the established order of society, any particular law or policy, actual or proposed, must be judged upon its specific merits and as part of the entire existing system of things; and to pretend that that system rests, or can be made to rest, upon any abstract doctrine of social justice is to indulge in a confusion of thought which may be highly mischievous. Everybody, of course, wishes the system to be as beneficial as possible to all the people; but to judge a proposal from the standpoint of the greatest attainable *benefit* is a wholly different thing from judging it from the standpoint of ideal *justice*.

The present chapter deals with a similar question; a question, indeed, which might be regarded as merely a particular instance of the broader question of social justice. And I am afraid that many of my readers, even if they admit the difficulties concerning the general concept of social justice pointed out in the foregoing chapter, will be shocked at the idea of there being any difficulty at all about the much simpler and more circumscribed concept with which the present chapter has to do. "What!" they will say, "does not everybody—certainly every good American—maintain the doctrine of Equality of Opportunity? Inequality of wealth, inequality of reward, inequalities of various kinds due to superior ability, superior industry and energy, or even to the vicissitudes of chance—these may be all right; but can any good American deny that we are all entitled to equal *opportunity* to gain the rewards of ability and energy and the prizes of Fortune?"

Now, shocking as it may at first blush seem, the fact is that not even in regard to opportunity is the existing order based upon any abstract doctrine of justice or equality; and the phrases so generally current, and so glibly used, about equality of opportunity must be understood in a very restricted and qualified sense if they are to correspond to the truth. Let us look into this matter a little; only in its broadest aspects, to be sure, and without entering into detail, but yet with our eyes open and our minds unafraid.

In what Sense we do have Equality of Opportunity

Let us begin by realizing that in one sense the doctrine of equal opportunity is a basic principle of American democracy; and that, indeed, one of the most signal fruits of the establishment of our Republic has been the influence of its example in spreading the doctrine of equal opportunity—understood in this sense—throughout the world. That sense is not, however, that the Government and the laws provide that every human being shall *actually have* an equal opportunity with every other for the good things of life; but only that the Government and the laws shall *interpose no obstacle* to his having such opportunity. The population is not divided into fixed classes, some being born to greater privileges than others; a child born in the humblest family may aspire to the highest position in State or nation, to the greatest professional honors, and to the most magnificent business success, without encountering any obstacle in the shape of discriminating laws. And more than this is true. Not only the laws of America, but the spirit of American life, has favored a free opportunity for the development of every man's possibilities. We have always pointed with pride to countless examples of the rise of poor boys to the summits of political and financial eminence; and until within the last few decades, our country presented in this respect a shining contrast to the nations of the Old World.

All of us, then, are sincerely devoted to the doctrine of equal opportunity understood in this restricted sense; but there are many who, through a failure to distinguish between this restricted doctrine, this negative doctrine, and a much broader positive doctrine of equal opportunity, fall into a confusion of thought similar to that which was dwelt upon in the preceding chapter, in relation to Social Justice in general.

Educational Facilities and Welfare Laws

The nature and consequences of that confusion of thought will be considered presently. But first it must be observed that in our desire to open the door of opportunity to the great mass of the people, we do actually go much beyond the merely negative principles above discussed. Free public schools, free libraries and museums, compulsory-education laws, laws forbidding child labor—all these are designed largely for the purpose of assuring to the people in all stations of life, and especially to the children of the poor, a far nearer approach to equal opportunity than would fall to their lot if the community did not positively intervene for their benefit. One after another (and in countries far less democratic, as well as in our own country) these things have been instituted, as higher and higher standards of life have become recognized, and have come to be regarded as essential; and we all rejoice that this is so.

But all this may be so, and the process may go on much farther still, without at all involving the abstract doctrine of Equality of Opportunity. And it is of not merely theoretical but practical importance—just as we saw was the case with the general question of Social Justice—that we should honestly and clearly recognize the difference. To adopt measure after measure of *extension of opportunity*, each upon its specific merits, is one thing; to adopt them as measures demanded by the abstract doctrine of Equality of Opportunity is quite another.

A single illustration may suffice to make the distinction clear. During the past twenty years or more, enlightened people in this country have been practically unanimous in the desire to bring to an end the evils of child labor, as that term has been understood in the past. There may have been some difference of opinion as to whether the limit of age to which the term "child" is applicable should be fourteen or sixteen; this is a matter of detail. Recently, however, there has been started a movement to raise the limit to eighteen years; and this proposal is advocated on the express ground of its being demanded by the doctrine of equal opportunity. The great force behind the movement to abolish child labor has hitherto been something very different from this. Although there is no doubt that a desire to equalize opportunity has been a contributing factor, the movement has rested in the main upon the instincts of common humanity and right feeling. Now, however, it is proposed that the government shall guarantee to young people up to the age of eighteen time for pleasure and for intellectual advancement; and this proposal is urged not simply as a thing that is desirable, but as an inevitable conclusion from the abstract doctrine of equal opportunity.

Unlimited Scope of the Abstract Doctrine

But obviously that doctrine, if accepted, carries vastly farther. I do not mean merely that, for youths free from the need of earning a living, educational opportunities continue to unfold beyond the age of eighteen; I mean especially that *time* is by no means all that is required to place these opportunities within their grasp. To wipe out these differences of opportunity, it would be manifestly necessary to abolish inheritance and bequest; and even this would be far from sufficient, for the *living* parent who is wealthy,—or, for that matter, who is wise, even if he is not wealthy—is in a position to give his children immeasurable advantages from which children less favored are debarred. Unless we are prepared to go the length of putting the state in place of the parent as provider of all that is desirable for children and youths, we must judge the question of child labor by concrete practical standards and not in the light of a dogmatic principle of equal opportunity.

The subject of the inheritance of property has come up here as incidental to the question of equal opportunity; but it will be well, before closing this chapter, to devote a few words to the discussion of that subject on its own account. Once in a while, some young man who has inherited wealth announces that he will not accept what has thus fallen to him because he does not regard it as right. That such a young man is animated by generous ideals may safely be assumed; and, in case he is an avowed Socialist, his course is respectable from the intellectual standpoint also, whether we agree with him or not. But if he is not a Socialist—if he acts merely upon some crude, vague, undigested notion of Social Justice or Equality of Opportunity—his action, however creditable to his heart, does little credit to his head. It proceeds not from a deeper, but from an infinitely shallower, view of existing institutions than that which, consciously or unconsciously, is entertained by his fellow-citizens generally.

What Abolition of Inheritance Would Mean

If inheritance is to be abolished, if the accumulation of wealth by the exertion of energy and talent is to be discredited, then some other spring of action must be found which will supply not only that incentive to effort, but also that zest of life, of which, in the existing order, the motive of material gain is so great a source. One of the great incentives to effort—and especially so among the poor and those in modest circumstances—is the desire to give to one's children better opportunities than those which are taken for granted as within the reach of all who live in a given community at a given time. To remove that incentive—unless it were replaced by one equally stimulating—would reduce to the plane of sordid selfishness what is now a high and generous, even if by some it may be regarded as a narrow, impulse to daily endeavor. In a state of society in which work was inspired solely by zeal for the common good, men of high gifts and noble ambitions might find in the desire to contribute all that was possible to the general well-being ample inspiration for the utmost exercise of their powers. But no such impetus to ardent exertion could be felt by the ordinary man. Now to do his utmost means, for himself and his family, the difference between success and failure, between advancement and retrogression, between self-respect and shame. Then it would mean simply the difference between a contribution a little greater or a little less, but in any case insignificant, to that vast ocean of human productivity in which his own output is but as a drop of water.

CHAPTER XXXIV

SOCIALISM (*First Part*)

BEFORE discussing Socialism, it would be highly desirable to define the term. Unfortunately, however, that is an extremely difficult thing to do. It would be difficult, even if there were no very great variations in the use of the word among the Socialists themselves; it is made almost impossible by the fact that there are such variations. I shall therefore not attempt to lay down a definition either of Socialism in general, or of any one particular form of Socialism; but I shall try to state briefly what may be regarded as common to all the forms of Socialism which are now prominent in public discussion. With this understanding, we may say that the system which Socialism proposes is one in which there would be *no private ownership of the instruments of production* (natural resources, factories, machinery, etc.; or, more briefly, land and capital); in which, accordingly, *the control and management of all industry would be in the hands of the state* (that is, of the government); in which *the income of individuals would be obtained solely as compensation for labor* (profits, interest, and rent being abolished); and in which *the compensation of labor would be fixed by the state*, in accordance with rules based upon some general principle or principles.

Socialist Systems and the Socialist Ideal

But difficult as it is to define *Socialism*, it is not very difficult to define *the Socialist ideal.* Although there are great differences between the various Socialist proposals, there is one result at which they all aim, one purpose by which they are all animated: that Society as a whole shall provide for the welfare of all its members; that our working life shall not be a struggle to obtain the necessaries, comforts, and luxuries that we individually desire, but simply the performance by each man of his proper share in the promotion of the general good; and that each man's share in the total that all have produced shall be determined not by bargaining, or strategy, or any chance advantage or disadvantage, but by fixed principles of social justice.[1]

Socialism presents a large and profound human issue, which it would be unprofitable to discuss as a mere question of Economics. Even in its purely economic aspect, it involves the question of how human beings would act under a system of which

[1] What those principles ought to be is itself a subject that opens up a large field for discussion, which cannot here be gone into. The three leading possibilities have been compactly stated in the maxims To each according to his work, To each according to his need, To each according to his sacrifice.

we have had little or no experience; and its larger human aspects are vitally connected with its economic aspect. Broadly viewed, the issue of Socialism turns on two cardinal questions. First, *Is the Socialist system workable:* can it be established and successfully maintained? Second, *Is the Socialist ideal desirable:* would the life of man under Socialism be a better, happier, higher life than that which is attainable under the existing order? These two questions we shall consider successively.

Is Socialism Practicable?

As to the question whether Socialism is workable or not, it was quite the fashion in this country thirty or forty years ago—it is still the fashion in many quarters—to dispose of it by a mere wave of the hand. "Socialism will never work, because it is contrary to human nature"—that was the simple formula which was most in vogue. But by many generations of men, including the most intelligent among them, democracy was honestly thought to be unworkable for the same reason—it seemed to them contrary to human nature. Nobody knows whether Socialism is contrary to human nature or not; and nobody is likely to know for a long time to come. Nowadays we don't hear so much of this easy-going method of disposing of the question, and nothing more need be said of it here.

Coming to more specific arguments against the

possibility of making Socialism work, we have to begin by noticing two that are manifestly unsound or inadequate.

Some people think that the case of Socialism is completely disposed of when they point out that capital is as essential as labor to high productivity. Undoubtedly it is; and undoubtedly, too, many Socialists completely overlook this cardinal fact—they talk as though labor were everything and capital nothing. But intelligent Socialists do nothing of the kind; they know that capital is indispensable, but they deny that *private ownership* of capital is necessary to its creation or to its maintenance. They say that, just as to-day a certain part of the total product of labor is taken by the government for what are now regarded as proper governmental undertakings, so it would be perfectly feasible for the government to undertake to build and maintain factories and machinery, to provide stocks of raw materials, etc.; that it would find the means of doing so by reserving for these purposes a certain part of the productive energy of the nation, instead of devoting the whole of that energy to the supplying of the immediate wants or desires of consumers. Capital cannot, indeed, be created or kept up except by saving; but it is perfectly conceivable that *collective saving*—saving by the government, as just indicated—could provide capital just as abundantly as it is now supplied by *individual saving*. Whether this is likely actually to happen under Socialism is, of course, quite another question; the point here made is only that you can't dispose of the possibilities of capital under Socialism by assuming that there can be no capital without capitalists—no saving for the purposes of future production except under the incentive of individual advantage.

The other argument that I have reference to is that which points to the experience of Russia as a complete demonstration of the impossibility of Socialism, or at least of any thoroughgoing form of Socialism. The Russian experiment in Socialism has, indeed, been a most dismal failure. It ought to serve as a crushing rebuke to those who glibly denounce the existing order as a mass of evil, and imagine that Socialism is a magic cure for the world's distress. But the failure of a single experiment, however impressive and however disastrous, cannot be regarded by sober thinkers as conclusive. How much of that failure may be due to faults special to the Soviet régime, how much to the backward condition of the Russian people, how much to the particular circumstances of the time—these and similar questions may justly be raised by intelligent Socialists who object to the Russian failure being regarded as demonstrating that Socialism can never be made to operate successfully.

The Mainspring of Productivity

From the standpoint of efficiency, the strongest argument against Socialism is that which rests on the conviction that neither governmental compulsion nor the desire to promote the general good can ever be expected to put into the work of production anything like the energy, the ability, and the close adaptation of means to ends, which are supplied under the existing system by individual interest and ambition. Of course such a proposition as this cannot be demonstrated like a theorem in geometry; but it can be supported by very powerful arguments. We cannot say that a Socialist system is "contrary to human nature," in the sense that it would be sure to be a disastrous failure; but there is every reason to believe that its efficiency would fall far short of that of the existing system. Under the stress of competition every man who undertakes or manages an enterprise, every man who orders a stock of goods, is actuated by most powerful motives to use the best possible judgment and the greatest possible skill, the most constant vigilance and care and energy. To fall short means loss and very possibly disaster and ruin; to do well means prosperity; to excel means fortune, and very possibly dazzling success. And all this is emphatically present to his mind; it is a wholly different thing from the mere prospect of criticism or displacement as the result of a government investigation which may or may not come and which may or may not be just and impartial. And the energy and watchfulness thus present among those at the head is transmitted all along the line. The subordinate who shirks or is careless, the workman who does not come up to a proper standard of quality or quantity, knows that his employer will not tolerate his shortcomings because he cannot afford to. Nor is this all; for not only is each man under constant and automatic pressure to do his best, but there is a constant and automatic tendency of men of exceptional ability to rise to the top—to become the managers of industry, the heads of enterprise. It seems almost certain, from what we know of human nature, that nothing comparable in effectiveness to all this would be possible under a system of government control of industry; and so far as experience of such control has gone, it offers very strong confirmation of the conclusion.

A Socialist Counter-Argument

It may be said, and indeed it *is* often said, in reply to this argument, that under Socialism we might fairly expect the desire for the general good to become so universal and so powerful that it would do all that is now done by individual interest and individual ambition. But, apart from any instinctive feeling we may have that this is not at all likely, there is a very strong reason for disbelieving it which has received less attention than it deserves. The question is not merely one of altruism versus egoism, of unselfishness versus selfishness; it is a question of the possibilities of the human imagination. Under a Socialist régime, with the general welfare as the motive for exertion, to do well would mean (except in the case of a few extraordinary persons) merely to add an infinitesimal amount to the total production of the community; even to do extremely well would simply mean to add a somewhat bigger, but still infinitesimal, amount. Under the individualist régime doing well or doing ill means the difference between success and failure, between self-respect and humiliation, perhaps between prosperity and ruin. It is true that the sum of all those infinitesimals is an important total; but no man can keep this fact vividly enough before him to make it dominant over his whole life and conduct; and indeed even the augmentation of the total is not a thing to inspire intense joy, nor its diminution a thing to cause tragic grief.

The unselfish devotion of millions of people to their country's service—civil and industrial as well as military—in time of war is often pointed to as a proof that desire for the general good may be as effective a spur to effort and labor as is individual interest or ambition, and that under Socialism we might expect this desire to be as ardent in time of peace as it now is in time of war. But in fact the conduct of people in war time instead of weakening the argument above presented, actually strengthens it. In war time, the question, is not whether the nation shall be somewhat better off or somewhat worse off; the question is whether it shall be victor or vanquished; and everybody feels that this tremendous and dramatic question is going to be decided for or against the nation according as its people do or do not their full duty. When war ceases, we don't suddenly become more selfish than we were the day before; this, if you come to think of it, you must see to be an absurdity. What does happen is that there is no longer any tremendous and dramatic significance in our doing our best for the country on the one hand or falling short of it on the other; and that is precisely what would happen in regard to our ordinary activities when Socialism took the place of individualism.

The Waste of Competition

On the Socialist side, however, it is urged that the competitive system, however stimulating it may be to energy and efficiency, involves enormous waste. And the charge cannot be denied. A very large portion of our activities is directed not to increasing the total output, or satisfying the general needs, but to promoting the interests of one person as against another in the great competitive contest. One of the most striking illustrations of this, and perhaps the one most frequently pointed out by Socialists, is the vast expenditure for advertising, which runs high into the hundreds of millions every year in such a country as the United States.[1] But besides advertising there is, of course, an enormous amount of energy and ability devoted in other ways to winning a victory or an advantage over competitors, rather than to the increase or improvement of production. Moreover, there is often

[1] It is only fair to note, however, that advertising, while in large part wasteful, is in large part distinctly useful; namely, in so far as it takes the place of other forms of salesmanship, which are a necessary part of the process of distribution.

duplication—or multiplication—of services which, under a non-competitive system, might be avoided by using a single agency where now we use two, or perhaps many. A standard illustration of this is the delivery of milk by several different companies in the same city block, where all parties could be served at a considerably less total cost in time and labor by a single company.

But, while all this must be admitted, there are two considerations which go far to break the force of it as an argument for Socialism. In the first place, if the competitive system really does bring about so much efficiency as seems to be justly claimed for it, we should not be too greatly distressed by the fact that a big price has to be paid for that benefit. You can't have intense competition without active rivalry; and active rivalry, whether it takes the form of advertising, of needless duplication, or what not, is necessarily a diversion of effort from directly productive activities. There are cases where the waste of competition is obviously out of all proportion to its benefit; but these are the exception, not the rule. By far the greater part of competitive effort in most fields is expended not in taking away other people's business by advertising or other devices, but in managing your own business with energy, skill, and good judgment. Advertising and some other forms of "competitive waste" are conspicuous and striking; but there is no reason to believe that they bear any very large proportion to the results which are brought about by that same competitive spirit, as it manifests itself unobserved, every moment of the day, in the efficient conduct of business and the constant improvement of production.

The Waste of Socialism

The second consideration has reference not to the waste which takes place under competition, but to the waste which would take place under Socialism. I do not refer to the question of *inefficient* production; that would be counting the same argument twice. What I have in mind is the waste involved in *misdirected* production. Under the competitive system, nothing is more essential than the adaptation of supply to demand. You must produce the things that people want, and in the proportions in which people want them; to have things left on your hands is fatal. And even more important than the correct adjustment of supply to demand in the case of ordinary commodities is correct judgment in putting capital into fixed forms—factories, machinery, etc. An enormous amount of waste may occur in these ways unless it is prevented by the best judgment and the keenest foresight. Under Socialism the attempt would, of course, be made to exercise correct judgment; but miscalculation would not be checked by any such prompt and decisive penalty, nor correct calculation stimulated by any such signal reward, as attaches to them under the system of individual enterprise. Accordingly, we may feel sure that there would be, under Socialism, an incomparably greater amount of waste in the shape of misdirected production than takes place in the existing system. It must in fairness be stated, however, as an offset to this, that the great waste caused by unemployment (to say nothing of the hardships of the unemployed) could be in large part avoided under Socialism; not being (like private enterprises) under the imperative necessity of finding demanders for what it supplied, the government might keep work going at one time as well as another. But on the other hand, this very circumstance would tend still further to increase waste in the shape of misdirected production; if the misdirection is checked neither by the prospect of commercial loss nor by the fear of unemployment, it may well go to very great lengths—wasting, it should be noted, not only the labor but the raw materials, fuel, etc., involved in the process.

On the question of the *workableness of the Socialist system*, these remarks will have to suffice; and in the next chapter we shall take up the question of the *desirableness of the Socialist ideal.*

CHAPTER XXXV

SOCIALISM (*Second Part*)

No remark, perhaps, is more frequently made about Socialism than that it is a beautiful ideal, but not a practical possibility. It would, in my judgment, be much nearer right to say that Socialism may, for ought we know, be a practical possibility, but that it is not a beautiful ideal. On either half of this proposition there is room for difference of opinion; but we are in much better position to judge of the second half than of the first. For while the question of the *practicability of the Socialist system* turns on economic considerations of some remoteness and some complexity, the question of the *desirableness of the Socialist ideal* turns on a contemplation of the most elemental facts of human life and human nature.

The Elimination of Struggle

The preëminent aim of the Socialist order is the elimination of the *struggle* of life. Everybody, except those who were criminally idle or refractory, would be assured of a comfortable living; anxiety for the future, one of the besetting evils of life as we know it, would thus be completely got rid of. Moreover, though there might be considerable inequalities of compensation for work, there would be no great acquisition of wealth; and accordingly little or none of that feverish desire for worldly success, those exaltations and depressions, those triumphs and heartburnings, which play so large a part in the life of today.

It may seem to many that this complete freedom from anxious care on the one hand, and from goading ambition on the other, would be an unmixed good for the world. But for my part—and I think the same is true of the great majority of normal human beings when once they have given their minds to a clear realization of the question—this ideal of a care-free and struggle-free world is neither attractive nor inspiring; desirable neither in its effect on happiness nor in its effect on character.

It is given to few men greatly to distinguish themselves above their fellows, or greatly to promote the general welfare; and this, in the very nature of things, must be the case under any system of society. But under the individualist system, to every man there is one object of keen and constant interest, both upon selfish and unselfish grounds. That object is to maintain himself and his family in decent comfort; to rise in the world if possible, but at least to do this. The mere fact that he has achieved this when he might have failed is a constant source of satisfaction to him, even though it be not constantly present to his thoughts. He knows that if he had been less industrious or less thrifty, he and his family would have suffered both materially and in the estimation of their friends and neighbors; and that it might even be possible that they would have become objects of charity instead of a self-supporting family. It is the fulfilment of this humble but vital purpose—the maintenance of his family in comfort and independence—that is, for all but a small fraction of mankind, the great source of manly endeavor, the great builder of sturdy character. Robert Burns was not a groveling materialist; yet it was Robert Burns who said:

> To make a happy fireside clime
>   To weans and wife,
> That's the true pathos and sublime
>   Of human life.

With everybody assured of moderate comfort, with each person's stint of work determined by government rules, with no fear of want and no hope of wealth, there could be nothing of either the "pathos" or the "sublime" which the poet's insight perceived in the homely strivings of the everyday man.

The Pleasures of Possession

Nor is it only through its bracing influence upon character that struggle plays a commanding part in the enrichment of life. Nearly everything we have derives a large part of its value to us from the fact that the possession of it is not a matter of course. And here I am speaking of value in a more absolute sense than that in which it was used in our discussion of the economic laws of value in the early part of this book; I mean not value as a mere ratio—the ratio in which one thing exchanges for other things—but value as it is understood in our habitual thoughts. I mean the satisfaction we get out of a thing.

Now of this pleasure and satisfaction that we get out of things an enormously large proportion arises out of the possession of them not being a matter of course. There are scores of conveniences and comforts which are accessible to almost everybody today, and which one or two hundred years ago were either absolutely unknown or were the luxuries of the rich. To be free from mud and dirt in the streets; to get a hot or cold bath by merely turning on a faucet; to be able to communicate instantly with anybody at a distance by merely lifting a receiver off a hook; to spend the evening in a brilliantly lighted room, and to walk out in the night upon streets almost as light as day; these and a multitude of other things that might easily be named are now the possession of nearly everybody, while a few generations ago any one of them was beyond the reach of any but the very rich and some were altogether inaccessible. Now it would be absurd to say that we do not get any good out of these things; we do get a great deal of *good* out of them. But hardly anybody gets a keen *pleasure* out of them. We take the telephone for granted, just as we take the bathtub and the electric light for granted; and nobody ever stops to think how fine it is to be able to cross the street dry-shod instead of floundering in the mud as his grandfather or great-grandfather had to do. The things in the possession of which we take a keen interest, the things from the possession of which we derive a lively satisfaction, are things which are not within everybody's reach as a matter of course. Whether we get them as the result of working and planning, or through some stroke of luck, or because of inherited wealth, the possession of them is something pertaining to us individually; and this gives them a value and an interest which they would not otherwise have.

Even that aspect of the matter which some critics of the existing order look upon as so distressing, the desire to possess things as a symbol of prosperity, an outward sign of our place in the social scale, is by no means so evil as those austere moralists think it. It has, of course, a contemptible, even a disgusting side;—it can range all the way from decent pride and honest ambition to degrading snobbishness and heartless luxury. But in all classes it is one of the chief sources of interest and satisfaction—in the workingman's family which strains every nerve to have its lace curtains and its piano and its parlor furniture as good as its neighbor's, as well as in that of the business or professional man which aims at a high standard of beauty in its domestic appointments and distinction in its social activities. It is not the highest possible manifestation of human nature, to be sure; but if you were to take it away altogether—and Socialism would come very near to doing so—you would wipe out one of the chief elements in the zest of life.

Socialism and the Family

In all this I have said nothing about the effect of Socialism upon the family itself, the family as a human institution, as the very corner-stone of our life. Yet nothing is more generally admitted by even the friendliest commentators on Socialism than that it would profoundly alter the character of the family relation. Under any thoroughgoing Socialist régime, the State would necessarily assume either the whole or a large part of the responsibility for the welfare of children—would see to it that they were properly fed and clothed, as well as educated, and that their education took the form of such training as not only their own welfare but the general welfare required. In regard not only to immediate comforts and satisfactions but also to the prospects of the future, the family would no longer be a unit, bound together by a common stake in the common welfare. The responsibility of parents for the present welfare of their children and for their future progress would be reduced to a mere shadow of what it now is; and it is absurd to suppose that removal of this vital bond of mutual duty, this constant source of mutual solicitude and reciprocal obligation, would leave the ties of family loyalty and family attachment unimpaired. Greatly as Socialism would diminish those motives for exertion and ambition which are now at once the most effective and the most inspiring, there is every reason to believe that it would have a still more disastrous effect on the character of the family relation. And for that warm and deep human attachment which their common struggles and cares and hopes keep constantly alive between husband and wife, between parents and children, the sense of obligation to a remote and abstract concept—call it the state or call it the general welfare—would be but a chilly and soulless substitute.

Socialism and Liberty

But of all objections to the Socialist ideal, the one that is to my mind the most fatal is that Socialism is incompatible with liberty. Every form of social organization, indeed, demands a sacrifice of liberty; some elements of personal freedom must be sacrificed to the common good. But it is only under Socialism that this loss of freedom pervades the whole of life. Of the tree of liberty we willingly cut off some of the branches; Socialism would strike at its root. Socialism may possibly be made to function efficiently; but hardly anybody claims that it can be made to function efficiently without what has aptly been termed regimentation. Just how complete that regimentation would have to be, just what form it would take, may be open to question; but certainly, in the main, our ways of working—what we shall do, how much we shall do of it, how well we shall do it—would be determined by government rules and would be supervised by government officers. To live under a régime like this is to surrender the very citadel of liberty—the right to order in our own way the essentials of our daily life. And it is idle to imagine that, with our daily life ordered for us by the state, the spirit of liberty would retain its vitality in any direction. It is not to reason or reflection that any deep and primal human sentiment owes its vitality; it can be kept alive only by exercise, by habit, by the familiar practice of daily life. Make regimentation the basis of life, and liberty must become, to most of us, a mere word, a metaphysical abstraction.

In reply to the assertion that Socialism is incompatible with liberty, Socialists are fond of saying that a large proportion of all the people have no freedom now; that as a practical fact they have no choice but to go on making their living by the one kind of work to which they are committed; that the wage-worker is really a "wage-slave." And indeed many who are not Socialists admit the soundness of this contention. Nevertheless it is thoroughly unsound; it rests on a confusion of thought, on a failure to grasp the essential nature of liberty. That the wage-worker may be *as badly off* as though he were a slave is a tenable proposition, but to say that he *is* a slave is mere nonsense. The wild Indian who has no choice but to hunt game and endure the severest hardships in order barely to keep alive may be far worse off than many slaves, but everybody sees that he is a freeman; on the other hand the black servant in a Southern family before the Civil War may have been far better off than many freemen, but nobody would deny that he was a slave. When every little farmer got his living out of his own acres—his food by his own hard toil, his clothing by the women's spinning and weaving of the wool of his own sheep—he had no choice but to keep on working from sunrise to sunset in order to maintain himself and his family; but only a fool would say that he was a slave. The compulsion of circumstances may be hardship, but it is not slavery, nor even any impairment of the spirit of liberty; nowhere has the spirit of liberty been more intense and indomitable than in mountain countries where comfort was almost unknown, where to extract a living from the soil meant the most unremitting and most scantily rewarded labor—countries like Switzerland and Scotland and Montenegro. It is true that under the existing economic order millions of people have little choice as to how they shall earn their living; but each of them has nevertheless the feeling of a freeman. No man, and no government, has ordered him to do what he is doing; and it rests with him to decide whether he shall continue to do it. If there are thousands who fare better, there are also thousands who fare worse; and whether he fares well or fares ill is his own business and nobody else's. If he has succeeded in keeping his head above water, if he has maintained his family without outside aid, he may justly feel that in the face of difficulty and temptation he has played a man's part in the struggle of life. And he has always the spur of hope that his children, like the children of so many of his fellows in like station, will attain a higher place in the struggle.

The Ordinary Man and the Exceptional Man

With just one more remark, I must bring this discussion to a close. One of the chief claims made for Socialism is that, while it may make life less attractive or interesting for the few, it will raise the life of the many to a higher plane. But this claim, too, rests on a very unsound foundation. One thing must, of course, be admitted; and it should be freely and frankly admitted. Under a Socialist régime, if it worked at all, there would be no such thing as extreme poverty; and the abolition of extreme poverty is an object which we should all heartily desire to accomplish. Great progress in this direction has been made in the past hundred years, in the past fifty years, in the past thirty years;[1] yet a great deal remains to be done. But while extreme poverty is an evil that exists under the present system, it is a highly exceptional condi-

[1] Of course the frightful poverty caused by the Great War throughout a large part of Europe is here left out of account.

tion; and it is not in regard to the abjectly poor but in regard to the great mass of the people that the claim above referred to is made—the claim that though Socialism may make life less attractive or interesting to the few, it will raise the life of the many to a higher plane. This claim has already been replied to in part, in the remarks made above about the zest of life for the everyday man; but there is one aspect of the claim to which those remarks do not apply, and which therefore demands our attention here. The point has been made thousands of times; let us look at it as stated quite recently by one of the most brilliant of Socialist writers, Mr. Bertrand Russell. Here is his picture of the general uplift of life which we must look to Socialism to accomplish:

> Man's true life does not consist in the business of filling his belly and clothing his body, but in art and thought and love, in the creation and contemplation of beauty, and in the scientific understanding of the world. If the world is to be regenerated, it is in these things, not only in material goods, that all must be enabled to participate.

This is very pretty indeed; but it is as unreal as it is pretty. There is no way of enabling "all the people to participate" in a large and vital way in the joys of the "creation" or even the "contemplation" of beauty, or "the scientific understanding of the world." Nothing that Socialism can possibly achieve could enlarge the access of *all* the people to these joys one tenth as much as that access *has* been enlarged for something like half the people by the printing press and the railroad and the enormous increase of wealth; but it takes something more than access to them to make them the stuff out of which life and the joy of life are made. They are for the few, not because they are shut out from the many, but because it is only the few that are capable of them. As for Mr. Russell's remaining category, love, it is perhaps worth while to consider what love would be like in the familyless world to which, it may be noted, he looks forward with calm complacency. The zest of life comes to only a few from the things which seem to be the exclusive object of his thoughts; and yet the many, for whom he believes himself to be so deeply solicitous, have found life to be not without zest, and still find it so even in this industrial age. And that zest comes from the sense of personal independence and personal responsibility and personal attachment; from the need of holding one's own in the world, and doing one's best for one's family; from the possibility of rising in the world or having one's children rise in it. These joys and sorrows, these strivings and ambitions—with that access to art and literature and music and science which adds greatly to the content of life, but cannot for most people form its staple—are nearly all men's portion under the existing order, with all its faults. Let us preserve as much as we can of individual freedom, of individual variety; let us fight against a benumbing devotion to standardization and "efficiency"; but let us not throw away what we have of individuality in the vain hope that Socialism, while destroying it in the only domains in which it has been a real part of the lives of ordinary men, will make amends by throwing open to them domains in which their individuality can find no exercise and their life can have no savor.

CHAPTER XXXVI

ECONOMICS AND LIFE

In the opening chapter of this book, it was stated that "the paramount object of Economics is to discuss the *causation* of economic phenomena." But the questions which the economist discusses are so closely related to human welfare, and so intricately bound up with great political, social, and moral issues, that it is almost impossible to avoid the error of supposing that the results at which he arrives are to be regarded as a conclusive judgment on these issues. When the physicist tells us about the path of a projectile, or the chemist determines the character of an explosive, everybody understands that this information tells only what will happen if we do certain things, and nothing at all about whether or not it is desirable to do them. But when the economist points out that in the existing system of society certain results will flow—or at least tend to flow—from competition or monopoly, from free trade or protection, from private ownership of land or the single-tax system which virtually abolishes such ownership, from unrestricted increase of population or its prudential restraint, etc.,—we are all so interested in the immediate bearing of these things upon human life that we are prone to think that Economics has passed judgment upon these alternatives, and decided which of the two is best for mankind.

Limitations of Economics

Now it would be idle to deny that Economics does in fact do something that is not wholly different from this; it does make an important contribution toward such decision, and indeed it is chiefly because it does so that Economics is one of the great subjects of human interest. But we must constantly bear in mind that in every case what Economics furnishes is only *one element* in the determination of the issue; the economist has no more authority than anybody else to pass upon the final question of what is right and what is wrong, what is wise and what is unwise, what is desirable and what is undesirable. In every instance in which it was particularly important to bear in mind the distinction between the *economic aspect* of a question and *the whole* of the question, it has been the endeavor in this little book to impress that distinction upon the reader's mind. But a few concluding remarks upon the general subject of that distinction will not be amiss.

Economics and Ethics

To begin with, let us look at the relation between Economics and Ethics. No charge has been more frequently made against Economics than that it inculcates a spirit of selfishness. It considers men as engaged in seeking to get, each for himself, the greatest possible material reward: buying in the cheapest and selling in the dearest market; employers paying no more wages than the state of the supply of labor compels them to pay; workers exacting from employers all the wages that the state of the demand for labor enables them to exact; landowners obtaining all the rent that the special advantages of their land over other land are worth; capitalists getting as high a rate of interest as anybody can be found willing to pay for the use of their capital; and so forth. The pursuit of individual self-interest which runs through all this, the economist takes for granted; and many people are shocked at the thought that he should give his tacit approval to such a vast exhibition of human selfishness.

It might be considered a sufficient answer to this charge to say that this "tacit approval" is no approval at all; that all that Economics does is to seek to understand *what is*, and that the question of *what ought to be* is outside its province. But in a certain sense, and by no means an unimportant one, Economics does give not only a tacit but an express approval to many practices which the uninstructed are prone to condemn as inhumane or unscrupulous. Indeed, perhaps the most vital part of the teaching of Economics is that which points out that through the pursuit by each man of his own self-interest—not, of course, without limitations, yet throughout almost the entire field of ordinary economic activities—the general good is served as it could hardly be served by any other means. And this is brought out most strikingly in the very instances in which the "man in the street" sees in the pursuit of individual gain the most inexcusable selfishness. That what is indiscriminatingly condemned as "speculation" or "profiteering" may be a most useful—indeed an almost indispensable—form of business activity; that the prohibition of "usury" harms most of all the very class of persons it is intended to benefit; that the cause of high rents is to be found not in the greed of landlords but in the unwillingness of other people to build houses without an assurance of profitable investment;—such are a few of the instances in which the economist not only fails to condemn, but actually approves, the exercise of the desire for gain in matters in which the unthinking see in that desire no aspect but that of conscienceless greed. When he points out the truth in these things instead of indulging in sterile condemnation that takes no account of consequences, the economist may well say "If this be treason, make the most of it."

But the economist, if he keeps within his proper limits, does not presume to say that the ethical standards which are dominant in the existing order of society, and which in large part are inextricably bound up with that order, are the highest that any social order could attain. Still less does he wish to discourage any individual from devoting his life, or his money, to purposes of a wholly altruistic character. There is nothing about the teachings of Economics that is in the smallest degree calculated to chill the ardor that results in such noble work as that of the Near East Relief, the Red Cross, the numberless philanthropic enterprises which high-minded men and women the world over, and especially in our own country, have supported by their means, and—what is infinitely more creditable—by personal exertion and self-sacrifice. A clear understanding of the principles of Economics does not interfere with high aspiration or noble endeavor, but only with the futilities of unthinking sentimentalists and the self-satisfaction of dilettante reformers. And even in the domain of business, it is only a narrow-minded person who sees in the principles of Economics a justification for ignoring the clear promptings of humane sentiment or disregarding the ordinary decencies of human intercourse. Economics has to do with general laws, not with the special relations that arise under particular circumstances between individual human beings; it offers no more warrant for the ruthless discharge of old employees by a business concern the moment their services are not wanted, or the exaction of the last farthing from a debtor in distress, than it does for any act of heartlessness or brutality in private life. It does recognize that "business is business," and that to insist that it shall be something else is calculated to do infinitely more harm than good; but it does not erect the maxim "business is business" into a sacred doctrine that overrides all the other principles of human conduct.

The Higher Charms of Life

But the higher side of life is not exclusively ethical, it includes the pursuit of æsthetic and intellectual aims for their own sake; and apart from anything consciously pursued, it includes the enjoyment of leisure, and variety, and serenity of mind. And in regard to all this a charge may perhaps be made against Economics which has more substance than the charge that it is unethical. For the constant preoccupation of the economist with the increase of productivity, and even with questions relating to the better distribution of the results of that increase, is unfortunately calculated to magnify in his mind, and in that of his readers, the importance of the material factors of life as distinguished from its less tangible elements. One of the notable works on Economics of the past generation has on its title-page the quotation:

'Tis the day of the chattel,
Web to weave and corn to grind;
Things are in the saddle,
And ride mankind.

It may be set down as quite certain that Henry Sidgwick no more meant to express his satisfaction with this state of things when he placed the quotation on his title-page than Ralph Waldo Emerson did when he wrote the lines half a century earlier; he simply recognized the fact. But, however this may be, we have to admit that, in concentrating our minds upon any particular aspect of life, we are prone to elevate it to an importance beyond its due; and this exaggeration is calculated to intensify whatever of evil accompanies the good of the thing upon which our interest is thus centered. And in the modern devotion to material progress there is, along with a great deal of good, a great deal of evil. This is true even as regards the end aimed at; it is doubly true as regards some of the inevitable accompaniments of the means by which that end is pursued. That multitudes of people have in the depth of their hearts and in the recesses of their minds a feeling of the folly and emptiness of our blind pursuit of material things, was strikingly evidenced by the immense popularity of Father Wagner's little book on *The Simple Life*, some twenty years ago; but how slight is the control which that inward feeling has upon our conduct was even more strikingly evidenced by the contrast between the number of those who read the book and the number of those who followed its teachings. And not only are we prone to exalt the increase of the material appliances of comfort or happiness above their due place, but we suffer the mechanization of life, the standardization of all our ways of living and working, to go to lengths which a real feeling for the beauty and variety of life would condemn as intolerable.

Obsessions of the Specialist

This exaggeration of the importance of material things is not, however, at all a necessary consequence of the study of Economics; the danger of it does not inhere in that study, but in a human weakness against which we have to guard in connection with any study that deals with an important aspect of life. Concentration upon the study of health, of heredity, of crime, of "intelligence," of "efficiency," is apt to breed an exaltation of the particular subject, a loss of the sense of proportion, full of the possibilities of serious mischief. The only safeguard is the preservation of a sane and comprehensive outlook on life as a whole; and that safeguard can be furnished only by one's own common sense and intellectual balance.

Great Value, Nevertheless, of the Spread of Economic Truth

But let us come back from these broad themes for a final word—not a defensive word to rebut a charge, but an aggressive word to assert a claim. Economic errors have been the source of enormous evil; and that evil has often been not only material, but also moral and spiritual. Of the disastrous possibilities of such evil, material and moral and spiritual, there could hardly be a more impressive example than that presented by the appalling conditions into which unsound money has, in these last years, plunged the populations of half the countries of Europe. On a scale less gigantic, but still most serious, lack of knowledge of the essential principles of Economics is constantly producing, in our own country as well as in others, a vast amount not only of economic mischief but of bickering and ill-will and political confusion. All this is going on, to be sure, in face of the fact that Economics has now, for more than a century, been a subject of abundant research and of somewhat widespread knowledge. But no one who is acquainted with economic history can doubt that the spread of that knowledge, far too limited though it is, has averted errors, and mischiefs, and futile struggles, which but for that knowledge would have afflicted us in a degree quite beyond estimate. There is in Economics much that remains doubtful or obscure, and much that admits of controversy as to its true significance. But there is also a core of truth, of which economists have gained command in its essentials, and of which the command is precious both as an intellectual possession and as a practical guide in some of the largest questions of our present-day life. If this little book shall have helped to make such truth more accessible, and more vital, to those who have had the patience to read it, it will have served the purpose for which it was written.

INDEX

A

Ability to pay, and taxation, 178–9
Abundance, hoarding in time of, 31–2
Adjustment of production, 26–7
Advertising, expenditure for, as an example of the waste of competition, 316–17
Agricultural land, rent of, 12; rental value, 80–1
Agriculture, the margin in, 10–11; law of diminishing productiveness and, 118 ff.
Allen, Henry J., Governor of Kansas, and Court of Industrial Relations, 298
American Sugar Refining Company and price of sugar, 149–50
Anti-trust laws, 147–8; and policy of *laissez faire*, 285–6
Arbitration, compulsory, failure of, in Australia, 298
Assessments for special benefits, 173–4
"Assignats," French, 266, 269
Australia, failure of compulsory arbitration in, 298
Average of prices, 62, 243–4
Averages of quantities, 9; and deviations, 10

B

Bad money drives out good, 267–8
Balance of trade, 256 ff.
Banking system, the, 73–5
Bank-notes, Federal tax on, 194
Banks, labor, 168
Barter, 38–9; difficulties of, overcome by money, 55–6
"Basing" of paper money of no avail without convertibility, 265–6
Bastiat's broken window-pane, 135–6
Bills of exchange, 254
Birthrate, lowering of, 125
Bolshevik régime in Russia, 269–70
Bonus for working gold mines asked for, 65 n.
"Booms" in business and alternate periods of depression, 237 ff.
Boycotting, 159
Building, cost of, rise in, 36
Building enterprise and the single tax, 209–13
Burns, Robert, quoted, 322
"Business cycles," 133, 237–40
Business profits, taxes on, 181, 186 ff.
Business psychology, 133–4

C

Calamity averted by clear thinking, 7–8
Capital, and production, 16 ff.; definition of, 17–18; the result of saving, 18–19, 94; possible without capitalists, 19–20, 102; performs an essential service, 20; service of, in production, 47–8; meaning of term, 94; and interest, 94 ff.; are interests of labor and, identical? 99; division of proceeds between labor and, 101–2; Socialists deny that private ownership of, is necessary, 311

Capitalist, not indispensable, 19–20, 102; and the risk of enterprise, 96–7
Causation of economic phenomena, principles of, 4, 5
Certificates, gold, 71–2
Changes in the value of money, 233 ff.
Character, bracing influence of struggle on, 322
Child-bearing, change in habits of, 124–5
Child-labor legislation, 285, 303–5
Clear thinking averts a calamity, 7–8
Colbert, minister of Louis XIV, and origin of phrase "*laissez faire*," 277
Collective bargaining, and trade-unionism, 154–5
Collective saving, supply of capital by, 19–20, 102, 311
Commodities, taxes on, 182
Compensation, inequalities in, 49; depends on scarcity, 50–1
Compensation laws, workmen's, 290–2
Competition, and law of demand and supply, 29; supposition of, 141; the check of potential, on monopoly, 148–50; not dead, nor dying, 150–1; the waste of, as an argument for Socialism, 316–18
Compulsory arbitration, failure of, in Australia, 298
Compulsory education, 285; 303
Confiscation, single tax equivalent to, 200; ethics of land confiscation, 203–6
"Continental" paper money, 73, 264, 269
Convertible paper money, 261
Convertibility, "basing" of paper money of no avail without, 265–6
Coöperation, profit sharing, etc., 163 ff; coöperative production, 164–6; coöperative distribution, 166–8; labor bank, 168–9; profit sharing, 169–71; shareholding, 171–2
"Corn laws" in England, 230
"Cornering" the market, 33
Corporations, a word about, 91–3; do not affect the essentials of the question of profits, 93
Cost of living, 51–3
Cost of production, and the margin, 11; normal value proportional to, 42–3; not uniform, 43–5; money cost and real cost, 46 ff.; real cost consists of services, 47; the service of capital, 47–8; the service of labor, 48–9; real, and foreign trade, 113
Cotton, price of, "fixed at Liverpool," 30–1
Court of Industrial Relations, Kansas, 297–9
Credit system, 74–5
Cultivation, margin of, 11
"Cycles, business," 133, 237–40

D

Debtors and creditors, change in value of money brings about injustice between, 234–6
Debts, impossibility of adjustment with changes in the value of money, 237
Demand and supply, 23 ff.; hoarding and, 31 ff.; forces that determine, 41
Depression, periods of, in business cycle, 238
Deviations from the average in incomes, 10
Diminishing productiveness, law of, and the problem of population, 118 ff.
Direct taxes, 181, 186 ff.
Distribution, coöperative, 166–8
"Diversity of employments" argument, 116; and protective system, 228–9
Division of proceeds between capital and labor, 101–2
Doctrine of *laissez faire*, 277 ff.
Doctrine of rent, 11
Doctrine, the single-tax, 195 ff.
Dollar, stabilizing the, 234, 241 ff.; purchasing power of, effect of fiat money on, 263–5
Duties, effect of import, 182–4
Duty, protective, 215
Dwellings and law of demand and supply, 35–7

E

Economic independence argument in case for protection, 116, 229–31

Economic phenomena, principles of causation of, 4–5; outcome of definite causation, 8
Economic truth, great value of the spread of, 340–1
Economics, method and spirit of, 3 ff.; paramount object of, 4; Economics and life, 333 ff.; limitations of Economics, 334; Economics and Ethics, 334–7; the higher charms of life, 338–9; obsessions of the specialist, 339–40; general value of the spread of economic truth, 340–1
"Economics of Destruction," article in London *Spectator*, 134 ff.
Economist, the, how he thinks, 4–5
Economists' meaning of "value," 39–40; meaning of rent, 79; view of overproduction, 130 ff.
Education, compulsory, 285, 303
Education, principle of state, 175
Educational facilities and welfare laws, 303–5
Effort, material gain incentive to, 307
Emergency rent laws, 35–7, 287
Emerson, Ralph Waldo, quoted, 338
Employment and the tariff, 217–19
Employments, separation of, 54–5; diversity of, and protective system, 228–9
England, and free trade policy, 230–1; opposition to factory laws in, 283–4; minimum wage laws in, 295
English coöperative stores, 166–8
Enterprise, and production, 16, 17; the risk of, and the capitalist, 96–7
Enterprise and profit, 86 ff.; no standard rate of business profit, 87–8; analogy between profit and rent, 88–90; prices not raised by rent of best land or profit of ablest manufacturers, 90–1; corporations, 91–3
Entrepreneur, the, 87; success depends on ability of, 88–90; and the capitalist, 96
Equality of opportunity, *see* Opportunity, equality of
Ethics, of land confiscation, 203–6; and Economics, 334–7
Europe, monetary condition of, as the result of issuance of fiat money, 264; fiat-money plague in, 268–72
Excess profits tax, 188
Exchange, money the medium of, 58–60
Exchange, par of, 254; bills of, 254; "triangular," 259–60; inconvertible paper money and the rate of, 273–4
Exchange, foreign, *see* Foreign exchange
Existing order, maintenance of fundamentals of, 300
Exporting, 109–11
Exports and imports and the rate of exchange, 256–8

F

Factory laws, mistaken opposition to, and policy of *laissez faire*, 283–4
Facts, relative importance of, known by the economist, 4, 6
Family, Socialism and the, 325–6
Farmer, and price fixation by margin, 11; may combine the four factors of production, 16; prices of produce "fixed at Liverpool," 30–1; and holding crops, 32; and his land and the single tax, 213–14
Federal tax on State bank-notes, 194
Fiat money, 261 ff.; defined, 261; what governments can and cannot do about, 262–5; prices affected by amount of, 263–5; "basing" of no avail without convertibility, 265–6; why bad money drives out good, 267–8; the fiat-money plague in Europe, 268–72; inconvertible paper money and rate of exchange, 273–4; essential vice of fiat money, 275–6
Fisher, Professor Irving, of Yale, index-number plan proposed by, 241 ff.
Fixed incomes, in relation to cost of living, 53; effect on, of changes in the value of money, 236

Ford, Henry, and automobile prices, 45, 91
Foreign exchange, 251 ff.; exchange and the gold standard, 251–3; normal fluctuations of the rate of exchange, 253–6; exports and imports and the rate of exchange, 256–8; "triangular" exchange, 259–60
Foreign trade, 109 ff.; importing and exporting done by individuals, not by countries, 109–11; baseless fears about flow of gold, 111–12; true nature of, 112–15; free trade and protection, 115–17
Free silver agitation, 236
Free trade, and protection, 115–17; and policy of *laissez faire*, 280; *see also* Protection and free trade
French Revolution, 266

G

General property tax, 189–90
General taxation, purposes of, 174–6
George, Henry, *Progress and Poverty*, 195, 196, 204, 205; and single tax, 195–203, 206; candidate for Mayor of New York, 214
Germany's debauch in fiat money, 270–2
Gold, and silver, how they came to be the world's money, 57–8; value of, 62–3; cost of production of, and value of money, 63–5; bonus for working mines asked for, 65 n.; substitutes for, in money system, 70–1; certificates, 71–2; notes redeemable in, 72; the banking system, 73–5; baseless fears about flow of, to other countries, 111–12; as the basis of all money, 233–4; and the index-number plan for stable measure of value, 245–6; avoidance of actual shipment of, in international exchange, 254–6; drain of, automatically checked, 257; hoards of, 265 n.
Gold standard, 70, 74; and exchange, 251 ff.
Government, functions of, and taxation, 175–6; *laissez faire* the doctrine of non-interference of, in matters of industry and trade, 278
Government ownership of public utilities, 144
Grades of workers, different, 49–50
"Greenbacks," 269
"Gresham's Law," 267

H

"Hard times," 130, 131
High prices, real cause of, 6
Hoarding, in time of abundance, 31–2; in time of scarcity, 33–5
Holding land out of use, 199, 207–9
Hours of labor, 154 ff.
Houses, and law of demand and supply, 35–7; taxes on, 190 ff.
Housing problem, 36

I

Ideal, Socialist, and Socialist systems, 309–10; question of desirableness of, 320 ff.
"Ill wind that blows nobody good" adage applied to matter of production, 129, 134, 136
Import duties, effect of, 182–4
Importing and exporting, 109–11
Imports and exports and the rate of exchange, 256–8
Improvements, land and, 84–5
Income tax, 186 ff.; progressive rates of, 187
Incomes, deviations from the average, 10
Incomes, fixed, in relation to cost of living, 53; effect on, of changes in the value of money, 236
Inconvertible paper money, 261 (*see also* Fiat money); and the rate of exchange, 273–4
Index-number, the, and "the stabilized dollar," 241 ff.; Prof. Fisher's plan for stable measure of value, 241 ff.; meaning of price level, 242–44; the index-number, 244; "the stabilized dollar," 244–6; a legislative danger, 246–8; some of benefits of index-number obtainable by voluntary agreements, 248–50.

Indirect taxes, 181 ff.
Individual interest the mainspring of productivity, 312–15
Industrial Relations, Kansas Court of, 297–9
Infant industries argument in case for protection, 116, 224–7
Inheritance, abolition of, necessary to establish equality of opportunity, 305; what abolition of, would mean, 306–7
Inheritance tax, 186 ff.
Interest, and capital, 94 ff.; rate of, 95–6; true, and compensation for risk, 97–9; what determines rate of, 100–1
Interest rates, laws on, and policy of *laissez faire*, 280–2
Inventions, labor-saving, results of, 140
Irredeemable or inconvertible paper money, 72–3, 261 (*see also* Fiat money)

J

Justice, taxation and the sense of, 177
Justice, social, 289 ff., 300; vagueness of the term, 289–90; workmen's compensation laws, 290–2; minimum-wage laws, 292–4; specific merits versus abstract doctrine, 294–7; self-delusion or false pretence, 297–9

K

Kansas Court of Industrial Relations, 297–9

L

Labor, and production, 16, 17; service of, in production, 48–9; trade-union control, 49 n.; are interests of, and capital identical? 99; division of proceeds between capital and, 101–2; and wages, 103 ff.; share of, 104–5; grades of, and wages, 105–6; trade unions and labor scarcity, 106–7; highly paid labor not necessarily dearly paid, 107–8; fundamental causes of the advancement of, 160–1; compensation of, under Socialism, 309
Labor banks, 168
Labor-employment fallacy in the tariff controversy, 217–19
Labor legislation and policy of *laissez faire*, 284–5
Labor-saving inventions, results of, 140
Laissez faire, 277 ff.; a practical maxim, not a scientific doctrine, 278–80; protection, usury laws, "speculation," 280–3; mistaken opposition to factory laws, 283–4; labor legislation, 284–5; anti-trust laws, 285–6; strong presumption in favor of, 286–8
Land, value of, and the margin, 11–13; doctrine of rent, 11–13; and rent, 78 ff.; rent the landowner's share, 78–9; rent and value of land, 79–80; what makes rental value, 80–2; speculative value of land, 82–4; land and improvements, 84–5; limited amount of cultivable, 118; taxes on, 190 ff.; and single-tax doctrine, 195 ff.; property in, unlike property in the products of labor, 197–9; holding land out of use, 199, 207–9; single tax equivalent to confiscation of land, 200; ethics of land confiscation, 203–6; the "unearned increment," 206–7; the farmer and his land, 213–14; case of mining land and single tax, 214 n.
Landlords and emergency rent laws, 36
Landowner, rent the share of, 78–9
Large-scale production and tendency toward monopoly, 145–7
Law of demand and supply, 24; regulates quantity of commodities produced, 26–7; controls relative numbers of persons engaged in the various occupations, 27–9; in relation to houses, 35–7
Law of diminishing productiveness and the problem of population, 118 ff.
Laws, anti-trust, 147–8, 285–6; usury, 280–2; factory, 283–4;

Laws—*Continued*
emergency rent, 287; workmen's compensation, 290–2; minimum-wage, 292–4; minimum wage, in England, 295; welfare, 303–5; compulsory education, 303; child-labor, 303–5
Legal tender, making paper money a, 262
Legislation, tariff, actual character of, 231–2
Liberty, Socialism and, 326–9
Life, Economics and, 333–41; the higher charms of, 338–9
Lincoln, Abraham, alleged quotation from, 221
Liquor, tax on, 194
Liverpool, prices fixed at, 30–1
Living, cost of, 51–3; standard of, 124–6

M

"Making work," 129, 134, 138, 140, 158
Malthus, *The Principle of Population*, 121–3; controversy over, 123–4; 284
Man, the ordinary and the exceptional, 329–32
"Man in the street," view of, compared with that of the economist, 4; what he does not do, 6; idea of cause of price fixation, 11; and market and normal values, 42
Manufacturing industries, law of diminishing productiveness does not apply to, 120 n.
Margin, the idea of the, 9 ff.; in agriculture, 10–11; and the value of land, 11–13; connects "value" and "utility," 13 ff.; and rise and fall of prices, 25; and adjustment of supply to cost of production, 44
Market, "cornering" of, 33
Market value, 42
Marks, preposterous quantities issued, 253
Marriage and child-bearing, change in habits of, 124–5
Meaning of words, difficulty of bearing in mind the real, 46
Measure of value, money the, 58–60; imperfection of money as, 233–4; index-number plan for stabilizing, 241 ff.
Medium of exchange, money the, 58–60
Merchandising, 20–2
Merchant, the, part in production, 21
Messina, earthquake at, used by London *Spectator* for a lesson on political economy, 134 ff.
Method and spirit of Economics, 3 ff.
Mill, John Stuart, and the unearned increment in land values, 206–7
Minimum-wage laws, 292–4; in England, 295
Mining land and the single tax, 214 n.
Money, use of, in buying and selling, 38–9; and real cost of living, 52–3; 54 ff.; as wages, 55; difficulties of barter overcome by, 55–6; what is money? 56; how gold and silver came to be the world's money, 57–8; medium of exchange and measure of value, 58 ff.; value of, and value of gold, 62–3; value of, and cost of production of gold, 63–5; general purchasing power of, 65–7; the quantity theory of, 67–9; other things than coin that play the part of, 70–1; paper money, 71–2; notes redeemable in gold, 72; irredeemable paper money, 72–3; the banking system, 73–5; and prices, 75–7; represents capital, 94; changes in the value of, 233 ff.; imperfection of money as measure of value, 233–4; debtors and creditors, 234–6; salaries and wages, 236–7; the business cycle, 237–40; index-number plan for offsetting changes in value of, 241 ff.; fiat money, 261 ff. (*see also* Fiat money); token money, 268 n.
Money cost and real cost of production, 46 ff.
Money fallacy, the, in tariff controversy, 219–23
Monopoly, and law of demand and supply, 29; 141 ff; natural, 142–5; large scale production

Monopoly—*Continued*
and tendency toward, 145–7; trusts and anti-trust laws, 147–8; the check of potential competition, 148–50; competition not dead, nor dying, 150–51; case of, and taxation, 184–5

N

Natural advantages and cost of production, 44
Natural monopolies, 142–7
Natural resources, and production, 16, 17; exhaustion of, cause of increase in real cost of living, 53; rent as price paid for, 79
Normal value, 42; proportional to cost of production, 42–5
Notes, governmental and bank, 71–2; redeemable in gold, 72; irredeemable, 72–3; the banking system, 73–5

O

Occupations, relative numbers of persons engaged in the various, controlled by law of demand and supply, 27–9
Opportunity, equality of, 300 ff.; in what sense equality exists, 300–3; educational facilities and welfare laws, 303–5; unlimited scope of the abstract doctrine, 305–6; what abolition of inheritance would mean, 306–7
"Out of use," holding land, 199, 207–9
Overproduction, 129 ff.; purchasing power keeps pace with production, 130–2; in reality only maladjustment of production, 130; not overproduction but misfit, 132–3; business psychology, 133–4; a long-lived fallacy, 134–9; fundamental truth of the matter, 139–40

P

Paper money, 71; notes redeemable in gold, 72; irredeemable paper money, 72–3; *see also* Fiat money
Par of exchange, 254
Patents, monopolies conferred to stimulate invention, 141–2
Physiocrats, the, 278
Population, problem of, and law of diminishing productiveness, 118 ff.; Malthus, *The Principle of Population*, 121–3; the controversy over Malthus, 123–4; and standard of living, 124–6
Possession, the pleasures of, 322–5
Poverty, abolition of, 329–30
Price, representative of value, 60; and value compared, 61
Price-level, 61–2; determination of, 65; meaning of, 242–4
"Price," "value" and, 40–1
Prices, cause of high, 6; minimum, of wheat fixed by Government during world war, 7–8; in agriculture fixed by the margin, 11; why prices go up and down, 24–6; how prices regulate production, 26–7; 61 ff.; the price-level, 61–2; value of money and value of gold, 62–3; value of money and cost of production of gold, 63–5; general purchasing power of money, 65–7; the quantity theory of money, 67–9; three factors that determine the general course of, 75–7; not raised by rent of best land or profit of ablest manufacturers, 90–1; as affected by trusts, 149–50; rise and fall of, produce injustice between debtors and creditors, 234–6; effect of high, on fixed incomes, 236; influence of, in business cycle, 239; average of, 243–4; affected by amount of fiat money in circulation, 263–5
Principle of Population, The, Malthus, 121–3
Principles of Political Economy and Taxation, Ricardo, 13
Private ownership of instruments of production, Socialism would abolish, 308, 311
Problem of population and the law of diminishing productiveness, 118 ff.
Proceeds, division of, between capital and labor, 101–2

Production, cost of, and the margin, 11; the four factors of, 16 ff.; nature and scope of, 20–2; how prices regulate, 26–7; normal value proportional to cost of, 42–3; cost of, not uniform, 43–5; money cost and real cost, 46 ff.; overproduction, 129 ff.; purchasing power keeps pace with production, 130; overproduction maladjustment of, 130; large-scale, and tendency toward monopoly, 145–7; coöperative, 163–6; instruments of, no private ownership of, under Socialism, 308, 311; misdirected, under Socialism, 318–19
Productiveness, law of diminishing, and problem of population, 118 ff.
Productivity, individual interest the mainspring of, 312–15
Profit, and enterprise, 86 ff.; no standard rate of business profit, 87–8; analogy between, and rent, 88–90; prices not raised by that of ablest manufacturers, 90–1
Profit sharing, 169–71
Profits tax, 186 ff.
Progress and Poverty, by Henry George, 195, 196, 204, 205
Property, taxes on, 189 ff.; in land unlike property in the products of labor, 197–9
Protection, 115–17
Protection and free trade, 215 ff.; the tariff controversy, 216–17; the labor-employment fallacy, 217–19; the money fallacy, 219–23; the infant industries argument, 224–7; social and political arguments, 227–9; economic independence, 229–31; actual character of tariff legislation, 231–2; and policy of *laissez faire*, 280
Protective duty, 215
Protective tariff, 215
Public utilities, 143–4; government ownership of, 144
Purchasing power, of money, 65–7; keeps pace with production, 130–2

Q

Quantity of commodities produced regulated by law of demand and supply, 26–7
Quantity theory of money, 67–9

R

"Race suicide," 125
Ransdell, Congressman, and alleged quotation from Lincoln, 221
Rate of exchange, normal fluctuations in, 253–6; exports and imports and, 256–8; inconvertible paper money and, 273–4
Rate of interest, 95–6; what determines, 100–1
Real and money cost of living, 52–3
Real cost and money cost of production, 46 ff.; and foreign trade, 113
Real cost of living, cause of increase in, 53
"Rebates" stopped by law, 148
Redeemable or convertible paper money, 261
Regimentation under Socialism, 327
Rent, of land, 11–13; is landowner's share, 78; the economist's definition of, 79; and value of land, 79–80; what makes rental value, 80–2; analogy between profit and, 88–90; of city houses, 191–3
Rent laws, emergency, 35–7, 287
Reserve for redemption of notes, 72
Resources, natural, and production, 16, 17
Ricardo, David, doctrine of rent, 11, 12, 80, 84; *Principles of Political Economy and Taxation*, 12
Risk, of enterprise, the capitalist and, 96–7; true interest and compensation for, 97–9
Rochdale Pioneers' Society in England, 166–7
Rockefeller, John D., 185
Roosevelt, Theodore, 125
Russell, Bertrand, quoted, 330

Russia, Bolshevik régime in, 269–70; failure of Socialism in, 312

S

Salaries, slowness of adjustment of, with changes in the value of money, 236–7
Saving, capital the result of, 18–19, 94; supply of capital by collective, 19–20, 311
Scarcity, hoarding in time of, 33–5
Scarcity of labor, compensation depends on, 50–1; trade unions and, 106–7
Selling value of land, 82–4
Servant girl, case of, in matter of wages, 51
Services, real cost of production consists of, 47
Shareholding by wage-earners, 171–2
Sidgwick, Henry, 338
Silver, and gold, how they came to be the world's money, 57–8; as money, 70; discontinued as money basis, 233 n.
Simple Life, The, Father Wagner, 339
Single-tax doctrine, the, its basis, 195–201; proposed by Henry George in *Progress and Poverty,* 195 ff.; property in land unlike property in the products of labor, 197–9; holding land out of use, 199, 207–9; single tax equivalent to confiscation, 200–1; objections to single-tax doctrine, 202–14; the ethics of land confiscation, 203–6; the "unearned increment," 206–7; single tax and building enterprise, 209–13; the farmer and his land, 213–14; single-tax scheme wrong from standpoint of Ethics and open to fatal objections from standpoint of Economics, 214; single tax and mining lands, 214 n.
Skill and business ability and cost of production, 44
"Slavery" of wage-worker, alleged, 327–8
Smith, Adam, *The Wealth of Nations,* 12; on rent of land, 12; and doctrine of *laissez faire,* 278
Social and political arguments in case for protection, 227–9
Social justice, *see* Justice, social
Socialism, versus Individualism, 20; and social justice, 289–90, 300; 308 ff.; aims common to all forms of, 308–9; Socialist systems and the Socialist ideal, 309–10; is Socialism practicable? 310–12; efficiency compared with present system, 312–14; a Socialist counter-argument, 314–16; the waste of competition, 316–18; the waste of Socialism, 318–19; question of desirability of, 320; the elimination of struggle, 320–2; the pleasures of possession, 322–5; Socialism and the family, 325–6; Socialism and liberty, 326–9; the ordinary man and the exceptional man, 329–32
Socialistic view of overproduction, 130
Soviet régime in Russia, 312
Specialist, obsessions of the, 339–40
Spectator, London, uses Messina earthquake for lesson on political economy, 134 ff.
"Speculation" and policy of *laissez faire,* 282–3
Speculative value of land, 82–4
"Stabilized dollar, the," and the index-number, 241 ff.; actual working of the plan, 245–6
Stabilizing the dollar, 234
Standard of living, 124–6; improvement in, 284–5
Standard Oil Company, 148, 185
Strike, the, 159–60
Struggle of life, elimination of, preëminent aim of the Socialist order, 320–2; elimination of, undesirable, 321–2; bracing influence on character, 322; pleasure of possession as result of, 322–5
Sugar, scarcity of after the world war, 34–5; price of, and American Sugar Refining Company, 149–50
Supply and demand, relations between, 130–1; *see also* Demand and supply *and* Law of demand and supply
Sympathetic strike, 159

T

Tariff, protective, 215; the tariff controversy, 216–17 ff.
Tariff legislation, actual character of, 231–2
Taxation, 173 ff.; assessments for special benefits, 173–4; purposes of general taxation, 174–6; distribution of the tax burden, 176–7; and the sense of justice, 177; a discarded view, 177–8; and the ability to pay, 178–9; practical effects must always be considered, 179–80; various forms of, 181 ff.; taxes on commodities, 182; effect of import duties, 182–4; the case of monopoly, 184–5; income tax, profits tax, inheritance tax, 186–7; progressive rates of income tax, 187–9; the general property tax, 189–90; taxes on land and houses, 190–3; other aspects of taxation, 193–4; the single tax doctrine, 195 ff. (*See also* single tax doctrine)
Taxes, direct and indirect, 181 ff
Tenant and law of demand and supply, 35
Token money, 268 n.
Trade, balance of, 256 ff.
Trade, foreign, *see* Foreign trade
Trade-unionism, 152 ff.; trade unions not necessarily monopolistic, 153–4; collective bargaining, 154–5; benefits of, 155–7; evils of, 157–9; the strike, 159–60; fundamental causes of the advancement of labor, 160–1; the reasonable attitude toward, 161–2
Trade-unions, control of labor, 49 n.; and labor scarcity, 106–7; rules designed for "making work," 129, 134; not necessarily monopolistic, 153–4
Traffic, principle of making price as high as it will bear, 149
Transportation, 20–2
"Triangular" exchange, 259–60
Trusts, and anti-trust laws, 147–8; the check of potential competition, 148–50; competition not dead, nor dying, 150–1

U

"Unearned increment," the, in value of land, 206–7
Unemployment, cause of, and means of preventing, fallacies regarding, 131 ff.; fundamental truth about danger of, 139–40
United States Steel Corporation, 150
Uplift of life, picture of, by Socialists, unreal, 330–2
Urban land, rental value of, 81
Usury laws and policy of *laissez faire*, 280–2
Utilities, public, 143–4; government ownership of, 144
"Utility," the margin connects "value" with, 13 ff.; definition of, 14

V

Value, theory of, 13; connected with "utility" by the margin, 13 ff.; 38 ff.; what economists mean by, 39–40; and price, 40–1; normal, 42; normal, proportioned to cost of production, 42–3; cost of production not uniform, 43–5; money the measure of, 58–60; price representative of, 60; and price compared, 61; of money and of gold, 62–3; of money and cost of production of gold, 63–5; of money, changes in, 233 ff.; imperfection of money as measure of, 233–4; index-number plan for stabilizing measure of, 241 ff.
Value of land, and the margin, 11–13; and rent, 79–80; what makes rental value, 80–2; speculative, 82–4
Voluntary agreements in adjusting measure of value, 248–50

W

Wage-boards in England, 295
Wage laws, minimum-, 292–4; in England, 295
Wage-worker, alleged "slavery" of, 327–8

Wages, effect of lowering, 28; cf servant girl, 51; and labor, 103 ff.; meaning of term, 103 n.; equality and differences in and between grades of labor, 105–6; high, not necessarily dear, 107–8; and trade unionism, 154 ff.; and the tariff, 218–19; slowness of adjustment of, with changes in value of money, 237; sliding scale of, in Great Britain, and index-number, 249

Wagner, Father, *The Simple Life*, 339

Walker, Francis A., view of business profits, 86 and n.

Waste, of competition, 316–18; of Socialism, 318–19

Wealth of Nations, The, Adam Smith, 12, 278

Welfare laws, 303–5

Wheat, minimum price of, fixed by Government during world war, 7–8; price of, and the margin, 11; price of, "fixed at Liverpool," 30–1

Window-tax in England, 193–4

Women, minimum-wage laws for, 292

Words, difficulty of bearing in mind the real meaning of, 46

Work, making, 129, 134, 138, 140, 158

Workers, excess or deficiency of, 28; different grades of, 49–50; limitation of numbers of, in certain trades, 153; benefits and evils of trade-unionism to, 155–9; and coöperation, 163–9; profit sharing, 169–71; shareholding by, 171–2

Workmen's compensation laws, 290–2

From the Press of G·P·Putnam's Sons

1923

New York
2 West 45th Street
just west of 5th Ave.

London
24 Bedford Street
Strand

NOVELS

Title	Price
Lew Tyler's Wives *by* Wallace Irwin	$2.00
Tetherstones *by* Ethel M. Dell	$2.00
Suzanne and the Pacific *by* Jean Giraudoux Translated by Ben Ray Redman	$2.00
Mainspring *by* V. H. Friedlaender	$2.00
The Shining Road *by* Bernice Brown	$1.75
Desolate Splendour *by* Michael Sadlier	$2.00
Mine of Faults *and* Ashes of a God *by* F. W. Bain	$2.00
Bubbles of the Foam *and* Substance of a Dream *by* F. W. Bain	$2.00
Helen of London *by* Sidney D. Gowing	$2.00
The Sun Field *by* Heywood Broun	$2.00
The Ungrown-ups *by* "Rita"	$2.00
The Grays *by* Charlotte Bacon	$2.00
The Seven Hills *by* Meade Minnigerode	$1.90
Echo *by* Margaret Rivers Larminie	$2.00
The Barb *by* William J. McNally	$1.75
Ponjola *by* Cynthia Stockley	$2.00
Up and Coming *by* Nalbro Bartley	$1.90
The Sign of the Serpent *by* John Goodwin	$1.75
The Clients *by* Melville D. Post	$1.75
The Corrector of Destinies *by* Melville D. Post	$1.75
The Charing Cross Mystery *by* J. S. Fletcher	$2.00
Rippling Ruby *by* J. S. Fletcher	$2.00
Fighting Blood *by* H. C. Witwer	$1.90
The Luck of the Kid *by* Ridgwell Cullum	$2.00
Dan Barry's Daughter *by* Max Brand	$1.90
Garden of Peril *by* Cynthia Stockley	$1.50
The Golden Book of Venice *by* Mrs. Lawrence Turnbull	$2.00
The Royal Pawn of Venice *by* Mrs. Lawrence Turnbull	$2.00

SHORT STORIES

Title	Price
Georgian Stories, 1922	$2.50
With the Gilt Off *by* A. St. John Adcock	$2.00
The Little Tigress *by* Wallace Smith	$2.50

HISTORY, BIOGRAPHY, AND MEMOIRS

Title	Price
The Veiled Empress *by* Benjamin A. Morton	$5.00
Wonders of the Past. Each volume Edited by J. A. Hammerton	$5.00
The Life and Times of Akhnaton *by* Arthur Weigall	$5.00
The Glory of the Pharaohs *by* Arthur Weigall	$5.00